MOCK STARS

INDIE COMEDY AND THE DANGEROUSLY FUNNY

BY JOHN WENZEL

speck press
golden

Published by Speck Press
An imprint of Fulcrum Publishing
4690 Table Mountain Drive, Suite 100 • Golden, Colorado 80403
800-992-2908 • 303-277-1623 • speckpress.com

ISBN-13: 978-1-933108-23-0

This publication is provided for informational and educational purposes. The information herein contained is true and complete to the best of our knowledge.

Library of Congress Cataloging-in-Publication Data

Wenzel, John, 1977-
Mock stars : Indie comedy and the dangerously funny / by John Wenzel.
    p. cm.
Includes bibliographical references and index.
ISBN 978-1-933108-23-0 (pbk.)
1. Stand-up comedy--United States. I. Title.
PN1969.C65W46 2008
792.2'30973--dc22
                            2008036374
Printed on recycled paper in Canada by Friesens Corp.
10 9 8 7 6 5 4 3 2 1

Book layout and design by Margaret McCullough

Photographs on pages viii, 80, 134, 188, 228, and 278 courtesy of Seth Olenick, author of the upcoming photo book *A Funny Thing Happened...*, setholenick.com; 28 courtesy Amelia Handscomb, Sub Pop Records; 50 courtesy of Geoffrey Brent Shrewsbury; 62 courtesy of Henry Owings; 244 courtesy of Simone Turkington; 266 courtesy of Cyrus McCrimmon, *The Denver Post*; author photo courtesy of Mat Luschek

To my mother and father,

for my sense of humor...and everything else.

ACKNOWLEDGMENTS

My deepest thanks to everyone who lent me their time for interviews and assistance:

Aziz Ansari, Fred Armisen, Scott Aukerman,
Donna Ayers, Maria Bamford, Todd Barry,
Greg Baumhauer, Matt Belknap, Doug Benson,
Matt Besser, Shonali Bhowmik, Adam Cayton-Holland,
Margaret Cho, Tommy Chong, Neil Cleary, David Cross,
Andrew Earles, Christian Finnegan, Ross Flournoy,
Zach Galifianakis, Neil Hamburger, Chelsea Handler,
Tim Heidecker, Jim Hickox, Rob Huebel, Tony Kiewel,
Ben Kronberg, Aimee Mann, Eugene Mirman,
Bob Mould, Rian Murphy, Tig Notaro, Bob Odenkirk,
Patton Oswalt, Henry Owings, Tom Papa, B. J. Porter,
Brian Posehn, Ben Roy, Kristen Schaal, Tom Scharpling,
Paul Scheer, Dan Schlissel, Robert Schneider,
Michael Showalter, Brendon Small, Robin Taylor,
Jesse Thorn, Paul F. Tompkins, Gregg Turkington,
Eric Wareheim, Geof Wills, Lizz Winstead,
and Jon Wurster.

And my unending gratitude to everyone who helped during the research, writing, and editing process, whether by offering advice, correcting errors, facilitating interviews, graciously lending photos, or simply being patient and kind:

Kathleen St. John (for everything), Derek Lawrence
and Susan Hill Newton (the opportunity and guidance),
Lori Smith (the title), Ricardo Baca (the inspiration and
encouragement), Andrew Earles (the contribution and
innumerable suggestions), Seth Olenick (the photos),

Mat Luschek (more photos), Eva Magdalenski
(publicist extraordinaire), Michelle Baldwin, Ken Beegle,
Angie Carlson, Paul Custer, Kambri Crews,
Elizabeth Derczo, Rick Dorfman, Emily Goldsher,
Alexandra Greenberg, Gerry Hart, Sara Hays,
Catherine Herrick, Joan Hiller, Kate Jackson,
Dawn Lach, Pam Loshak, Karen Malluk, Rebecca Many,
Stacey Mark, Arlen Marmel, Annissa Mason,
Daisy May, Brian McKim, Jamie Mercer, Greg Moore,
Michael O'Brien, Tonya Owens, Erin Palmiter,
Ken Phillips, Loren Pomerantz, William Porter,
Dave Rath, Drew Reifenberger, Erin Roberts,
Will C. Rogers, Ray Rinaldi, Tim Sarkes,
Rebecca Silverstein, Ed Smith, Keri Smith,
Haley Wallace, Justin D. Williams, Jesse Wingard,
Nicole Yalaz, Paul Young, Wendy Zocks,
all my friends and family, and anyone I may have missed
in my eminent forgetfulness.

Contents

★★★★★★★★★★★★★★★★★★★★★★★

Comedians of Comedy veteran Maria Bamford contemplates
hydration in downtown Los Angeles. *Photo by Seth Olenick*

Introduction

NOTES ON A SCENE

I know what you're thinking.

Really, I'm psychic. I can read your mind despite the fact that you're sitting all the way over there in that folding chair with the crappy, uncomfortable seat. My brain can grasp your boiling psychic energy regardless of physical distance. Someone should write a screenplay about me and sell it to a J-horror company, because bespectacled, telepathic, midlevel journalists are all the rage with the kids these days.

You're thinking about indie comedy, and the brazen culture hound in you wants to know: "What in God's name is indie comedy, and who needs it? Is it a form of racing that takes place in the hinterlands of Indiana on an oval-shaped track, featuring insect-shaped vehicles and an audience of fat midwesterners wheezing their way through trays of nachos? But funnier?"

No, that's *indy* comedy. The unintentional kind.

"Is it that cute little *Garden State* movie? Or *Juno*, the one about the non-abortion-having teen? Or whatever other piece of life-affirming celluloid crap that's oozing from my local art house theater this week?"

No. Those are indie *comedies*. Films. Low- to mid-budget Hollywood droppings. Romantic fantasies with magical female characters and catchy, nonthreatening soundtracks. Not living, breathing humans performing stand-up and sketch routines. Not indie *comedy*.

I'll delve into what the questionable term *indie comedy* is shortly, but as for "Who needs it?" well, pull up a chair, little Billy and Susie. It's for anyone who finds most mainstream comedy boring, irrelevant, insulting, or worse—soul-destroying. It's for people tired of passively ingesting cultural hegemony via flaccid, middle-of-the-road Clinton jokes on late-night talk shows (yes, even they persist in the twilight days of this wretched decade) or who have grown numb to the litany of ways in which white people are not like black people, or black people are not like white people, or women like men, or husbands like wives, etc. It's for anyone who savors the visceral, unpredictable jolt of watching quality stand-up comedy but prefers not to be deposited into a sea of *According to Jim*-loving, cat-calendar-collecting, McMansion-dwelling mouthbreathers (i.e., the stereotypical audience at a traditional comedy club).

It's also for anyone who loves *Mr. Show*.

If you want to get historical about it, what I'm generally calling indie comedy owes its existence to countless entertainers stretching back to the dawn of modern stand-up, not the least of which were (and are) the fearlessly progressive orators, writers, and thinkers of the last century, and certainly the contemporary entertainers who share a similarly absurdist, painfully self-aware, or cynical ethos. The uniquely American writing of authors from Mark Twain to Kurt Vonnegut Jr.; the unabashedly political material of Mort Sahl; the boundary-shredding, abrasive humor of Lenny Bruce; the anti-humor of Andy Kaufman; the caustic wit of Bill Hicks; the 1990s alternative comedy movement; the social milieu of these post-9/11 years; and the prescient bookers and managers of various stand-ups and musicians also play significant roles in the birth and growth of this hipster-leaning offshoot.

But really, a chunk of the comedians who can be called independent—who have in some way distanced themselves from the mainstream club circuit, forged their own path, and/or aligned themselves with the underground music world—can often trace some measure of experience or inspiration back to *Mr. Show*, that woefully underwatched sketch program that ran late nights on HBO from 1995 to 1998.

Mr. Show's short-attention-span pieces played like a mash of *Monty Python's Flying Circus*, *SCTV*, *Kids in the Hall*, *Saturday Night Live*, and presumably whatever drugs the writers had stashed in the glove boxes of their rusty Nissan Stanzas. *Mr. Show* cocreators Bob Odenkirk and David Cross (and their able staff) violently resisted cheap laughs and bow-tying punch lines. They challenged the audience to come to them, instead of pandering or enticing them with safe, low-calorie humor. They dropped references like breadcrumbs, never stopping to see if anyone had picked them up, and relied on smarter audiences' knowledge of comedy conventions to forge material. *Mr. Show*, like so many others rightfully lauded as years ahead of their time, ran to great critical acclaim and little ratings notice.

Alas.

My obsession with it began innocuously enough: I spied a DVD promo in the mail bin at a temp job some years back and decided to snatch it, if only because HBO's hit-to-miss ratio for quality screeners was higher than most. It wasn't intended for me, but whatever; it probably would have ended up in the giveaway pile or swiped by another destitute, overeducated dayjobber. I remembered my high-school friend Steve mentioning *Mr. Show* while I was home from college one summer, and since he had already introduced me to a lot of the literature, film, and music I loved, I figured it couldn't hurt. Like many people born in the 1970s, I was also primed to appreciate a certain type of comedy, exposed over the years to touchstones like *Saturday Night Live* and *SCTV*, and—practically from birth—my father's unending string of one-liners. (A jeweler and consummate salesman, he often deals with Hasidic Jews, which only reinforces his existing love of old schoolers like Henny Youngman and Jackie Mason, and latter-day masters Mel Brooks and Larry David. I still occasionally receive random greeting cards from him congratulating me on my bar mitzvah, which makes perfect sense, since I'm of Irish-German descent and was raised Catholic.)

Prone in my early twenties to boredom and smoking far too much pot, I watched a few episodes of *Mr. Show* in my neighbor's Capitol Hill apartment in Denver, noting that bald, grinning cocreator David Cross would occasionally introduce episodes wearing concert T-shirts from indie rock bands. "Sweet," I thought when a Superchunk shirt appeared. "I fuckin' love those guys." Another episode opened with Cross sporting a Creeper Lagoon shirt (remember them?), cocreator Bob Odenkirk attired in his usual gray suit and sneakers. I dot-connected and remembered that Cross had emceed a New Year's Eve concert at the Apollo Theater in 2001 with indie-rock godheads Guided By Voices and then-upstarts The Strokes, further hinting at a connection between the comedy and music to which I was drawn. I even remembered seeing Amy Poehler sport a Yo La Tengo shirt during an episode of the now-defunct *Upright Citizens Brigade* sketch show on Comedy Central. These badges of coolness impressed me, but only to the extent that I would also notice someone on the street wearing a hip, funny T-shirt, prompting me to think such deeply philosophical things as "Sweet" and "Nice."

Of course, the relationship between indie rock and this certain brand of comedy has evolved rapidly since I first noticed Cross and Poehler's choices of wardrobe— about as rapidly as my bottomless, unnatural zeal for *Mr. Show*. And what is this certain brand of comedy? It's many, actually. I've been calling it indie comedy, but it also has the ability to encompass and overlap with sub-genres such as alternative comedy (itself an imprecise term), rock 'n' roll comedy, political comedy, avant-garde comedy, confrontational/experimental comedy, awkward comedy, pain-as-humor, and whatever unfortunate nouns we're saddling with the term *post* these days.

Like most subcultures, it tends to define itself by what it is *not*, pointing out (and ridiculing) the fact that the anodyne stuff of most mainstream comedy effectively doubles as mind control. Independent voices often teach us that the messages emanating from the mainstream have a vested interest in reinforcing traditional roles and institutions, soothing us to their injustices by negating the need for thought or dissent. The indie-comedy scene isn't necessarily out to topple any corporate giants by tossing verbal bricks at the neighborhood Starbucks. It mostly originated as a loose network of performers disenfranchised with—or simply bored by—mainstream comedy offerings. Nonetheless, it has come to serve a growing audience similarly repelled by the cloistered environs and messages of the traditional club scene, with its two-drink minimums, disruptive bachelorette and birthday parties, hot wing/potato skin specials, and patrons whose heads often seem alternately filled with air, meat, and shit. Generally speaking, this new comedy movement more accurately reflects its audiences' and performers' values, and does so without compromising the intellectual and cultural hallmarks they hold dear—at times by completely destroying them.

The term *subversive* has mutated into a clichéd badge of approval in these post-9/11 days, but much of this cerebral, reference-heavy, surreal humor really does subvert the norm, twisting cultural and comedic conventions into logical pretzels, often eschewing punch lines for thought-provoking pauses or stream-of-consciousness rants. Occasionally these comedians' bits also fulfill the same role as the establishment-fucking, disaffected political screeds and nihilistic essays that populated fanzines and mix tapes in the 1980s and early nineties. The difference is that instead of getting passed around backstage at hard-core shows or popping up in college-town record stores, they're getting posted on YouTube, MySpace, AdultSwim.com, and FunnyorDie.com, offered as podcasts on artists' websites, peddled as ten-minute chunks of humor on iTunes, or linked through comedy sites like ASpecialThing.com.

But is there some nugget of truth at the center of the term *indie comedy*?

Not really. Like any tag, it's inherently limiting, potentially meaningless, and more than a bit condescending. It's a placeholder, just as *alternative* was in the nineties, a word that heralded the crest of a new wave (or, if you prefer, one that attached a glib handle to an unwieldy package). For the purposes of this book, I'm pegging indie comedy as the progressive, ever-expanding, tech-savvy scene of comedians who have evolved from the alt-comedy movement of the nineties and taken the do-it-yourself ethic to heart. Much of that includes allying themselves with the underground music circuit, taking inspiration from that scene's ethos and practices, and speaking directly to an audience long afraid of paying an expensive cover to watch some asshole tell jokes onstage. "Several years ago they called us alternative comedy, but indie fits better to me because a lot of us are on indie labels and we do have our indie music fans," says *Mr. Show* alumnus Brian Posehn.

"But what's the big deal?" you might ask. "Why does it matter that comedians are playing underground rock clubs, dive bars, and music festivals, that they're breaking from the now-standard club format familiar to most of us through endless *Seinfeld* reruns?" Well, reader, it's because any art form needs regular infusions of new blood to prevent its creative muscles from growing weak. (If you don't believe me, look at the mediocrity of most sitcoms, stand-up specials, and *The Tonight Show* guests of the past twenty-five years.) "But I still don't see how this is anything revolutionary," you might want to interject. "Don't young, cutting-edge artists of any discipline tend to run in the same circles, gravitating toward each other like metal filings toward a cartoonish, U-shaped magnet?" Sure they do, but this scene is decidedly different, partly because there's some disagreement as to whether it even *is* a scene, and partly because most of its members resist being labeled indie, alternative, punk, or nontraditional for assorted (and potentially obvious) reasons.

This new comedy movement arrives with all the attendant positives and negatives a scene implies, from the sense of openness and community scenes engender to the mindless hipsters who care little for the art of stand-up and sketch comedy and more about being noticed by other flesh mannequins with the same haircut and glasses.

Mock Stars loosely traces stand-up and sketch comedy's evolution from the 1970s renaissance through the 1980s comedy boom and bust, on through the rise of alternative comedy in the 1990s (chunks of which went semi-mainstream and brought us a slew of cable-TV, *Saturday Night Live*, and talk-show regulars), and into the present. Because, really, the indie-comedy movement, as I'm defining it, barely existed ten years ago. Outside of places such as New York, Los Angeles, San Francisco, Boston, and Chicago, most people had no idea you could even *see* comedy outside of a comedy club or theater. By and large, indie musicians and audiences formerly only rubbed shoulders with comedians, sharing stories and passing each other in the hallway on their way to stages, greenrooms, or disgusting, dimly lit bathrooms.

But thanks to a growing number of tours, record labels, websites, and venues, independent comedy is infiltrating the rest of the country. Now comedians and indie musicians ransack each other's wardrobes, trying on the others' fraying, tight-fitting, ironic T-shirts, corduroy jackets, and black plastic-frame glasses. In some rare cases, they even take each other's shape, hybridizing or trading melodic and comedic talents to greater cumulative effect (*Saturday Night Live* regular Fred Armisen and indie-rock drummer Jon Wurster of the Scharpling and Wurster comedy team provide sterling examples).

Musicians, hipsters, technophiles, intellectuals, comic-book slaves, shut-ins, druggies, critics, and other self-aware smarty-pants are both indie comedy's progenitors and its primary consumers, although comedians like David Cross, Patton Oswalt, Maria Bamford, Brian Posehn, and dozens of others pop up—usually in character-actor mode—in mainstream films, TV shows, stage productions, commercials, and your mom's chili cook-off from time to time.

This movement's virility and relevance springs from its multiple entertainment and artistic virtues: snarky, unapologetic, boundary-pushing humor that reflects underground music's propensity for taking chances with its audience and itself. It doesn't mind heading down a dark alley, especially if that leads to new creative avenues. And like most progressive art, it cares little about offending existing sensibilities. If that means having audience members walk out of a show in anger or disgust, well, that's okay too. Hell, that might even be the point.

The knowledge that only *you* are aware of a certain artist, that only *you* understand the joke, is often central to underground art's appeal, and indie comedy is no different (particularly when it strays into its more elitist, exclusive, or experimental strains). On the one hand, its recent growth has shown that like-minded people can get in on the joke without sacrificing its unique intimacy, but really it's that same satisfaction you feel in a tiny club when it hosts an obscure, mind-blowing act—like when I was lucky enough to catch a fresh-faced TV on the Radio at Denver's Larimer Lounge in November 2003, opening for the relatively languid Ladybug Transistor. (Don't get me wrong. I like them too. Get off my back, okay? Jesus.) It's the thrill of feeling that something is yours and yours alone, although, since most comedians of any persuasion just want steady work, it's a feeling they may not always share.

These stand-up, improv, and sketch practitioners are often smart, book-learned ladies and fellows to be sure, but they're also painfully aware of comedy clichés. Many of them trade in typical mock-shock topics like rape, AIDS, abortion, racism, incest, and homophobia, skewering their subjects by taking them to ridiculous extremes and pushing buttons you didn't know—or didn't want to know—you had. Critics have variously labeled them absurdist, confessional, anti-humor, deadpan, or meta (that last term skirting how they implode the means by which we communicate, and the hackneyed aural and visual vocabulary we employ in doing so; see Neil Hamburger, or Tim and Eric of Cartoon Network's late-night Adult Swim programming). These folks didn't invent conceptual humor, but they're taking it in bracing new directions.

The indie-comedy movement has only gained momentum as it has evolved over the last decade, paralleling the growth of other art forms that hungrily sank their teeth into the Internet, eschewing or toying with old models of communication and kinship. Even in 1996, *New York Times* writer Neil Strauss witnessed the stirrings of New York's DIY comedy scene as it mutated from what was then considered alternative comedy. "This is an evolution of a new kind of comedy, and it's time for it to happen," Rick Newman, owner of the legendary comedy club Catch a Rising Star, told Strauss. "It's still in the early stages, but you're going to see people who in two years are going to be your new Seinfelds and Paul Reisers and Steve Martins."

An overstatement, perhaps, but in order to understand the concept of indie comedy, we need a coherent definition of indie rock. That proves difficult, since savvy corporations and crappy musicians have since the turn of the century drained indie rock of its once-positive connotations. The phrase didn't begin life as a hipster signifier, but rather as a term that crawled out of the Reagan era, an abbreviation of *independent* as that phrase related to underground, post-punk rock 'n' roll. Problem is, the indie rock of today is a different animal than it was twenty years ago. It's a far more mainstream, diverse, co-opted, and confused beast than when it was first slapped on the ass and named, back when seminal acts such as The Minutemen, Hüsker Dü, Dinosaur Jr., Sonic Youth, and Mission of Burma were synonymous with its catchall, fanzine-and-college-radio-perpetuated usage.

New York writer John Sellers was forced to confront the creature early in his 2007 book, *Perfect from Now On: How Indie Rock Saved My Life.* "The phrase has become nebulous in this relatively recent era in which Borglike conglomerates have swallowed up labels once considered too insignificant to matter," he wrote, "and also because indie rock may be defined differently depending on whom you ask. Back in the early 1980s...things were relatively simple: you were either on an independent label or you weren't—and if you weren't, then you probably sucked, at least to die-hard fans of the genre. But then R.E.M. got popular. And Nirvana. So now confusion reigns."

It's true that indie music increasingly looks and acts like mainstream music, gaining acceptance from the same people who used to beat up its artists in high school (much like the commercial turn of alt-rock audiences in the nineties, when popularity both diluted and soured what made the music so good to begin with). It's not uncommon to hear formerly obscure acts like The Shins, Feist, Cat Power, Death Cab for Cutie, Modest Mouse, or Spoon on corporate radio stations and insipid TV commercials—acts who defined themselves in underground terms until ramming headfirst into walls of mainstream approval. Subsequently, many bands these days identify themselves as indie based purely on their sound, not on the way they do (or do not do) business.

Fortunately, the indie-comedy scene still takes legitimate creative chances, certainly more so than much of what's being marketed as indie rock and punk these days.

"Part of the energy I felt from punk rock as a kid was like, 'Wow, this seems dangerous. It's nothing I can buy in a store, it's nothing my parents approve of, and they're saying stuff that I can't believe they're saying,'" says Matt Besser, a founding member of the influential Upright Citizens Brigade troupe and theaters. "When

I saw Dead Kennedys' single 'Nazi Punks Fuck Off,' I couldn't believe that was the name of a band. These people were doing what they wanted and saying outrageous things! But independent music has lost a little bit of that, and I don't think anyone's amazed by music in that way anymore. They might be amazed by the musicality and the inventiveness of the band, but in terms of what they're doing and saying onstage? That whole aspect of it's gone away. I see that a lot more in stand-up and sketch videos these days. That kind of cool vibe that used to be in punk and indie rock is now in comedy." As Besser hints, indie rock has been reduced to a genre tag these days, not an implication of business practices or commercial nonaffiliation. It usually implies sensitive, smart, arch-melodic, willfully obscure, slacker, contrarian, guitar-based, lo-fi, college-rock, or, in many cases, self-indulgent and shitty, but not quite as shitty as emo.

However meaningless and occasionally hated indie has become as a musical descriptor, indie comedy is meant to convey the DIY ethic that has led to the practice of stand-up and sketch comedy on and around the indie-music circuit. As you'll read in these pages, other culture hounds are now getting their music fix from comedy, discovering the same pleasures of buildup, hold, and release in punch lines instead of riffs and melodies. Just like the best new music, the finest examples of this new comedy have either found a way to reinvigorate classic forms or have kept the experimental, fuck-all, punk rock ethos alive, as opposed to stumbling into a quirky romantic comedy soundtrack or car ad.

Certainly, just lending your song to a commercial or Hollywood enterprise doesn't make you a sellout. Everyone needs to eat, and holding onto some misguided notion of authenticity for its own sake is impractical and irritatingly idealistic. But the comedians in this scene who refuse to compromise their art, such as David Cross, also tend to get labeled as having more punk-rock cred—for better or worse. The larger world of which they're a part also enjoys warranted credibility for its general ambivalence toward sitcom stardom and regular spots on *The Tonight Show*.

These comedians have taken matters into their own hands, partly inspired by the ill-defined alternative music and comedy movement of the early 1990s, opting to work outside sanctioned institutions and root for new audiences on their own provisos. This diverse, growing segment appropriates and vertically integrates indie music's means of production, distribution, and exhibition without edging out its product, using indie rock's tool belt to conquer new environments in its own creative frontier. In other words, indie comedians often play music venues instead of (or in addition to) comedy clubs, speaking directly to an audience who specifically came to see them—an audience who follows them as one would his or her favorite band. These comedians increasingly release their albums on respected independent music labels such as Sub Pop, Drag City, Relapse, Matador, and Suicide Squeeze. They perform at and emcee showcases at music festivals like South by Southwest, Bonnaroo, Coachella, Bumbershoot, and Sasquatch.

And they often tour and play with bands. Duh.

The Hipster Handbook, Robert Lanham's tongue-in-cheek illustrated guide to all things cool (or "deck," as he wrote at the time—what a shame that hideous term never caught on outside Williamsburg, Brooklyn, after 2003), noted Janeane Garofalo and Sarah Silverman among the top twenty-five female celebrities on which hipsters have crushes. The list also included musicians PJ Harvey, Meg White, and Miho Hatori of Cibo Matto, plus various actresses and filmmakers. (Oddly, no male stand-ups made the list, but we'll let Conan O'Brien, Jon

Stewart, and Ben Stiller count anyway. If the book were written today, it's a good bet David Cross and Michael Cera of Fox's ill-fated *Arrested Development* would be on there, as well as moppy Comedy Central regular Demetri Martin, Jemaine and Bret from HBO's *Flight of the Conchords*, and maybe even Zach Galifianakis, our very own Fat Jesus.)

The point of the list was that it was safe for hipsters to have comedy idols, to obsessively discuss and dissect comedy as they would their favorite music. This has always been true within certain segments of the music-loving world—especially among musicians themselves—but for many years, being infatuated with most of what passed for stand-up comedy in the United States was about as cool as masturbating to Pat Boone.

To understand this loose, expanding scene of performers, we'll look at their historical context and the media disseminating their work, because the general relationship between comedy and music goes back farther than many of us realize (even to the dawn of Western culture, if you want to get macro about it). In some ways, stand-up comedy has always been inextricable from other genres of modern stage entertainment, particularly the vaudeville tradition. But more and more, the subculture this book studies has utilized information-age mainstays like social networking sites, digital video, and podcasts to spread and reinforce its message, or to subtly blur the boundaries between traditional commentary and parody. The comedy profiles on MySpace, for example, allow Maria Bamford fans in Casper, Wyoming, or Xenia, Ohio, to connect virtually with the comedian herself or create their own humor and post it for every last mother to see.

The bite-sized forms that comedy has increasingly taken are also influencing its content and accessibility.

For guidance, we can look to Bill Ivey and Steven Tepper's excellent *Engaging Art*. The book takes a broad view of contemporary performing arts participation, asserting that new inventions inevitably change the way artists operate, begetting new styles (impressionism, dime novels, rock 'n' roll) and forms (photography, synth music). "But perhaps even more far reaching," wrote Tepper, Eszter Hargittai, and David Touve in the book's "Music, Mavens, and Technology" chapter, "new technologies have dramatically changed the market for art, typically leading to expanded audiences with access to more diverse cultural fare." For people who take their comedy seriously and consider it an art form as much as entertainment, it's significant that our instant, 24/7 access to diverse styles of comedy (both new and old) has created not only a marketplace to exchange that cultural capital, but has also encouraged people's own responses to it, whether by engaging in dialogue about said content or crafting their own videos with their laptop's shitty digital video software.

Of course, funny is funny, regardless of some notion of a preferred audience or technological gateway. The best comedians transcend their environments, keeping the focus squarely on the material or concept, not on whatever scene an overzealous Denver-based writer is attempting to nail them to. The ultimate goal for comedians who truly love performing is to be able to play anywhere—preferably with some regularity and financial guarantee. If that's a rock club, fine. If that's a theater, fine. As long as people are creating an environment conducive to appreciating the art. "Any comedian's dream is to be able to show up in any city and every person's there to see them, specifically," says comedian Christian Finnegan, who has played mainstream comedy clubs, alternative rooms, and music festivals. "That's really when you can do the purest version of yourself. People already assume you're funny, and you can do what you want. Whereas when you're coming up, you have to let people relax right off the top of the bat. It's like, 'Sit back and enjoy yourself, 'cause you're not going to be uncomfortable for the next hour.' You want to hit them hard and quick right up top."

Most mainstream comedy clubs took that approach too much to heart, becoming factories where people are herded into seats to guzzle booze and have comedy "administered" to them, as *Chunklet* editor and *Comedians of Comedy* tour manager Henry Owings has said. Founded by stand-up veteran Patton Oswalt, the *Comedians of Comedy* tour played rock clubs instead of comedy clubs in the mid- to late 2000s, acting as an equal-opportunity showcase for some of Oswalt's favorite talent, and swiftly earning all involved enough indie-rock points to win the hipster equivalent of the giant stuffed bear at Chuck E. Cheese. (The giant stuffed Stephen Malkmus, perhaps?)

And though I risk ghettoizing certain performers by pegging them as indie, or at least identifying them as overlapping with that scene, it's undeniable that a certain swath of stand-up comedy has moved into a new phase in the later years of this decade. Something legitimately different has been happening since the alternative-comedy movement of the nineties, and it has successfully picked the lock that mainstream clubs formerly enjoyed on the stand-up world. Wherever you look, from music festivals to record labels, websites to late-night TV shows, a certain type of smart, gleefully warped comedy has begun to assert itself as the new vanguard. "The type of performers [comedy clubs] book are safe, and some very gifted performers aren't getting work at those venues," says Geof Wills, president of Live Nation Comedy. "So you could say some of the comics coming up feel more comfortable in a bar or a drinking atmosphere than they would in a comedy club. There's no bachelorette parties sitting around. It's a bit freer for them to do what they want to do...they're coddled a bit more, because that audience is there just to see them. Whereas with a comedy club you've got a bunch of morons showing up just for laughs or to heckle someone. Which isn't to say they don't book great acts, [just that] they're not particularly nurturing places. They want every seat full."

Wills offers that many of the comedians he has booked—including Dave Chappelle, Janeane Garofalo, Sarah Silverman, and Demetri Martin—have been willing to take pay cuts in order to chase a better vibe at a nontraditional venue. "They find [comedy clubs] a bit sterile, and they don't want to be put in the same boat as everyone else that comes through. To me it's part of their identity. You've heard that cliché that all comedians want to be musicians and all musicians want to be comedians? I know a lot of stand-up comics, alternative and mainstream, and a large amount of them wish they were in a rock band. Dave Chappelle said the other day, 'Man, I just want to do a show where I just sing.' In *Block Party* [a movie that features Chappelle's favorite hip-hop acts] you can see how he always plays "Round Midnight.'"

Even as comedians are leaking out of comedy clubs and into nontraditional venues, some things haven't changed quickly enough. Like all stand-up of the last several decades (and much of the indie and punk world that indie comedy emulates), the most visible members of this movement are largely young and middle-aged white males. Of course, the group I'm studying here is notably more self-conscious about its lack of racial and gender diversity, owing to its generally liberal and, occasionally, libertarian political beliefs. Progressive male comedians of color such as Aziz Ansari, Reggie Watts, Jasper Redd, and Ian Edwards might be less visible on the scene, but they're there, and a growing number of women such as Maria Bamford, Morgan Murphy, Kristen Schaal, Jen Kirkman, Natasha Leggero, Chelsea Peretti, and Melinda Hill are stealing some of the spotlight from contemporary go-to female stand-ups like Sarah Silverman, Chelsea Handler, Lisa Lampanelli, and Kathy Griffin— and they're encouraging other voices in the process.

The taboo of being unladylike, whether it's in Silverman's shock-value material or Lampanelli's salty, Don Ricklesesque approach still possesses a certain cultural cachet, trading on stereotypical ideas of what it means to be a proper woman. But by breaking down and inverting that cachet, the more visible female comedians are making it safe for up-and-comers to say whatever they please—and not be chided for it. If that means talking about "women's topics" like their time of the month, what huge assholes guys can be, or the vicissitudes of motherhood, then so be it. "I think it's not as much of an issue," says comedian, writer, and *E!* regular Chelsea Handler. "Women are getting away with so much more than we were ever getting away with before. You look at people like us going out and saying things ten or fifteen years ago that we wouldn't have been able to get away with. Yeah, there is a stigma to it. Some people are totally put off by it. But now more than ever female comedians are saying the things they want to."

Of course, backward cultural critiques like Christopher Hitchens's January 2007 *Vanity Fair* article, "Why Women Aren't Funny," don't exactly chip away at the perception that there are fewer female comedians because women are naturally unfunny. Hitchens blithely cites a Stanford University School of Medicine report that studied how women's brains respond differently to comic stimulus than men's. "Slower to get it, more pleased when they do, and swift to locate the unfunny—for this we need the Stanford University School of Medicine?" he wrote. "And remember, this is women when confronted with humor. Is it any wonder that they are backward in generating it?"

Hitchens's essay is part of a larger problem, subconsciously reinforcing notions that women should be dainty, quiet creatures who observe more than they create, or who at least shouldn't bother trying to go into fields that men have seemingly mastered. "There are more terrible female comedians than there are terrible male comedians," he continued, "but there are some impressive ladies out there. Most of them, though, when you come to review the situation, are hefty or dykey or Jewish, or some combo of the three."

Right. What year is this?

Hitchens's not-so-subtle misogyny is part of what makes female comedy or women comedians a subcategory on many comedy websites, tossing them in with other groupings such as dick jokes, religion, and bathroom humor. It's abundantly obvious that men and women are different, and that there are fewer popular, visible female comedians than male. Yes, ladies, we want to fuck you. That's nature. But does that automatically mean we require an unequivocal approach to every other aspect of our personalities? Does that mean my girlfriend doesn't love a show like *Tom Goes to the Mayor* as much as I do, or that your daughter doesn't possess the same basic mental tools to craft a hilarious joke? Only the myopic and self-obsessed fail to see that theories of gender and race inferiority are self-sustaining, culturally and historically specific figure eights.

"Female comedians are out there, they're just not recognized," says Maria Bamford, who recently enjoyed a surge in popularity due to the *Comedians of Comedy* tours and films. Her website includes links to nearly eighty female stand-up comedians—and those are just the ones she can name off the top of her head. "People are like, 'Why aren't there more Native American or Asian comedians?' There are, it's just that they're not chosen. Which sucks."

It doesn't help when popular female comedians like Lisa Lampanelli gleefully celebrate their Howard Stern–style lack of political correctness by agreeing with Hitchens and asserting that there are, in fact, fewer funny female comedians as a matter of course. She has charged that most female stand-ups' subject matter is exclusive, boring, or relationship-oriented, which tends to alienate male audiences (and which also implies that it's all women really want to talk/hear about). What she and others don't see is that the generalization ignores any type of female comedy that isn't touchy-feely or that deals with subjects outside stereotypically female topics. What's worse, it's akin to noting the scarcity of black politicians a hundred years ago or gay middle school teachers today, and interpreting that lack as an inherent genetic failing instead of a cultural and historical one. Stand-up pioneer Elayne Boosler may have been the only female headlining club comic of the 1970s, but she did it "without putting down her sex or playing into men's stereotypes," as Richard Zoglin wrote in his book *Comedy at the Edge.*

Boosler chopped away at the inanity of cultural detritus we already took for granted as dumb, but that we never bothered to articulate as such. Take her pithy rendering of *Playboy* magazine during a TV appearance on *The Comedy Shop* in the 1970s:

"They never want you to think the pictures are posed, right? 'We just happened to catch Kathy typing—nude on top of a Volvo in a field this morning...' Maybe I'm sheltered. I just don't know anybody who takes a shower in a baseball cap and kneesocks. See, the bad thing about

Playboy [is that] it gives men the wrong idea about what women do when we're home alone. Makes you think we all sit on the couch, very introspective, like this [pretends to cup her right breast while stretching her jaw suggestively]. And the captions are *so* believable. Underneath that it always says: 'Kathy likes to read to orphans and is studying to be a dental hygienist.' What kind of job can she get later on? 'Hi, I can type with one hand!'"

And this is to say nothing of the countless female stage comedians who influenced popular culture in ways we're still only beginning to appreciate, such as Elaine May, Joan Rivers, Phyllis Diller, or Lily Tomlin, or the contemporary ones working largely outside the stand-up circuit, on TV and in film (Tina Fey, Amy Poehler, Amy Sedaris, etc.). "Stand-up comedy was always harder for women, because it is aggressive—comedians have to dominate their audiences and 'kill,' by common metaphor," wrote Alessandra Stanley, the television critic for *The New York Times*, in her *Vanity Fair*–published response to Hitchens's essay. "Women either had to compete—head-on, in the aggressive style of Paula Poundstone or Lisa Lampanelli—or subvert the form and make themselves offbeat and likable, the way that Whoopi Goldberg and Ellen DeGeneres do. As Elaine May used to say regarding improv, 'When in doubt, seduce.' By and large, however, stand-up comedy is tougher and meaner, and the women who do it play by men's rules."

I'm not proposing that the indie-comedy scene or stand-up in general has made great strides in the arena of gender rights, or that it even needs to. Political correctness and speechifying are the downfall of good humor, and the comedians I'm writing about are not interested in delivering group hugs or finger-wagging sermons on inclusiveness and tolerance. If anything, their progressive attitudes are more implied than stated, serving as staging grounds for attacks on hypocrisy, inanity, and everyday bullshit of any stripe. Anyone with a basic understanding of stand-up knows that comedy with a sacred cow is not good comedy.

But more so than at any time in the past, the current indie-comedy scene has leveled the playing field by removing preconceptions about material and presentation and by jettisoning all rules and restrictions but one: just be funny.

At its heart, *Mock Stars* is less a historical account of the indie-comedy scene's birth and growth than a collection of profiles on the artists who have made it safe for the newcomers, the ones just beginning to gravitate toward the profession without having to climb the typical club ladder and get out in front of the potato skins night after night. These are the people carrying the spark from the alt-comedy torch, cauterizing the wounds from stand-up's painful 1980s boom and bust (the same cycle that gave it such a stale reputation to begin with), and the ones helping to keep the art form vital by, mercifully, speaking to an audience in its own language.

It wasn't always this way. Until the mid-1960s, the most visible, popular forms of stand-up comedy typically existed as soft, reassuring radio and TV programming or nightclub entertainment. It had the potential to be subtly smart and conceptual, and pockets of experimentation existed throughout the country before and during that time period. But overall, the most readily accessible forms of stand-up and sketch comedy failed to challenge their audiences' expectations or provoke much thought. During the later part of the 1960s and throughout the

1970s, however, we began to associate edgy voices such as Richard Pryor and George Carlin with the larger world of stand-up; personalities influenced by the stream-of-consciousness style of Lenny Bruce; people who talked openly about race, sex, drugs, and anything else on their restless, coke-addled minds. Experimental sketch and improv troupes in Chicago, Toronto, New York, San Francisco, and elsewhere began to offer relatable, democratic takes on everyday life and politics that didn't require a cocktail, dinner jacket, or upper-tax-bracket status to access. Improv geniuses such as Del Close, first with the Compass Players and then at various times with The Second City, cemented a performance and teaching aesthetic that came to define the current approach to improvisational comedy.

"Originally theater was considered cultural and effete, and experimental theater was Communist," says Matt Besser of the Upright Citizens Brigade. "That vibe got switched around in the 1960s by The Committee and The Second City. Improv started out as working-class theater, and I really believe it is that way. Much of improv theater throughout the US is still affordable and accessible to most people."

It wasn't a notion conjured from thin air: when producer David Shepherd founded the Compass Players in Chicago in 1955, he gathered inspiration from the concept of commedia dell'arte. That form had its footing in Renaissance Europe, particularly in Italy, as performers worked their way across the countrysides like the troubadours before them, putting on outdoor shows that traded in subjects familiar to followers of Greek and Roman comedies (mistaken identities, infidelity, etc.). The difference was that commedia shows did not stop at lighthearted clowning and slapstick. "They also had a satiric edge, burlesquing the venality, hypocrisy, cowardice, and stupidity of such traditional authority figures as doctors, merchants, and military officers," wrote Jeffrey Sweet in *Something Wonderful Right Away*, an oral history of early US improv troupes. "In their desire to connect with each particular audience, the cast would ad-lib topical references to local figures and issues. The commedia was popular theater in the truest sense." Indeed, members of the commedia-inspired Compass Players would eventually break off to form The Second City improv theater in 1959, which in turn helped birth a slew of 1970s comedy icons via television sketch shows such as *Saturday Night Live* and *SCTV*.

Stand-up's popularity explosion in the 1980s put the brakes on this democratic, progressive-leaning momentum by meeting demand with a lesser supply of quality, both in comedy clubs and on television. The rush of mediocre talent to the commercial gold mines embalmed a safe, bland performance aesthetic that still reigns in many people's minds. When that boom went bust in the late 1980s, the mainstream stand-up scene essentially resembled a ghost town. Some critics have charged that stand-up comedy is still that shuttered, wind-whipped burg it was twenty years ago, or that quality comedy has nowhere left to go these days, other than to the history books. They prefer to hail the times when comics sold millions of albums, topped charts, and held the same pop-culture renown as The Rolling Stones and Andy Warhol, or enjoyed as much sway over the perception of race and gender issues as social justice movements in the black, female, and gay communities.

But hearing someone assert that comedy has nowhere left to go is akin to hearing your grandpa cry, "Shut up!" from the living room while you play noisily with your cousins in the basement. Excitement, risk, and innovation are alive and kicking in comedy, whether some critics recognize it or not. And while it's easy to take shots at *Time, Rolling Stone, The New York Times,* and other media outlets for their occasional obliviousness to whatever's beneath the surface of a given art form, it's also important to remember they help supply and shape many Americans' cultural predilections. Which is to say don't believe the hype that stand-up comedy begins and ends with Jerry Seinfeld, or with relative upstarts/commercial phenoms Dane Cook, Dave Chappelle, and Carlos Mencia. If anything, the larger world of comedy has experienced a surge of popularity over the past decade thanks to the efficient branding of cable network Comedy Central, the multiplicity of online humor channels and offerings, and the larger sociocultural cynicism at the hands of an inept, corrupt, self-interested White House.

Disavow yourself from the notion that cutting-edge humor is all about cheap fireworks and profanity, or that men are the only ones telling good jokes. Taking a classic approach to skewering absurdities (Louis C. K., Paul F. Tompkins), pushing the limits of logic and coherence while indulging one's own sense of humor (Kristen Schaal and Kurt Braunohler, or Adult Swim's *Tim and Eric Awesome Show, Great Job!*), or crafting inclusive, painfully hilarious, deadpan bits (Morgan Murphy, Tig Notaro, Reggie Watts) rarely requires a loud voice or filthy vocabulary.

Before you throw rotten fruit at my apartment window, there is also this potentially obvious caveat: there are dozens of established and emerging comedians of every type whom I failed to interview or include in this book because it's simply too gargantuan a task, people who could easily pack a rock club, art gallery, theater, or chat room or who would fit the progressive and possibly experimental definition I've laid out. The deeper you dig, the more examples you find of the seemingly endless overlaps of indie music and a certain swath of comedians. These are people who conduct quality comedy nights in hot spots like New York, Los Angeles, Chicago, San Francisco, Seattle, and elsewhere—people who have every right to a loving audience and critical appreciation, and who in many cases are starting to find one. The comedy world is rich and diverse, and this book only focuses on one segment of it. I'm just profiling the biggest, most recognizable names of the current independent-comedy scene in the United States, as well as those upstarts who have grabbed some of the national spotlight (even if that light's shining out from a blog or digital video site).

Mock Stars is not meant as a gap-filler for any particular historical account of comedy, nor does it assert that the comedians profiled within its pages have changed popular culture in the same way that icons Lenny Bruce, Richard Pryor, Steve Martin, George Carlin, or Jerry Seinfeld did. The comedy scene I'm writing about is a largely underground one, and unless the ill-defined heartland starts snapping up David Cross and Patton Oswalt albums by the truckload, it will likely stay that way.

But I am arguing that the comedians who have emerged from the creative wreckage of the past twenty years are equally as fearless and relevant to stand-up as the trailblazers of the 1970s, reshaping the art form in their own image and for their own purposes. "There was a time in the late eighties where anything like what we're doing now was alternative," says *Mr. Show* cocreator Bob Odenkirk. "But I do think over the last ten years there's just been a gradual spreading out of attention for comedy so that it's not all focused on a few little places. Some of what we call alternative just has more venues now, like the Internet, alternative rooms, the *Comedians of Comedy* tour, and *Tim and Eric* on Adult Swim. It's still very much a niche market, but the niche has gotten big enough to be noticed."

Call it what you want, but whatever's bubbling underneath the surface one day often empties into the mainstream the next. My aim with this book is not to flash-freeze particular performers or stamp their foreheads with a cutesy logo. This is a compositional reading of the comedy world's fertile underground, which in turn nourishes the rest of stand-up by sprouting strange, colorful new organisms who hungrily seek out new brains for sustenance—yours, preferably.

Bret McKenzie (left) and Jemaine Clement (right)
of New Zealand comedy-music duo Flight of the Conchords.
Photo by Amelia Handscomb, courtesy of Sub Pop Records

1

SHAKING HANDS WITH MUSIC

Whether we realize it or not, we're culturally hardwired to equate popular stand-up comedians with rock stars. Outlaws, icons of cool, antiestablishment voices—all hallmarks of a distinctly American attitude from cowboys and jazz musicians to the US side of the punk-rock movement. But it was during the 1970s stand-up renaissance that we were acquainted with the concept of comedian not just as star, but *rock* star, with the attendant screaming fans, picturesque stage silhouettes, and sex- and drug-fueled lifestyles. When comedians play to thousands of amped-up souls on a gigantic stage normally reserved for pyrotechnics and fog machines, it's difficult to see them any other way.

"To me [Richard Pryor] was as significant in comedy as Bob Dylan and Paul Simon, or The Beatles or The Rolling Stones," *Saturday Night Live* creator Lorne Michaels told Richard Zoglin in *Comedy at the Edge*. "It elevated the seriousness, the importance, of what we were doing in comedy." Of course, back then it was a much dicier proposition for a comedian to open for a musician, the audience set up to passively absorb or (in some cases) dance and sing to a wall of aural stimulus, not pay attention to some lone schlub talking about whatever was bugging him at the moment about airplane food, race relations, or blowjobs.

"Comedians were sacrificial lambs," says Bob Mehr, a music writer at *Commercial Appeal* in Memphis, Tennessee. He notes that the worst examples of comedy-music pairings have made it seem that the two were somehow antithetical. And there's truth in that separation: countless comedians have related the considerable perils of opening for a musical act. If audiences are not expecting jokes with their riffs, they won't pay the same attention that they would at a club or theater, often turning against the stand-up and souring the mood for the rest of the night. There are obvious differences between either art form that work to keep them apart.

Nirvana fans, for example, pelted Bobcat Goldthwait with M-80s, shoes, beer-soaked blue jeans, miniature Bibles, and even an unlucky audience member when Goldthwait attempted to open for the band in Chicago. "No amount of comedy-club heckler training could ever have prepared me for the sight of a pie-eyed teenager flying toward me," he wrote in 2006's *I Killed*, a compendium of road stories edited by comics Ritch Shydner and Mark Schiff. "He struck me square in the back and the crowd roared." After the set, security guards were forced to place a towel over Goldthwait's head and ferry him to a waiting van, which rushed him to O'Hare Airport. "I remember passing Kurt Cobain, who was watching from the side of the stage," Goldthwait continued. "He was laughing his ass off. Of course, he hired me for the rest of the tour. It always paid to make the band laugh." (See also comedian

Neil Hamburger's rocky stint opening for Tenacious D in 2006, detailed in chapter seven.)

A glance at comedy-music pairings over the last century, however, reveals that comedians were not always so incompatible with musicians. Often they were considered as important to the meal as the main dish, providing a valuable contrast that emphasized the headliner's unique flavor (or that acted, in some cases, as a palate cleanser). The variety show approach that vaudeville codified in the late nineteenth and early twentieth centuries worked well when the comedy complemented the music. The widening leisure class in the mid-twentieth century supported breezy—and spectacularly popular—comedy-music pairings such as Jerry Lewis and Dean Martin, and Don Rickles and Frank Sinatra. *The Smothers Brothers Comedy Hour*, helmed by mild-mannered musical-comedy duo Tommy and Dick, welcomed The Doors and Pete Seeger onto their slyly subversive program during the Vietnam era. Peter Sellers recorded a parody of The Beatles' "A Hard Day's Night" in the *Richard III*-style of Laurence Olivier (a bone-dry version that became an improbable Top 20 hit in the UK in 1965). Even before that, Richard Pryor, George Carlin, Robert Klein, and other stand-ups would perform at folk-music clubs in New York's Greenwich Village. Richard Zoglin noted in *Comedy at the Edge* that David Steinberg, a prolific comedian who went on to direct episodes of *Curb Your Enthusiasm* and other shows, used to open for musicians Carly Simon and Tom Paxton in the 1970s.

The rock-comedy gig seemed ubiquitous in the seventies: Albert Brooks sometimes preceded Neil Diamond or Sly and the Family Stone, Jay Leno opened for Kris Kristofferson and Linda Ronstadt at jazz clubs, and Steve Martin opened for The Nitty Gritty Dirt Band (among many others). Zoglin went as far as to propose a "spiritual link" between rock music and comedy that epitomized their seventies-era pairing, with future rockers such as Pat Benatar getting discovered at open-mic nights at New York's Catch a Rising Star.

"Oh yeah, we opened up for The Rolling Stones," says Tommy Chong, one half of the wildly successful stoner-comedy duo Cheech & Chong. "That was our debut gig in LA at the Forum. We opened up for the Stones but we also used to share bills with Alice Cooper, Steely Dan, Santana, Harry Chapin—tons of people. Although we played with the Allman Brothers right after Duane died, and we got heckled by the crowd. They kept yelling, 'Where's Duane? Where's Duane?!'" Chong says the splintering of music into even more specialized genres helped stop the trend dead in its tracks. "What happened with music is that at one time there was just rock and blues, and then all of sudden there's everything: funk, rock, punk, and hip-hop. It was so diversified that a comedian wouldn't stand a chance opening. But it's probably going back, because everything is cyclical."

It wasn't surprising that comedians in the 1970s followed the lead of many musicians and styled themselves as antiauthoritarian rebels. Each took shots at corrupt people and situations, casting themselves as social justice warriors in causes ranging from racial and gender equality to marijuana legalization. The framework that separated comedy from music (and either from social activism) seemed more artificial than it was, failing to take into account that stand-up, regardless of where it was performed, only needed the proper context and expectations to be taken seriously—just like music.

"That's a big challenge for comedians," says Jesse Thorn, host of public radio's *The Sound of Young America*, a show that has welcomed hundreds of comedians and musicians over the years. "In music you're drawing people to hear things that they've already heard. They're getting an enhanced version of their favorite album. In comedy it doesn't really work that way. Comedy often needs to come from surprise."

Thorn offered the example of Cure fans listening to their favorite Cure albums hundreds—if not thousands—of times, whereas Richard Pryor fans may not derive the same satisfaction listening to Pryor's groundbreaking live albums, because the jokes will have been thoroughly memorized. "That's the key difference between music and comedy," he says. "Comedians who perform material on television, for example, often consider it to have been 'burned,' so it's done. They won't perform it again. As a comedian, you have to work really hard to create a brand for yourself so you can draw people to see stuff they haven't seen you do before."

Some unlikely comedians carry the rock-star status, even if most people don't think of them that way. Penn Jillette, one half of the morbid magic-comedy duo Penn & Teller, said that old-guard icon Don Rickles easily stands among his other rock-star champs. "After I'd seen Don, it turned out the people that were my heroes were like The Velvet Underground, Iggy Pop & the Stooges, Bob Dylan, Houdini, and Don Rickles," he said in the Rickles documentary *Mr. Warmth*.

Rickles is just one of a handful of fifties- and sixties-era comedians indelibly linked with music. He has frequently employed a touring musical band, including on his various stints opening for The Rat Pack. Some members of his band have even been with him for decades, as much a part of his act as the material.

Comedian Sarah Silverman also counts Rickles as an influence, saying he helped her feel less alien growing up Jewish in New Hampshire. Rickles's "nothing is sacred" comedy, as Mario Cantone calls it in *Mr. Warmth*, may have been offensive for its own sake, but crowds usually got an equal-opportunity drubbing, regardless of gender, race, and age. It was a scorched-earth approach to the crowd that hinted at a nihilism boiling just beneath the surface—just like in punk rock. "Billy West, a wonderful voiceover talent, said years later to me that there was one show business," Jillette continued in *Mr. Warmth.* "And Bach and porno stars and the guy in the Santa suit at the mall and Scorsese all have the exact same job. But seeing Don Rickles with that kind of intensity and that weird combination that you can see in the Sex Pistols and the vital need to please, coupled with the unwillingness to bend at all in order to accomplish that, was life-changing. And all of a sudden things just broke down to Iggy Pop, The Velvet Underground, The Ramones, and Don Rickles. (They) were the same. Identical."

To some, Rickles may represent a rock 'n' roll comedian; an artist who ignored barriers and plowed ahead with a fiercely individual (and offensive) sense of creativity and craft. But few, if any, sane stand-ups would identify themselves as rock 'n' roll comedians—and fewer still as indie comedians. Classifying something automatically limits it and, as my friend and colleague Ricardo Baca, the pop music critic at *The Denver Post,* likes to say, "Artists hate to have their art quantified." With good reason: they don't create it for overeducated, nitpicky writers to dissect and categorize, they create it to share with an audience, to forge a connection, to communicate some innate truth about the human experience—and millions of other god-awful reasons.

But classifications can be useful. Differences exist in the style and approach of, say, the music of Guided By Voices and Elliott Smith. Guided By Voices lead singer Robert Pollard never fully embraced his externally imposed designation as an indie rocker, preferring his project to be known simply as a rock band, whereas the late Elliott Smith hewed closer to the singer-songwriter camp (albeit a dark, fucked-up sleepover camp that managed to get its hands on some smack). But identifying them both as indie rock allows for a certain utility in discussion, especially in contrast to artists who they are stylistically antithetical to, such as Toby Keith (pop country), Kenny G (smooth jazz), Celine Dion (adult contemporary), or the myriad others who most hipsters would be loathe to embrace without a sweet, suffocating blanket of irony. Guided By Voices trafficked in melodic, guitar-based, sixties- and seventies-influenced rock (or the "four Ps," as Pollard liked to say when his band still existed—pop, prog, punk, and psychedelic). Elliott Smith's music came across like a mash of George Harrison, Cat Stevens, Nick Drake, and a bottle of Nyquil-spiked St. Ides. Different, sure, but both firmly in the indie-rock camp, and not just because the artists took it upon themselves to craft careers outside the mainstream.

But what exactly is a rock 'n' roll comedian? Is it someone who has watched *This Is Spinal Tap* fifty times? Clearly just having a guitar or singing ability does not make you a rock 'n' roll comedian, and just calling yourself one does not make it so. And if you do, well, you probably suck. To that extent, it's easy to find examples of what a rock 'n' roll comedian is *not*. Stephen Lynch plays acoustic guitar and skewers rock clichés in his songs, but his sensibility is less antiestablishment than it is goofy, playing off "tee-hee" moments in tunes about being Jesus' brother, who's *totally* not as cool as Jesus but who still likes to party. (All right! Yeah...oh wait. No. Sorry.) There's also the Musical Comedians of Comedy tour, which bears no relation to the Patton Oswalt–founded *Comedians of Comedy*. Michael Mack, Ron Feingold, and Kier (the last one has one name, just like Cher!) play middling, cheesy musical parodies and often employ audience clap-alongs and props, cardinal sins in many comedy circles.

Prior to the scene this book examines, comedian Bill Hicks probably enjoyed more credibility in punk and underground rock circles than almost any other. His act veered from philosophical, antireligious material to his drug experiences and loathing of fundamentalists, conservatives, hacks, and generally narrow-minded souls. ("The comedy of hate," as he called it.) His rants were meant to roil staid crowds and make the experience more participatory than passive and entertaining, and his expert inflection, timing, and body language made it seem effortless. "By the way," he said gently during one set, crossing the stage, wearing black pants and a black shirt, "if anybody here is in marketing or advertising, kill yourself...You are Satan's spawn filling the world with bile and garbage. You are fucked and you are fucking us. Kill yourself. It's the only way to save your fucking soul. *Kill yourself.*" Later in the same set, he rails against antidrug musicians, the kind approved by the government and soft drink companies: "And these other musicians today who don't do drugs and in fact speak out against them? Boooooy do they suck. What a coincidence! Ball-less, soulless, spiritless, corporate little bitches. Suckers of Satan's cock, each and every one of them." Perhaps unsurprisingly, his material got him banned from the Ed Sullivan Theater after an appearance on *The Late Show with David Letterman* in 1993.

A passage in Shydner and Schiff's *I Killed* recounts the time Hicks and fellow comedian Ron Shock dropped acid before a set at a "redneck discotheque" in Lake Charles, Louisiana. Even before taking the stage, various patrons flashed their firearms at the comedians, threatening that they'd better be funny—or else. As people's faces appeared to mutate into lizards and demons while Hicks stepped onstage, an audience member unplugged his microphone. "A sober Bill would have lost it at that point, but tripping Bill went past threatening them and into assaulting everything they held dear and their entire way of life," Shock wrote. "It was brilliantly funny, not that any of those people understood anything other than that they were fighting words." Hicks even tried his hand at music on the *Marblehead Johnson* album and went on to open for prog-metal band Tool during their Lollapalooza stops in 1993. (He often asked the audience to stand and look for a contact lens he had lost. Many obliged.) Tool and Radiohead have dedicated albums to him, and music label Rykodisc reissued a slew of his CDs.

Sam Kinison also affected a coarse, outsider persona during his 1980s heyday, appealing to druggies, bikers, and pissed-off fucks in general, handily earning him the rock 'n' roll comedian tag alongside people such as Andrew Dice Clay. Kinison, in fact, was often tagged as a heavy-metal comedian, sometimes performing with a touring band. His novelty version of The Troggs's "Wild Thing" included notable members of Aerosmith, Bon Jovi, Guns N' Roses, Mötley Crüe, and others.

But as much as people wanted to apply the rock 'n' roll comedian term to some stand-ups, it didn't always stick. "I think there's a reason why that stopped," David Cross told *The Stranger*'s Sean Nelson in 2002, "and it was a good reason, which is that it wasn't a good idea. It was embraced in the eighties because there was all this fucking bullshit talk in *Esquire* about comedy becoming the new rock 'n' roll...but it wasn't done right."

British DJ and BBC regular Phill Jupitus nodded toward the cyclical nature of the media proclamations in a 2008 piece for *The (London) Times Online* called "Comedy is the new rock 'n' roll (again)." Jupitus, who had performed poetry and comedy with UK musicians Billy

Bragg, Paul Weller, and others, noted that British funny-men Norman Lovett and Keith Allen also played with The Clash and Dexys Midnight Runners, respectively. "There has always been a symbiosis between bands and comedians," he wrote. "The Stones loved hanging out with comics such as John Belushi and comics loved hanging out with the Stones. You'd always see a comedian at rock parties." The current incarnation, according to Jupitus, is the "unbelievably hip" Noel Fielding of the British sketch show *The Mighty Boosh*. Fielding, he said, frequently looks like he should be fronting his own band.

During the peak of his career, American comedian Mitch Hedberg won considerable love in underground music circles—and not just because he looked the part. Scenes from a Comedy Central special at the Palace in Los Angeles offer insight into why geeks and rockers related to him: early in the set he talks about his neighbor banging on his apartment wall to get Hedberg to turn his music down. "And that made me angry," Hedberg says, "because I like loud music. So when he'd knock on the wall I'd mess with his head. I'd say, 'Go around. I cannot open the wall. I don't know if you have a doorknob on the other side, but over here there's nothin'. [pause] It's just *flat*.'" The material is funny enough on its own, but its repeat-listen value lies in the awkwardly deliberate delivery that Hedberg perfected. Mild jokes become unexpectedly brilliant when stamped out with the delicacy of a bricklayer: "I like an escalator, man, because an escalator can never break. It can only *become* stairs. [pause] There would never be an 'Escalator Temporarily Out of Order' sign. Only an 'Escalator Temporarily Stairs: Sorry for the Convenience.'" His careful pronunciation hybridizes a stereotypical stoner and a reformed nerd fighting a stutter. He doesn't slur or go slowly, he simply skips certain syllables and leans on others for effect. (He also looked the part, his wide, tinted sunglasses, long brown hair, and shaggy-thin beard often casting him as an errant member of The Allman Brothers Band circa 1973.)

Some of Hedberg's jokes use rock as a backdrop for fundamentally non-rock-related one-liners. Others poke fun at rock conventions, as when Hedberg invokes hard-rock band Monster Magnet: "I went to a concert in New York City where I live. It was a heavy-metal band called Monster Magnet. They were *heavy*, boy. The singer had no shirt on and leather pants and he was playing like a Flying V guitar, and he stood on the monitor and he yells at the crowd. He says, 'How many of you people feel like human beings tonight?' And then he said, 'How many of you people feel like animals?' And the thing is, everyone cheered after the animals part. But I cheered after the human beings part, because I did not know there was a second part to the question. [pause] I said, 'Yes, I do feel like a human. I do not feel like a tree.'"

Anyone could get the joke, but a Monster Magnet fan would both get it *and* appreciate Hedberg's taste, since he easily could have chosen another, more popular group. On his Palace special he relates the experience of playing in a death-metal band: "A lot of death-metal bands have intense names, like Rigormortis or Mortuary or Obituary. We weren't that intense. We just went with Injured. Later on we changed it to A Cappella...as we were walking out of the pawnshop. [pause] We became a death-metal barbershop quartet." He also balances the surreal with the scientific: "You know when you go to concerts, like punk rock, and the kids get onstage and they jump into the crowd—stage diving? People think that's dangerous. But not me, because humans are made out of ninety-five percent water, so the audience is five percent away from a pool."

Like Hicks and Kinison, Hedberg died relatively young, accidentally overdosing on drugs in 2005. Hicks succumbed to pancreatic cancer in 1994; Kinison was hit by a seventeen-year-old drunk driver in 1992. All were notorious substance abusers.

I remember watching Lou Barlow, of indie-rock band Sebadoh, play Denver's Larimer Lounge the night that news of Hedberg's death came out. Between songs from his recent solo album, Barlow called for a moment of silence for Hedberg. From where I was standing, it looked like Barlow was fighting back tears. I was only familiar with bits of Hedberg's material at the time, but the obvious reverence Barlow displayed for him immediately compelled me to seek out more. His love of Hedberg, in other words, was shorthand for: "Check this shit out. *Now*."

Indie-rock audiences have frequently been accused of having little or no sense of humor about themselves, and a survey of the scene ten to fifteen years ago would have left you with a similar impression. That reputation was cemented in part by the slacker aesthetic that paralleled indie rock in the late 1980s and early nineties—one that gradually came to overlap with early alt rock in general. That aesthetic left outsiders with the notion that indie-rock audiences were sullen, dance-averse, deadly serious nerds who used sarcasm as a shield and who couldn't be bothered to tune their instruments. In truth, many were just socially retarded and introverted. (Trust me.) But even in 1991, when Sebadoh issued its seminal *Gimme Indie Rock!* EP, the stifling, deprecating stance that the band had taken bordered on self-aware comedy. "Started back in eighty-three, started seeing things differently.

Hard core wasn't doing it for me no more," sang Lou Barlow, formerly the bass player for Dinosaur Jr., and the spitting image of many of the genre's fans with his pale, skinny frame, long hair, and oversized glasses. "Started smoking pot. I thought things sounded better slow...milk that sound, blow your load!"

The song not only reinforced the indie-rock scene's increasingly exclusive view of itself (name-dropping The Stooges, Sonic Youth, and Hüsker Dü), it also took a self-conscious jab at its own gut by calling it just "a new generation of electric white-boy blues." As *All Music Guide* scribe Jason Ankeny wrote, Sebadoh would soon make "a cottage industry of feigned indifference and self-reflexive indignation." Barlow's lash-out mockery effectively doubled as masochism.

Of course, sarcastic self-awareness does not equal comedy, and most musicians who attempt straight-up comedy—or vice versa—tend to fail. However, it's not uncommon for comedians and musicians to show open, mutual love for each other, and when progressive artists of either genre start communicating, that love only grows. When *Mr. Show* cocreator David Cross taped his cable special *The Pride Is Back* in Seattle in 1999, scores of "super hipsters" showed up, according to *Live Nation*'s Geof Wills, who promoted the show. "It's just the guys he was hanging with. It's the same with the *Comedians of Comedy* tours or Mitch Hedberg's stuff, which I did pretty much all of," Wills says. "You'd go to New York City and The Strokes were hanging out. I did the *Mr. Show* tour, too, and the real cool cats were showing up."

As Wills noted earlier, many comedians and musicians wish they could trade shoes. Even a glance at popular comedians of the past century shows how frequently they've used musical instruments in their acts, from the Marx Brothers' piano, guitar, and harp and Jack Benny's violin to Steve Martin's banjo. The two genres have long held an intense fascination with, and respect for, one another. "A lot of musicians really do want to be comedians; look at John Mayer," says comedian Patton Oswalt, creator of the *Comedians of Comedy* tours. "And a lot of comedians wish they were musicians, or just frustrated rock stars. But we also inspire each other. I'm always excited to have new music to listen to when I'm on the road, and so many musicians tell me, 'We play your CD in the van. It makes everyone laugh, so it's perfect.'"

The grass may be greener on the other side of the fence, but it's also harder to cut, says singer-songwriter Aimee Mann, who has played shows with comedians Patton Oswalt, David Cross, Morgan Murphy, and others. "Comedy is an incredible skill. It requires this ready wit and being fast on your feet. It seems to me like the toughest gig ever, and I have a whole lot of admiration for the people that do it. Comics really love music and musicians, and when musicians are sick of music they always go to the one thing that they can't do."

Indie-rock godfather Bob Mould, who formerly played in Hüsker Dü and Sugar, remembers seeing Bill Hicks in Austin, Texas, and being amazed by his downed-power-line energy. "It was like you were at a punk-rock show. He was changing the way people looked at things. Comedy can be very, very sharp social commentary when done properly. When done wrong, it can be a horrifying mess, but someone who's of a certain intelligence and has a certain understanding of pop culture can be a very sharp weapon to get inside people and get them to reconsider things. David Cross is a really good example of that. His stuff with Sub Pop...that makes perfect sense."

The emergence of Mould's extroverted social conscience has occasionally overlapped with comedy, says comedian Margaret Cho. "He's become a lot more political. We were on Wed-Rock together in New York, this big benefit for gay marriage that was put together by John Cameron Mitchell, who plays Hedwig of *Hedwig and the Angry Inch*. Bob and I had done a few different kinds of events over the years." (Cho also emceed the 2007 installment of the Cyndi Lauper–led *True Colors* music tour, which advocated on behalf of the gay, lesbian, bisexual, and transgender community.)

Lizz Winstead, cocreator of *The Daily Show*, knew Mould from their early days in Minneapolis. She tapped him to write the theme song for *The Daily Show*, and even opened for him. She wholeheartedly endorses the recent overlap of progressive comedy and music. "I really love Patton Oswalt, David Cross, Janeane Garofalo, Marc Maron, and people like that. That's my peer group, and we sort of all bore out the boom of the eighties. I came out of Minneapolis, and those guys came out of San Francisco and Boston. The scenes were similar in that music and comedy were very intertwined."

Robert Schneider, lead singer of indie-pop mainstay The Apples in Stereo, appeared on Comedy Central's *The Daily Show* spin-off *The Colbert Report*. He penned a tongue-in-cheek tribute to host Stephen Colbert and, in an instance of genius crossover marketing, appeared with guitarists from indie-rock band The Decemberists, power-pop legends Cheap Trick, and others in a "guitarmaggedon" face-off. "That's my favorite show," Schneider says. "I was going to send [the song] to the show as a Christmas present, but I wasn't trying to get on the show or anything. And like, I finished it on a Thursday morning and by that evening Stephen had heard it. I didn't know that, but on the next day he had a staff meeting and the meeting consisted entirely of him singing it over and over and dancing around. On that Monday, I met Peter Frampton and Rick Nielsen from Cheap Trick, who literally inspired me to become a musician...It's a fortuitous, karmic kind of little loop." Schneider later became the only musician invited back to *The Colbert Report* for a second appearance, after his band played their single "Can You Feel It?" on August 4, 2008. (During the song, Schneider proudly sports a Barack Obama T-shirt, running ostensibly counter to the program's mock-conservative tone.)

Creative types in general have a reputation for demented senses of humor, which makes it unsurprising that musicians such as Rob Zombie (White Zombie) and Les Claypool (Primus) would seek out comedy as another creative outlet. *The Haunted World of El Superbeasto*, Zombie's animated movie based on a comic book he wrote, features the voices of *Mr. Show*'s Tom Kenny and Brian Posehn, with comedian Tom Papa as the title character. The ease with which Zombie connected with the comedians seemed organic. "Rob had met me through a mutual friend and saw my stand-up and we just became friendly," says Papa. "He was going ahead with this project and asked if I'd help him write it and be the lead voice. There's certain things you push for in the biz and certain things that just kind of happen. I was always just pushing to be the best stand-up I could be. Then these things pop up...I guess that's why some people become game show hosts."

Claypool has penned theme songs for Comedy Central's long-running *South Park* and Adult Swim's stop-motion-animated *Robot Chicken*. He also directed *Electric Apricot: Quest for the Festeroo*, a *Spinal Tap*–style mockumentary that skewers the jam-band scene (and that includes *South Park*'s Matt Stone and Arj Barker from HBO's *Flight of the Conchords*). The tagline for the *National Lampoon*–sponsored film ("A band with no limits, no fear, and no clue") sounds more harsh than it is, as the film mostly lets the scene off without a real drubbing. Then again, even casual Claypool fans know that the man's reputation for stoned, twisted humor—apparent in his song titles and album art—is one that rarely turns as dark or pointed as, say, Bill Hicks, preferring to stick to an unabashedly cheesy aesthetic.

Even rarer are the musicians and comedians who make successful forays into each other's realms. And no, Robert Pollard's drunken between-song banter (collected on the vinyl-only albums *Relaxation of the Asshole* and *Meet the King: Asshole 2*) isn't what I'm talking about. The media loves to ponder the appropriateness of the jokes-music mixture: an article in the May 29, 2008 edition of *The Onion*'s *A. V. Club* subverted the title of a Frank Zappa album by asking, "Does music belong in humor?" It made no overt conclusions, but listing novelty singles of debatable quality by Rodney Dangerfield, Eddie Murphy, Billy Crystal, and others essentially answered the question. *Paste Magazine*'s May 2008 issue featured a sidebar with the mildly convoluted headline "Does 'LOL'='R.I.P.?'" in which musicians sound off on the dangers of novelty hits. Writer Hal Bienstock asserts that country music's tradition of tongue-in-cheek songs is in no danger of stopping, but that "when rock bands start to tell jokes, they usually find their careers languishing once the laughter dies down." He cites Les Claypool, Wayne Coyne of The Flaming Lips, and Ed Robertson of Barenaked Ladies as "artists who've managed to survive their novelty hit."

It's a rocky journey, then, from one profession to the other, and woe to those who undertake it without the proper footing. "People like Jon Wurster and Fred Armisen are exceptions that prove the rule," says Patton Oswalt. "I mean, those guys are fucking geniuses. They are truly multitalented."

Incidentally, both also happen to have started out as drummers. Wurster first gained notice drumming for Superchunk, a genre-defining indie-rock band whose leaders, Mac McCaughan and Laura Ballance, went on to birth the influential label Merge Records in Chapel Hill, North Carolina. Wurster got to know Tom Scharpling, publisher of the fanzine *18 Wheeler* (which had previously interviewed Wurster's band and released a single from its lead singer's side project, Portastatic), at a Superchunk show with My Bloody Valentine and Pavement in 1993. The two hit it off after discussing their shared love of Chris Elliot's surreal sitcom *Get a Life*. Wurster became a fan of *Mr. Show* in the midnineties and met David Cross and other cast members through it. He would also see members of Yo La Tengo and Sebadoh at comedy shows in New York whenever his band visited.

In that way, it wasn't strange when he and Scharpling started crafting extended call-in sketches on Scharpling's *The Best Show* on legendary New York–area radio station WFMU. "It was completely organic and kind of unplanned," Wurster says. "Coming from a band that toured all the time, you kind of sought stuff like that out just to break the monotony of listening to music all day." The Scharpling and Wurster duo (detailed later in chapter five) would go on to write for Adult Swim's *Tom Goes to the Mayor* and generally create a self-contained universe of smart, subtle, long-attention-span characters and jokes on their Stereolaffs label.

Fred Armisen formerly drummed for the punk band Trenchmouth, as well as Blue Man Group and Those Bastard Souls, at various times. In 1998 he unleashed the short film *Fred Armisen's Guide to Music and South by Southwest*, in which he passed himself off as various clueless journalists in order to poke fun at the self-importance of rock musicians and their annual meeting in Austin, Texas. (Sally Timms of

The Mekons handled video duties.) When the video became an underground hit, Armisen transitioned into stand-up comedy and eventually joined the cast of *Saturday Night Live* in 2002. Beside the fact that he regularly appears at hip comedy nights across the country, he has directed music videos (for the Helio Sequence), appeared in music documentaries (Wilco's *I Am Trying to Break Your Heart*), and written for indie-rock website Pitchfork. He also released the DVD *Jens Hannemann: Complicated Drumming Technique* on Chicago indie label Drag City in 2007. The twenty-eight-minute video parodies the mindlessly complex histrionics of Scandinavian progressive rock and metal drummers with nary a wink. "The reaction is better than I could have imagined," says Armisen via e-mail. "I've been obsessed with drum-instruction DVDs. Something about the format and camera angles just makes me smile. I just decided that I had to make one."

A fan of Devo and The Clash as much as he is of Andy Kaufman and Peter Sellers, Armisen seems reluctant to adhere to any particular format for his creativity or any limit to his bizarre characters. (His Hannemann DVD is billed as "Fred Armisen Presents," hinting at the separation of personas that Drag City label-mate Neil Hamburger affects.) Armisen crafts occasional online comedy shorts under the moniker Thunderant with Carrie Brownstein of the (sadly) defunct band Sleater-Kinney. The episodes cover such subjects as a quest to write the perfect song and the exclusivity of feminist bookstores. "We've been friends for a while," Armisen says of Brownstein. "We had some mutual friends years ago and I was/am a HUGE fan of Sleater-Kinney. I mean to say that I love them truly. We did this one video for a Democratic benefit. We liked doing it and eventually wanted to do more."

So what's the deal with drummers going into comedy? Even indie-comedy hero Todd Barry started out as one.

"I picked the drums because they were the loudest, showiest instrument," Armisen says. "When I was in a band I would play purposefully loud and did fills as much as I could. My hero was Keith Moon. He made a spectacle of playing the drums. Tito Puente [the inspiration for Armisen's *SNL* character Fericito] stood when he played his timbales, so it's all about attention."

"The drummer's always the funniest," says David Cross. "Always. I don't think it's a secret that a lot of musicians are frustrated actors or comics, and vice versa."

"I don't know why that is," puzzles Jon Wurster. "I mean, I think it's true that drummers are often funny, but a lot of times the drummer's the biggest asshole too." He pauses before adding, "Hopefully I don't fall into that."

Not likely. Wurster never left indie rock behind, continuing to drum for Superchunk and fill in with Robert Pollard, The New Pornographers, R.E.M., Ryan Adams, and, lately, The Mountain Goats and Bob Mould. His comfort in both comedy and music speaks to a classic breed of performer able to work in multiple genres. When he performs comedy onstage, however, it doesn't always translate as well as on record. Notable misfires include his appearance at *Magnet* magazine's tenth-anniversary show, where crowds nearly massacred him, and a poorly received South by Southwest show in 2007. That's the opposite of another musical-comedy hybrid that has recently made hipsters swoon.

The New Zealand duo Flight of the Conchords, composed of scruffy, mild-mannered singer-guitarists Bret McKenzie and Jemaine Clement, use subtlety as their weapon, approaching musical genre parodies with a pair of acoustic guitars and a wit so gleefully dehydrated it makes the BBC's *The Office* seem like a Japanese game show. They began as a college cult duo in 1998, working music and comedy venues before officially dubbing themselves

Flight of the Conchords. With seemingly limited appeal in the beginning, they developed into an international brand through festivals, talk show appearances, online shorts, and, eventually, an HBO series that paved the way for their current semi-stardom. The 2007 Sub Pop EP *The Distant Future* won them a Grammy, and their 2008 eponymous Sub Pop full-length opened at number three on the Billboard charts, outselling Ashlee Simpson and setting a new record for the best debut for a New Zealand band (the runner-up was Crowded House's 1986 self-titled debut). That they present themselves as a pair of struggling musicians playing low-key folk music is probably the biggest irony, considering that a recent US tour of large venues sold out quickly. Comedians who appeared on their show (Eugene Mirman, Aziz Ansari) and *Mr. Show* vet Karen Kilgariff joined them at select dates.

"They're huge," Mirman says. "They sold out the US tour they originally booked within an hour, and within a day they sold out the whole tour." Having appeared several times on their show (as their landlord), Mirman has gotten an intimate view of the pair, which leads him to attribute their success to their accents. "No really, they're just funny and charming guys. It's this sort of oddball sensibility that speaks to people."

"The last time they played in Seattle, well before the show aired, they sold out a 3,000-person room in hours," says Sub Pop A&R director Tony Kiewel. "I have no idea how that happens. The sales of their EP are around 90,000 now, and it's several months old. It still sells something like 1,200 copies a week."

Indie? Perhaps in name and approach, but the commercial potential of the music-comedy crossover has begun to reach a level of success not seen in thirty years. It's no stretch to think their handshake will soon turn into a loving, potentially pornographic, embrace.

Andrew Earles (left) and Jeffrey Jensen (right) of prank-call duo Earles & Jensen, at Neely's BBQ in Memphis, Tennessee.
Photo by Geoffrey Brent Shrewsbury

COMEDY FROM ANOTHER PLANET

BY ANDREW EARLES

In America, ground zero for several strains of *deregulated* comedy, for lack of a better phrase, is widely considered to be 1990, give or take a year. Of course, the future would hold many things, but here we're looking at a particular snapshot of mainstream adult comedy circa 1989. It would be impossible to thoroughly discuss the problematic nature of stand-up comedy in the late eighties within the constraints of a single sidebar.

Opening Night at Rodney's Place, an HBO special that aired almost twenty years ago, is a recommended eye-opener for those interested in how comedy as a whole has changed drastically over a two-decade period. It would be inaccurate to blame the special's content for the reactionary stance of what came to be known early on as "alternative" comedy. Conversely, *Opening Night* is exactly the type of comedy for which, say, *The Ben Stiller Show* provided an antidote. To say that the sketches and stand-up in *Opening Night* are archaic, different, and, more often than not, unfunny, is to state the obvious. But the years have added an element of the absurd to this and other comedy specials of the mid- to late eighties. With that in mind, we must ask: Is any of the material so unfunny that it's funny in an unconscious, post-comedy, Neil Hamburgeresque fashion? The answer is, for better or worse, yes. Viewed with hindsight intact, *Opening Night* plays like an alternate-reality fever dream created on another planet. It is a fascinating ride, and not only because we are now armed with the modern knowledge of where some of the comics ended up, but also where some of them did not.

Barring Johnny Carson, few old-school superstar entities nurtured mainstream stand-up comedy throughout the late seventies and early eighties quite like the sadly departed Rodney Dangerfield, or so it would seem on the surface. Along with several other series, Rodney's HBO and network television specials created a trickledown that went a long way toward fostering the ill-defined stand-up boom of the eighties in general. This phenomenon (or rather occurrence, since it is not exactly bizarre or surprising) has nebulous boundaries that no one seems to agree on. It might encompass the early to mideighties as a period, as well that many refer to as the "dark days" of stand-up—the late eighties. An appearance on a Rodney Dangerfield special was one of the golden eggs sought by the army of road comics/road dogs who nurtured the powerful comedy club network of the eighties. Even then it was hit or miss. It was not like getting a laugh from Johnny (which was also, as history has dictated, hit or miss).

The seldom-remembered *It's Lonely at the Top* (1992) closed the run of Dangerfield-helmed specials that began more than a decade earlier with 1981's *It's Not Easy Bein' Me.* Situated in the homestretch is *Opening Night at Rodney's Place.* Its 1989 airdate is significant to the eventual development of underground comedy. Some might say that traditional stand-up comedy has more or less remained in a perpetual state of creative bankruptcy for years before and since the show's debut, but that's not true, nor is it a discussion for this particular sidebar. One thing is certain, though: if *Opening Night at Rodney's Place* simply hints at the condition of mainstream midprofile stand-up in 1989, things were in a pathetic yet bizarre and disturbing state. A half-decade is an eternity in any form of entertainment; after examining *Opening Night,* it's astonishing to consider that *Mr. Show* debuted in close to the same HBO time slot only six years later.

Many comedy specials of the day were structured as sketch/comic/sketch programs, bookended by sketches with intro and outro themes. *Opening Night* followed this once-sturdy model. It's basically a variety show, without too much variety. Sketches were prerecorded far, far away from the nightclub and starred established comedians and actors. The sketches were shown to the live audience between sets, and canned laughter was probably overdubbed to fool those at home. *Opening Night at Rodney's Place* did not have the star-making power or historical significance of previous Dangerfield specials (which featured names such as Andrew Dice Clay, Jerry Seinfeld, Andy Kaufman, and Bill Hicks). Only two of "Rodney's Funny Friends," as they were termed in the intro, would leave *Opening Night* to achieve gradual fame.

From the late 1980s' saturation of comedy specials, why is *Opening Night* so interesting? Was *Opening Night* actually considered funny? Good questions. Ones that may or may not be answered, but an attempt is in order.

The opening sketch has Rodney begging his massively coiffed, absurdly endowed girlfriend Laverne to behave during his big night. According to Rodney's accusations, Laverne "fucked the maitre d', fucked the bartender, fucked the chef." Rodney notes that Laverne committed these acts before the club even opened, adding the final quip, "You even fucked my manager," to which Laverne replies in stereotypical, gum-smacking, stock upper-East-Coast dialect, "Why not? He's fwuckin' yooooou!"

The duality of Rodney-as-Cuckold + All-Women-Are-Whores = the punch line. That's it. Laverne smirks and does her nails as Rodney pleads and eventually ends up on his knees. The audience laughter is positioned not after jokes (there are none, really), but after lines when Laverne's debaucheries are highlighted and when it becomes apparent that Rodney will stick with Laverne no matter what she does. Sure, this plays on Rodney's venerable sad-sack loser persona that mainstream audiences still found hilarious, but the backbone is nothing more than Rat Pack–era sexism.

Upon watching it today, *Opening Night* is saturated with head-scratchers, the aforementioned "Was that actually considered funny?" being paramount. Case in point: for the opening credits, Rodney was cast as a blackjack dealer laying down cards that said "Sam Kinison" or "Rich Little" as rollicking Tin Pan Alley-by-way-of-eighties synthesizer music played in the background and the voiceover ran through the names. When the time came for Rodney's funny friends to be announced, they were physically ejected from a ladies' room by the sole female comic, Thea Vidale. It's vexing to think this sort of thing was amusing to even targeted mainstream audiences. Rodney then took the stage to cherry-pick from his bag of four gazillion bad-luck jokes.

This is a perfect time to take a closer look at the Rodney Dangerfield act circa late eighties. At this autumnal stage, two things must be noted about Rodney's jokes: first, most were purchased (yes, literally purchased) from less-famous comedians. This explains the wild inconsistency; secondly, their efficiency is rather awe-inspiring.

"Last night I found some guy's wallet. Inside was a picture of my two kids."

"The other day, I told my kid about the birds and the bees. He went out and knocked up a sparrow."

"The other day, my wife called to say she had a new position. I ran home. The position was already filled."

The special was front-loaded with Tim Allen and Jeff Foxworthy. Already in his midthirties, Allen had spent the eighties as a road dog, honing the single-premise act that would later bring him sitcom superstardom. All of the featured comedians spoke to the working-class, white, ham-n-egger demographic (even Vidale's "I'm a scary black woman!" routine), but none so much as Allen's. The flow was punctuated by his famous catchphrase—the impersonation of a grunting pig to suggest that men are simpletons who only need food, sex, and riding lawn mowers to achieve happiness. Allen's act leaned toward males but appealed to both genders with the venerable "that's so true!" agenda. The punch line that followed included Allen laughing maniacally then concluding that he was just kidding.

The first connecting sketch was so brazenly phoned-in that one might wonder what didn't make the cut. Or maybe that's what happened: every sketch shot was used. Like Rodney hanging out at a pool, presumably at a Las Vegas hotel, and verbally assaulting women until a family asks him to perform the famed high dive. And that's exactly what he does (using the footage from the movie *Back to School*, naturally). Other than the playful idea that a hotel pool has a high dive, not much else happens, aside from the audience's roaring applause. (As a side note: A young Tobey Maguire played the little boy who badgers Rodney into completing the dive.)

Hitting the "You might be a redneck, if..." bit less than a minute into his act, Jeff Foxworthy, like Tim Allen, also failed to deviate from the material that would make him famous in the next decade. Though simple and not necessarily clever, some of Foxworthy's jokes were (are) universally funny, which cannot be said for Allen. His warm wit no doubt assisted his subsequent success. Jokes about paying a repo man with a check and the fact that he and his wife had been trying to have a kid—"She's not pregnant, but I figure if you're going to be a failure at something, this is about as much fun as anything"—worked their pedestrian magic on the audience.

How about some period sketches? (No, they are not about a woman's time of the month.) The quick "The Adventures of Sherlock Holmes" sketches (three in all) played on one of the flimsiest premises in all of comedy: injecting modern profanity and physical humor/violence into a disparate, historic setting. Rodney played the cartoonish Holmes, gently playing a violin while Watson (played by character actor extraordinaire Chuck McCann) tried to grab his attention by saying, "Holmes, Holmes, Holmes, I was thinking..." Holmes responds with the lines, "Don't bug me when I'm into my music, you fucking asshole. And where do you get the nerve to think? You fucking moron!" and "Shut up, you nitwit cocksucker!" When the premise is revisited later in the show, Holmes calls Watson a "fucking retarded scumbag." Finally, Holmes smashes the violin over Watson's head, knocking him unconscious.

Another one-trick sketch involved Rodney interviewing prospective men's room attendants and cocktail waitresses to work in his new nightclub. Implausibility added to the viewing pleasure (with the gift of hindsight, naturally). Why would Rodney be interviewing these people? When asked why he was fired from his last job as a men's room attendant, an applicant replies, "Peeking" in a flamboyantly gay fashion and is kicked out of the interview. Two "hot" cocktail waitresses get the same treatment after giving Rodney an ultimatum: "I'm honest, I'll work hard, but if you want me to work here, Rodney, you're going to have to fuck me." Get it?! It's supposed to be the other way around!

Like several of the other performers, Thea Vidale had recently appeared in the movie *Comedy's Dirtiest Dozen* (1988) along with Bill Hicks, a young Chris Rock, and Jackie Martling. Vidale is the show's only African American performer, and her act is based around two basic concepts: (1) She's a big, crazy-looking black lady with a wild hairdo (a couple of Tina Turner references) and white people are scared of/fascinated by her, and (2) White people do this. White people do that. White people sound like this. White people's children are the spawn of Satan (she was a schoolteacher). Vidale would continue to dog-paddle the backwaters of stand-up comedy for a few years and score a number of bit parts on various network programs. African American comedians have continued to exhume the rotting corpse of "white people do this...white people talk like this" as if it's a brand-new, unheard-of cache of comedy gold. But for a real lack of progress, look no further than the unwritten no-no of a white comedian turning the tables.

Opening Night at Rodney's Place did contain two longer, more relatively complex sketches. The first arrived about forty minutes into the special and featured an odd, rather prescient choice for a cameo appearance. In 1989, Ron Jeremy was still years away from having the quasi-hip novelty capital he enjoys today. Even with his superstardom in the pornography genre, viewers would need to be patrons of the XXX-rated arts to be familiar with Jeremy during this time. The exhausting segment revolved around Rodney's desire to be in a porno because "he's done everything else in show business." The porno producers were cigar-chomping, plaid-suited sleazebags of hilariously stereotypical proportions. This is what middle America thought porno producers looked like: the evil characters from a Sunday night made-for-TV movie about missing children. The humor was as flaccid and predictable as Rodney's supposed erectile dysfunction that provided one of the punch lines. Ron Jeremy emerges from one of the rooms wearing a bathrobe, and everyone over the age of eight can guess the comic finale that ended the sketch: Jeremy opening his robe to show Rodney his infamous gift, Rodney saying, "All men are created equal, what bullshit!" Rodney loses again.

For the remaining comedians, *Opening Night at Rodney's Place* stands as the pinnacle of their respective careers. In the case of Larry Reeb, he had only been in the previous year's straight-to-video, self-explanatory *Truly Tasteless Jokes*. It's not fantasy to envision Reeb as a fairly successful mainstream comedian in the 1990s, or at least a regular in the sitcom trenches. Reeb's greasy hair, shiny complexion, and bad dress (even for the time) made him no more unattractive than 98 percent of the male contemporary comedians of today (particularly the indie ones). His set was the funniest of the whole bunch, though that claim carries fluctuating value. Some of his jokes have even stood the test of time, no easy feat for a creative venture that ages worse than any other. His "women do weird stuff" material was unsurprisingly pedestrian but perhaps a tier above the other male comics. On cleaning the house: "Men figure, if you can't see it, must not be dirty. Meanwhile, there's corn growing behind the couch." Reeb's catchphrase (variations of "Another tip from your Uncle Lar!") is terrible, yes, but it's hard to deny the general appeal and base wit of this joke: "When you wear glasses, people bug you. They come up and say, 'Oh, you have glasses, can I try them on?' Then they put them on and say, 'Jeez, you've got bad eyes!' That's why I wear 'em, call me kooky. Wearing glasses is a handicap. You don't see people going up to a guy in a wheelchair, 'Oh, you're in a wheelchair, mind if I take it for a spin? Jeez, you've got bad legs!'" Faint booing can be heard after that one. Reeb remains a road comic, living part of his life in Comfort Inns, enjoying the wonderful cuisine of America's urban sprawl, and turning up on local morning zoo-style radio shows. "The other day I dialed a wrong number, the guy on the other line asks, 'What number did you dial?' and I said, 'Well, did it ring at your house?'"

Greg Travis was the evening's token in-your-face performer, which suited his angle: he's a prop comedian with a flair for impersonations. With his voice perpetually raised, he asserted that the microphone stand was a giant roach clip, then launched into R-rated impersonations of Robin Leach and Casey Kasem. Before long, the act went straight into Travis's metal briefcase. The set was ruled by his pride and joy, "David Sleaze: The Punk Magician." Wearing a punk-rocker Halloween costume (giant purple mohawk, loud shades, ripped skull-and-crossbones tank top) purchased from a drugstore, Travis affected the type of god-awful fake accent normally (well, not *normally*) heard when a cast member of *Mama's Family* decided to impersonate a British person. When one of the devious magic acts failed to elicit a big laugh, Travis resorted to Sleaze's catchphrase: an extended "Fuck yooooooouuuu!!!" The ultrageneric, Hollywood-created punk-rocker caricature as comedic punching bag in 1989? Ten years prior, this may have made sense.

One particular sketch during *Opening Night at Rodney's Place* played out like a bizarre, catastrophic train wreck of indeterminate vintage. The plot, a dirty send-up of *The Tonight Show with Johnny Carson*, was simple enough. Dangerfield was known for his frequent *Tonight Show* visits, so the idea was a natural and was presented as a flashback to "the one night that things went wrong." Rich Little played Carson, Chuck McCann was the overblown, overstated Ed McMahon, and Heather Thomas was Joan Emery (a spoof on real-life zoo lady Joan Embery). Rodney made homoerotic come-ons to an off-screen Doc Severinsen, and Rodney, Little, and McCann chanted, "Fuck the commercial! Fuck the commercial!" at the prospect of breaking for the sponsors. Actor Kevin Peter Hall played Richard Small, the author of *Sex: Is a Big Dick Important?* He "leads a life of confusion" as a "big black man with a small dick." (Another side note: The now-deceased Hall was the actor inside the creature suit for the first two *Predator* movies.) Joan Emery arrives as the next guest and is subjected to a barrage of nasty dialogue. When asked by Little's Carson if he'd ever met Joan before, Rodney replies, "I don't know, tell her to get undressed." Rodney and the gang pant over Joan as she bends over to release a tiger cub, which turns out to be a normal kitten. Rodney loses his cool and engages in mock sex with Joan's backside. The Siberian tiger cub is a normal (and real) kitten that eventually attacks and pisses all over Rodney. In the closing scene, Rodney's face is covered in fake blood as he shakes, waves, and throws the kitten around. "I'll tell you one thing, I'll never go to another fuckin' cathouse, where's my fucking dog?" screams Rodney as the sketch ends. PETA's influence over the media in 1989 was clearly not what it is today.

John Fox is the last of Rodney's funny friends. As an introduction, Rodney skips the jokes and introduces Fox with, "Well, here he is. If you think I'm a loser, wait'll you see this fuckin' guy." A mulleted, disheveled, mustachioed everyman in jeans and a sweatshirt, Fox was the poster boy for the strain of 1980s road-dog comics who existed far below the level of fame—of any type. For his (unbeknownst to him) final cable television appearance, Fox steps onto the stage and in a commanding voice states, "Two firemen are butt-fucking in a smoke-filled room. The chief says, 'What're you doing?' The first fireman says, 'Sir, this man has smoke inhalation.' And the chief asks, 'Well, give him mouth to mouth.' 'I did, how do you think all this shit got started?'" Like the similarly destined Reeb, Fox was good at serviceable, somewhat clever mainstream stand-up...barring the lines lifted from a tattered copy of *Truly Tasteless Jokes*. With his look, a Tim Allen–style trajectory into sitcom hell could have been his calling. Instead, his next two appearances in front of a camera would be the straight-to-video specials *Redneck Comedy Roundup II* (2006) and *Comedy Ain't for the Money* (2007).

The sketch that ended *Opening Night* became famous partially by default of Sam Kinison's inclusion. Rodney and Sam sit in a bar as the latter plucks out a ditty on the piano. Addressed to Rodney and designed to ease his female woes, Sam's ballad devolves into just what audiences wanted: a profanity-laced screamfest about the extracurricular activities that Rodney's gal enjoys behind his back.

Opening Night at Rodney's Place is a fascinating time capsule, a mess constantly grasping at straws, an overdose of unaware noncomedy, and a rapid procession of crude for-the-sake-of-it humor. Its influences are telling—traditional comedy roots stretching back to the 1940s, when Dangerfield first tried his hand at making people laugh. Its causal ties to the topical inundation of what people consider alternative or indie comedy are nebulous but undeniably present. The marriage of music and comedy was largely unheard of in the late eighties, relegated to examples like Sam Kinison's flirtation with hair metal. The seemingly natural racism and homophobic humor in *Opening Night* is like hearing an elderly relative drop the n-bomb during Thanksgiving dinner, followed with a shrugging, "That's just how they're going to be...can't change 'em!" comment, unlike what might be heard on *The Sarah Silverman Program*, which attaches "post" to the front of all unsavory styles of humor and supposedly works to make fun of the real offenders. Both examples attempt to succeed with shock value, no matter how natural, reactionary, or funny any of it is at the end of the day.

Opening Night at Rodney's Place is available on the highly recommended *Rodney Dangerfield: No Respect* three-DVD set. The program offers a needed expansion to everyone's frame of reference regarding comedy and comedy history. Yes, everyone needs it.

Mr. Show's Brian Posehn enjoys the nightly special at the
Magnolia Café in Austin, Texas. *Photo by Henry Owings*

2

THE *MR. SHOW* EFFECT

I decided a few years back to separate the people of this fine planet into two categories: those who know *Mr. Show*, and those who do not.

If you're part of the latter group, I'm sorry. Sucks for you. You're missing out on one of the greatest television sketch comedies ever produced. Turn off that fucking *Malcolm in the Middle* rerun, get online, and order seasons one through four of *Mr. Show* on DVD immediately. It's not stuffy or hard to get into, or so-bad-it's-good. It's just really, really funny. Like quoting-it-for-years-to-come funny. Funnier than the time you literally shit your pants (although that was pretty funny too).

If you're part of the former subset of people who know *Mr. Show*, you probably comprise one of the two additional categories: the lovers and the haters (the latter of which tend to overlap with the indifferent). To you lovers out there, any words about the program are just more affectionate, drooling sermons to the choir. You probably bought Naomi Odenkirk's *Mr. Show* episode guide,

What Happened?!, and have preordered the commemo-
rative, hand-carved *Mr. Show* jade figurines. Your tattoo
looks good, too. That one above your ass even looks like
Jay Johnston. A little, anyway.

The haters and the indifferent, on the other hand, are
probably reading this with typical skepticism. "This guy's
obviously a fan, so everything he writes will be tainted
with that fanaticism. I've seen the show and it sucks—or
at least it's not as great as everyone says." Yeah, well,
you're an idiot. *Mr. Show*'s caustic humor can turn on a
dime, mutating from absurdist jokes to acerbic cultural
indictments as invisibly fussed-over as they are left-
field. The subtly intellectual, in-joke approach is not for
everyone, which, like most innovative things, can be its
greatest asset and its greatest liability. You have to possess a certain awareness of and distaste for hackneyed
comedy conventions to even gain entry to many sketches.
To paraphrase a cliché, you don't decide whether or not
to like *Mr. Show*; it decides to like you.

Taking cues from groundbreaking sketch comedies
such as *Monty Python's Flying Circus* and, to a lesser
extent, *SCTV*, *Saturday Night Live*, *Kids in the Hall*,
and the entire tradition of subversive comedy from the
Compass Players to Bill Hicks, *Mr. Show* began as a stage
show from ex–*Ben Stiller Show* writers Bob Odenkirk and
David Cross, who won an Emmy for their work on that
short-lived but star-launching Fox sketch comedy. You
might recognize the bald, bespectacled Cross from guest
spots on NBC's *Just Shoot Me!* and *NewsRadio*—shows
that seem to be many people's reference points—and
random appearances on talk shows (*Late Night with
Conan O'Brien*), and Comedy Central shows (*The Colbert
Report*). Cross is also a prolific character actor in films,
popping up in the margins of Hollywood flicks like *Men
in Black* and nabbing larger roles in kiddie films like

Alvin and the Chipmunks. He's also familiar to the art house crowd, in movies such as *Ghost World, Waiting for Guffman, The Eternal Sunshine of the Spotless Mind*, and the Bob Dylan biopic *I'm Not There* (in which he played an eerily spot-on Allen Ginsburg). He's often got a goatee, a fuck-you grin, or both, and his malleable pipes carry as much personality as his face (see his voice work in cartoons such as *Family Guy* and *Aqua Teen Hunger Force*). Of course, his longest-running and best-defined character is probably Dr. Tobias Fünke on Fox's *Arrested Development*. Like *Mr. Show*, that was another slice of brainy, endlessly watchable comedy heaven that many felt was yanked before its time.

Bob Odenkirk is the barely restrained yin to Cross's rubbery, gleefully contrarian yang. His boiling kettle of a personality cools down only long enough to shoot up and steam-clean your face. An actor even when he was writing for *The Ben Stiller Show*, Odenkirk has made appearances on *Seinfeld, The Larry Sanders Show*, and *Curb Your Enthusiasm*. He's also directed a few less-than-blockbuster movies, such as *The Brothers Solomon* and *Let's Go to Prison*. Odenkirk is a talented writer and producer more so than an actor, first getting his feet wet in the 1990 cult sitcom *Get a Life* with Chris Elliot and an early version of *Late Night with Conan O'Brien*. He's also a mentor to some of the best new comedic voices of the last decade, including Tenacious D's Jack Black and Kyle Gass, Adult Swim's Tim Heidecker and Eric Wareheim, and Derek Waters and Simon Helberg (formerly of the ill-fated SuperDeluxe website).

Really, Cross and Odenkirk's IMDB.com profiles read like a short list of every good show (and a few bad) that you've seen over the years. Just don't let those crude sketches of their talent taint your opinion. They're better than that when given the chance to stretch their talents to proper show length. HBO originally ran their thirty-minute *Mr. Show* episodes at midnight, from 1995 to 1998, during which time I was too busy in college getting drunk and stoned, feeling sorry for myself, or pining for unattainable girls' notice. (That, and who had cable at Bowling Green State University?) Luckily, *Mr. Show*'s release on DVD allowed us latecomers, and the vast league of cult devotees, to absorb and obsessively memorize each of its episodes.

But why, you ask, is *Mr. Show* so important to the indie-comedy scene? It's because the show's various writers, actors, and related friends have continued steering stand-up away from the dumbed-down, generic style of humor that indirectly threw them together in the first place, with people such as David Cross and Brian Posehn each taking part in a series of tours that would place comedy at the forefront of the indie-rock world, and B. J. Porter and Scott Aukerman founding the popular *Comedy Death-Ray* show in LA, which gives up-and-comers and vets a high-profile venue to test material. It's because Bob Odenkirk has continued to mentor new comedic voices and serve as an icon in the scene. It's because nearly all of *Mr. Show*'s alumni are still writing or performing stand-up and sketch comedy at clubs, theaters, and music venues and festivals. And it's because the show's now-canonized sensibility can be felt, even if subtly, in nearly every type of cutting-edge humor out there. It's almost unthinkable, in other words, that a smart comedian or comedy devotee wouldn't be at least familiar with *Mr. Show*, if not a rabid fan.

Then again, I'm what you might call "biased as hell."

★ ☆ ★ ☆ ★

Mr. Show's third season provides a good entry point into its twisted sensibility, since that's when the cast and crew began to hit their full creative strides. Some of the skits seem like ideas you and your friends would come up with in high school, the sort of pain-as-humor schtick that easily mutates into absurdism: replacing the product in a mindless television commercial with something vulgar or ridiculous (Mustardayonaise, Mayostard), or taking a cable televangelist screed and substituting "Satan" for "Jesus" while retaining the sickly, overearnest sentimentalism, forced vocal cadence, oblivious wardrobe, and public-access TV production values.

The sarcasm in sketches like these is thick and appropriately multilayered, and *Mr. Show*'s writing staff is well versed in the vocabulary of popular culture. Nothing is taboo: racism, sexual orientation, domestic violence, and mental and physical handicaps are all targets of its decidedly postmodern satire. The profanity is frequent, although self-consciously so, as in an episode where a swear jar nets millions of dollars for what turns out to be a ridiculous charity ("Evil Genius Telethon"). Other sketches take bizarre ideas beyond their logical conclusion and test assumed notions of what constitutes humor (the mercilessly funny "America Will Blow Up the Moon," the newscaster-skewering "Young People and Companions," or "Frankly Anne," which serves up a pair of college tourists like Thanksgiving turkeys). It cleverly contrasts outrageous subject matter with our knee-jerk response to it, and inadvertently broadens our comedic horizons by showing how alarmingly close they are.

The elaborate links between sketches also distinguish *Mr. Show* from other sketch comedies, tying together seemingly random ideas into a mostly thematic whole. Ingeniously combining pretaped pieces with studio-audience footage, the transitions are about as predictable as your average strobe-lit pinball match. At least upon first viewing—each episode's arc is actually a painstakingly constructed Möbius strip of logic. Take the link near the beginning of episode 302, in which a fake ad for the Marriage-Con and Boat Show at the tristate Globo Dome shows a map of a nearby biosphere, where cooped-up scientist Cross pathetically attempts to snag a date for New Year's Eve. Or the "Young People and Companions" link in episode 305, in which an already ridiculous news report bleeds into a newscast blooper reel, which whisks us to a boardroom-style fashion forecast that eventually involves the gay, eternal spirit of Nostradamus.

By that same token, even people on similar wavelengths as the show's creators are sometimes left confused by the transitions. The truly funny sketches contain more than enough material to make up for these head-scratchers, and realistically, if every sketch was as straight-ahead funny as "Blowjob," you'd have to acquire a new set of pantaloons after each viewing. But there are notable misses from time to time. Some of the bits feel creaky and dated, like the *Cops*-aping sketches with perpetual white trash arrestee Ronnie Dobbs, a roving-camera format that was later polished by Comedy Central's largely improvised mockumentary series *Reno: 911!* The sketch links on *Mr. Show* also reek of *Monty Python*, though there's always some larger point to it, as opposed to *Python*'s "Now for something completely different," which proudly proclaimed that program's lack of continuity.

What continually redeems each *Mr. Show* episode is its hermetic construction and interwoven themes, and the ways in which those subtly reveal themselves over repeated viewings. The versatile, spot-on cast clearly enjoys parodying newscasters, limelight prima donnas, and has-been celebrities as much as they do creating new characters. (Significantly, *Mr. Show* resisted recurring characters, considering it the creative crutch of shows such as *Saturday Night Live* and *MadTV*.) The writers clearly had fun plundering familiar archetypes, tossing stuffy Brits, nerdy scientists, pathetic game show contestants, neo-Luddites, surly service industry workers, cock-rock bands, rednecks, old-timey grocers, political separatists, and others into the mix. The wardrobe from a Spike Jonze video seems to have been raided and reworked, making the plethora of characters as visually distinct, intentionally cheap-looking, and ultimately memorable as the bits themselves.

Mr. Show's underlying political and social conscience is also impossible to ignore, especially if you're already a member of its target audience (i.e., educated, young, liberal-minded, un-PC types). The bits seemed tailor-made for cynical college students, sensitive indie rockers, pot-smoking academics, drunks, and all manner of art fags. In other words, most conservatives' worst nightmares. It's only a shame *Mr. Show* wasn't around to skewer the hysterical faux patriotism that infected our culture after 9/11, although many of its sketches had already alluded to that timeless subject, and several of its alumni mined it for material in their mid-2000s acts.

Fortunately, *Mr. Show*'s recurring themes generally resisted the sell-by dates that many sketch shows suffer from, taking on the idiocy of our TV-addicted society (via frequent infomercial parodies), the self-imposed gulf between illusion and reality, workplace double standards, canned nostalgia, and the futility of objectivism. If that all sounds a bit like a freshman philosophy paper, it's at least delivered with a heaping dose of sarcasm and burning disdain for clichés. And while it hits a few easy targets along the way, it's delightful to watch them crash and burst into lovely blue-green flames.

The inherent limitations of TV comedy are strong, and *Mr. Show* suffers a bit here, too. The laugh track, while live, can be distracting. The audience reacts with silence or polite chuckles to some of the more "difficult" material, which psychologically weighs on the flow of the sketches. Ideally, good comedy would be funny regardless of an audible response, but let's be honest: borderline stuff sometimes benefits from a laugh track. Look at 99 percent of sitcoms.

Still, this doesn't diminish the quality of the writing or acting. How the cast keeps from cracking up most of the time is unfathomable, and lesser-talented/disciplined comedians wouldn't even know what to do with the material (I'm looking at you, Jimmy Fallon, who couldn't keep a goddamned straight face to save his life on *Saturday Night Live*). Some of the more topical bits don't age well—references to *Forrest Gump* and *The Firm* seem especially spoiled—but considered in context, the overall construction is airtight. The confrontational nature of the humor is largely unmatched, and the bevy of wickedly funny, endlessly fertile, quotable lines helps *Mr. Show* stand as a document of inspired avant-garde sketch that was largely ignored by its contemporary audience.

Thank you, Satan, for DVD technology.

Blame Janeane Garofalo for introducing *Mr. Show* cocreators Bob Odenkirk and David Cross. She first met Odenkirk while auditioning for *Saturday Night Live*, which employed Odenkirk from 1987 to 1991. She also befriended him through her roommate Jeff Garlin (later of *Curb Your Enthusiasm*), who had known Odenkirk in

Chicago—back when Odenkirk was doing Second City shows and working with people like Robert Smigel (later of *Saturday Night Live* and *TV Funhouse*). It was on *SNL* that Odenkirk would not only meet Conan O'Brien and Ben Stiller, but also realize that many of his sketch ideas were too conceptual for people, leading him to eventually quit. His best-known *SNL* sketch is probably Matt Foley, Motivational Speaker, which Chris Farley made famous. Garofalo had already known David Cross through her open-mic days in Boston, where the cutting-edge comedy scene had coalesced around a handful of performers and venues such as Catch a Rising Star.

Even before they would work together on 1992's *The Ben Stiller Show* (on which Garofalo was also a writer-actor), Garofalo tried to set up Cross and Odenkirk to play basketball one Sunday afternoon in LA. Odenkirk, however, was too busy for such dalliances, so it never happened. The next time they met, Cross had just joined *The Ben Stiller Show* as a midseason replacement writer. The pair didn't click on that short-lived enterprise either, but they would eventually develop a respect for the other's sense of humor when they saw each other's stand-up acts—Cross first seeing Odenkirk at the Upfront Theater, and Odenkirk later catching Cross at the Santa Monica Improv.

Many of the edgier comics who moved to LA from Boston, San Francisco, and New York at the end of the eighties comedy boom had been performing at Beth Lapides' Sunday night Un-Cabaret shows at Luna Park. Founded in 1990, the critically lauded underground show defined the early alternative-comedy scene—a reaction to the sameness of eighties comedians and the relatively strict comedy club environment in LA that disenfranchised many talented performers. People such as Garofalo, Cross, Odenkirk, Dana Gould, Laura Kightlinger, Patton Oswalt, Andy Kindler, and Laura Milligan would perform at the Un-Cabaret nights, although Lapides was picky about whom she let onstage (stand-ups Brian Posehn and Mary Lynn Rajskub did not make the list). Comedy manager Dave Rath, who handled the careers of Garofalo, Oswalt, Posehn, Rajskub, and many others, eventually provided his *own* alternative to the Un-Cabaret by renting out the back room of a nightspot on Hollywood Boulevard called the Diamond Club.

So starting in 1994, the close-knit alt-comedy scene in LA had another reliable place to perform. Most of the aforementioned comics played there, collaborating on sketch shows and "character-based theme shows," as Naomi Odenkirk wrote in her *Mr. Show* book, *What Happened?!* Jack Black and Kyle Gass's comedy-metal duo Tenacious D often took the stage, and Dave Rath's crew generally hung out and partied together around the performances. Cross and Odenkirk overlapped on a few of the weekly Thursday-night shows and soon joined to create *The 3 Goofballz*, an early version of what would become *Mr. Show*. The pair's concept-heavy sketches betrayed a hatred of mind-numbing comedy fare, and their clever pretaped pieces fed into each show's larger theme. Comedian Brian Posehn, who had moved to LA from San Francisco with a wave of other stand-ups, joined the show as it went through a series of name changes (*Grand National Championships, The Cross/Odenkirk Problem*, and, significantly, *Mr. Show*).

Cross and Odenkirk quickly sensed the television potential in what they were doing, each person's writing and performance talents complementing the other's perfectly. Although they weren't as seasoned as some, they had already gathered enough writing experience to recognize their instinctively fertile working relationship. HBO development director Carolyn Strauss had taken notice of Odenkirk and Cross even before their proto–*Mr. Show* had moved from the Diamond Club to the larger, more formal Upfront Theater in Santa Monica. A series of appearances at the HBO-sponsored US Comedy Arts Festival in Aspen, Colorado, in 1995 didn't win over every crowd, but powerhouse manager Bernie Brillstein saw Cross and Odenkirk and took a liking to them, dispensing friendly advice between sets.

Brillstein's support meant a lot to HBO. He'd managed *Saturday Night Live* stars John Belushi, Gilda Radner, and Dan Akroyd and had a hand in seminal TV shows *Hee Haw*, *The Muppet Show*, and later, *ALF*, *NewsRadio*, *Just Shoot Me!*, and *Politically Incorrect*. He also executive-produced box office smashes such as *The Blues Brothers* and *Ghostbusters*. HBO was reluctant to fully get behind Cross and Odenkirk, because other than Carolyn Strauss and head of programming Chris Albrecht, the network considered them unproven. But thanks to Brillstein's endorsement and their in-house advocates at HBO, Cross and Odenkirk were given a shoestring budget to produce a two-episode pilot series. With the help of inventive, quick-witted director Troy Miller, Cross and Odenkirk were able to wring four half-hour episodes out of the cash, employing some of their favorite actors and writers they had worked with and watched over the years.

The early cast was composed of the portly, avuncular John Ennis (a friend of Cross's from his Boston days), the versatile Jill Talley (who had known Odenkirk in Chicago), lumbering man-giant Brian Posehn, square-jawed loudmouth Jay Johnston, rubber-faced vocal wiz Tom Kenny, the subtly unhinged Mary Lynn Rajskub, and the classically reserved Paul F. Tompkins. Nearly all were new to television. People who acted primarily as writers and producers, like Odenkirk's brother Bill or Odenkirk's compatriot from the Conan O'Brien days, Dino Stamatopoulos, would occasionally pop up in sketches, as would sometime performer-guests Sarah Silverman, Patton Oswalt, Dave Foley, Ben Stiller, and Maynard James Keenan of Tool. Later seasons featured cast members Scott Aukerman, B. J. Porter, Karen Kilgariff, Jerry Minor, Brett Paesel, Scott Adsit, and others. Jack Black also showed up in the first couple of seasons, bringing his uniquely throaty, prancing style to the material. Cross and Odenkirk later helped launch Black's career by producing three half-hour Tenacious D shorts for HBO, which aired just after *Mr. Show* starting in 1997. Tenacious D, of course, went on to open for bands such as Pearl Jam, Foo Fighters, and Beck, and Jack Black became the movie star we know (and sometimes love) today.

But before any of them became celebrities in their own right, the cast and crew of *Mr. Show* were busy revolutionizing sketch comedy—even if the general public took little notice. There's no such thing as a typical episode, but it usually went like this: a cast member introduced the show from a platform in the audience as the camera swung over to the main event. Cross and Odenkirk situated themselves on a small stage (first at the Hollywood Moguls nightclub, and later taped at various studios) before transitioning into a sketch, whether through a pretaped piece, elaborate link, or fourth-wall-shattering stage hop. Sketches rarely ended where they began, setting an early precedent for the unpredictable, smart, and often ridiculous subject matter that came to define the show's sensibility.

Mark Rivers, Cross's friend since they were teenagers, crafted the upbeat, ominous theme featuring a twisting, whistled melody set to a vaguely surf-rock backing track. Eban Schletter joined as music director/composer on the second season, taking over for Groundlings vet

Willie Etra. Early tapings were hot, cramped, and located in a dangerous part of town, often making it difficult to wrangle the necessary audience members (or rather, the right type of audience members—which is to say people who would actually get the jokes). After the first four-show season, and with help from supporter and HBO star Garry Shandling, the network gave *Mr. Show* more money and space to craft a six-episode second season. The critical response had been overwhelmingly positive, but the larger machine at HBO remained wary of getting fully behind it.

The breakneck pace of the work and various creative struggles within the show made the ten-episode third season both a reward and a challenge, with cast members shuffling in and out and guest writers materializing for brief periods. Fortunately, things calmed down by the fourth season, with a handful of performers moving into more assertive roles as writers and producers. The show's writing was nominated for Emmys and the tapings were see-and-be-seen hot spots for cutting-edge comedy fans. But for the fourth season, HBO made the decision to move *Mr. Show* to Mondays at midnight, which effectively zapped cocreator Odenkirk's enthusiasm. Cross was itching to get out of Los Angeles, and the occasionally nasty tension that had built over the years between *Mr. Show*'s writers was not dissipating, so it made sense for everyone to make the fourth season their last. It was also the show's overall best, allowing it to go out on a creative high note that few, if any, sketch comedies have matched.

Appropriately, the cast held a premiere party for the final season at LA's El Rey Theatre on October 13, 1998. Indie rockers Yo La Tengo joined Superchunk—a band Cross had long championed and worn T-shirts of on the show—in providing the music.

★ ★ ★ ★ ★

The end of *Mr. Show* on HBO did not mean the end of *Mr. Show* in general. HBO began releasing the seasons on DVD in June 2002, although Odenkirk and Cross never saw a penny from the sales. Odenkirk, Cross, Brian Posehn, John Ennis, and Stephanie Courtney (who appeared briefly in the last season) reunited in the fall of 2002 to tour a live stage version, bringing back old bits and unveiling new ones. Graphic designer Henry Owings, who handled Naomi Odenkirk's *Mr. Show* book, remembers the rigors and pleasures of the tour. He trekked along with the cast to sell merchandise as the sarcastically named *Hooray for America!* tour made its way from coast to coast. "I've toured a lot with bands, and this was hands down one of the roughest I've ever done," says Owings, who edits the snarky rock-humor magazine *Chunklet*. "Still, when I think about it, I'm so proud I did it. Getting to see the interplay between Bob and David every night was beautiful. They're both funny, but there's something very synergistic about them being together. No matter what I would be doing, setting up tables, selling merch, whatever, I would go out of my way to make sure that I saw that [show] every fucking night, because it was magical."

Odenkirk, Cross, Brian Posehn, Scott Aukerman, and B. J. Porter also wrote the movie *Run Ronnie Run*, which spun off one of the show's few recurring characters, the ignorant redneck Ronnie Dobbs (aka the "most arrested man" in TV history). Unfortunately, Odenkirk and Cross had a falling out with *Mr. Show* alum and *Run Ronnie Run* director Troy Miller over the film's editing, so New Line Cinema held it for nearly three years before dumping it to DVD in 2002. Since they did not have final say in the edit, Odenkirk and Cross both disowned it.

(The movie has its scattered moments, but only the most hard-core *Mr. Show* fans need apply. "It's like *Joe Dirt* meets *Cops*," one user wrote on the movie's IMDB.com page, which pretty much sums it up).

In hindsight, *Mr. Show* does not have the same things going for it that other sketch comedies do, such as being the most bracingly original, longest-running, or popular of the format. But ever since it went off the air, and certainly since it enjoyed new life on DVD, its name has popped up regularly in comedy and industry circles as one of the overall funniest and most cultish sketch shows on TV. "They were really just left alone to do something good," says musician Aimee Mann, who has performed with a good chunk of *Mr. Show*'s cast at her Acoustic Vaudeville nights and tours. "Having this underground scene with these great people, it really does have more of indie sensibility, and it dovetails wonderfully with the music. You've got to give *Mr. Show* credit for that."

But is it the show that defines the sensibility of an era? Patton Oswalt, creator of the *Comedians of Comedy* rock-club tour, notes that *Mr. Show* was one in a long line of benchmarks for the art form. "*Mr. Show* was a big launchpad, but then you think about how it kind of came out of *The Ben Stiller Show*, and that was parallel with *The Kids in the Hall*. So just like with *Comedians of Comedy*, there was always a way of tracing it back, an evolution," he says. "That was one of many awesome things that were happening around that time with Tenacious D and the Largo and *Mr. Show* and the Acoustic Vaudeville nights. But it was still a huge influence."

Comedian Doug Benson, who appeared in three *Mr. Show* episodes and writes movie reviews for BobandDavid.com, relates a story that reinforces the devotion of *Mr. Show* fans. He once ran into reality TV personality Jonny Fairplay (of CBS's *Survivor*), and they quickly got to talking about *Mr. Show*, which Fairplay counted among his favorites. "I recently got an invitation to his wedding," Benson says, "and that all comes from the fact that I wrote those reviews on BobandDavid.com."

Cocreator Odenkirk takes a less charitable view, asserting that *Mr. Show* is still very much a cult phenomenon. "I recently read an article about The Whitest Kids U' Know (a New York–based sketch series) in the *L.A. Weekly* and they didn't mention *Mr. Show* in referencing various sketch shows over the last twenty years," he says. "And I'm not saying that their show is derivative of *Mr. Show*, but the point is that there are still people who write reviews of sketch comedy that don't even know or mention *Mr. Show*." Odenkirk also admits that he's not as plugged in to the performance side of the underground comedy world now that he's in his midforties with two kids. But his assessment of *Mr. Show* as a largely cult, critical success isn't far off. Intelligent, rule-bending comedy still represents just a sliver of the larger entertainment world. "*The Onion* is probably the biggest thing for sort of smart alternative comedy, and it's got its legitimate niche," Odenkirk says. "Whereas back when I was doing the Un-Cabaret shows with Beth Lapides, Greg [Behrendt], Janeane [Garofalo], and Kathy Griffin, that was really relegated to a few tiny little rooms."

What Odenkirk may not appreciate is how large and interconnected the comedy underground has become in the years since *Mr. Show* went off the air and enjoyed rebirth on DVD. "The DVDs sort of stoked the fires for people who either remembered the show fondly and hadn't seen it for awhile, or for people discovering it for the first time," says Matt Belknap, founder of the popular comedy website ASpecialThing.com. "Around that same time Scott [Aukerman] and B. J. [Porter] started *Death-Ray* at the M Bar in LA and were booking a lot of people who had been on *Mr. Show* or were related to *Mr. Show*. So in my mind, running a website like AST that was focused mostly on *Mr. Show* and Tenacious D early on, it felt like *Mr. Show* was the Rosetta stone of comedy. It was this unique moment when two of the best guys in alternative comedy were doing arguably their best work. They brought together a very diverse and interesting group of, at that point, young talent from LA and other places, just pulling together the funniest people they could find. These people became my idols in their post–*Mr. Show* careers, people I aspired to be like in terms of comedy writers."

Tony Kiewel, head of A&R for David Cross's record label Sub Pop, said *Mr. Show* essentially helped reinforce sketch comedy as a relevant art form in a time when few programs were pushing the envelope. "Comedy wasn't cool for a long time. The eighties were such a bad time for comedy, and the idea of stand-up still carried a lot of baggage, at least in my community. Then it started to build back up in the nineties with things like *Mr. Show*."

Cast member/writer Paul F. Tompkins, who tours and performs regularly, thinks *Mr. Show* will only remain an influence as long as no one betters its brand of humor. "It has the potential to become stronger, but *Mr. Show* has already had such a life after cancellation with the DVDs and everything," he says. "That certainly buys us some time, but there will be other things coming along to supplant it, the things that have been influenced by *Mr. Show*, and those will become the influences, as inevitably happens."

David Cross, at his home in New York, would like you to
leave him alone so he can take a shower, for fuck's sake.
Photo by Seth Olenick

3

AT CROSS LAKE

Who would have thought that the unlikely backdrop of Shreveport, Louisiana, would further help me understand how a certain type of comedy had escaped mainstream clubs and taken refuge in the indie-music world?

Not I. But that's exactly where I found myself. I ended up in Shreveport because in order to interview David Cross—a busy man whom I spent months nailing down for an interview and a man often pegged as responsible for the indie-comedy movement—I had to visit him during one of his rare off-weekends while shooting the movie *Year One*. Cross was in Louisiana for a few weeks to play the character of Cain in the Harold Ramis–directed flick, the plot of which concerns a pair of lazy hunter-gatherers (played by Jack Black and Michael Cera) stumbling through the ancient world after getting banished from their village.

But still: Shreveport? *Shreveport*? What the fuck?

Believe it or not, the city has lately been a hot spot in the film and television industry. When *New York Times* reporter David Carr joined others in calling it "Hollywood South" in a May 2008 article, it was no idle boast. More than forty television and film productions have used the city as a stand-in for places that fail to offer the enticing tax incentives Louisiana does. In fact, it was recently (and somewhat loosely) ranked third behind California and New York for the number of screen productions it hosts.

During the early-March weekend that Cross and I agreed to meet, there were no fewer than six television and film projects under way in Shreveport, taking over classic movie theaters, courthouses, and hundreds of thousands of square feet of increasingly professional soundstages. The film industry in Shreveport has gone a long way toward helping the city recover from its mid-1980s slump, when the majority of its oil and gas jobs evaporated. Now it's not uncommon to see Samuel L. Jackson, Sharon Stone, or 50 Cent milling around the modest downtown, which has largely welcomed the productions with open arms (although it occasionally turns ugly, as on July 12, 2008, when actors Josh Brolin and Jeffrey Wright were pepper-sprayed and handcuffed after a melee at local hangout the Stray Cat). Local monthly magazine *CityLife* even features the "Film Reel" column, written by Chris Jay, director of Shreveport's brand-new $4.2-million Robinson Film Center. There's also a great deal of predictable river-city entertainment, such as the various glittering riverboat casinos along the Red River, Harrah's Louisiana Downs horse racing track, and Larry Flynt's Hustler Club, which beckons residents with its sickly neon signage.

And really, it's not so bizarre that Shreveport hosts such a glut of entertainment productions. It has always flirted with pop-culture celebrity as the birthplace of various sports stars (Terry Bradshaw, Joe Ferguson, Albert Belle) and musicians (Hank Williams Jr., Leadbelly,

Kenny Wayne Shepherd). Most significantly, the city hosted the weekly *Louisiana Hayride* radio show from 1948 to 1960. The program gave a young Elvis Presley his start—among dozens of others—which explains the terrifying life-sized Elvis statue that greets travelers by the baggage claim at the airport. An unexpected place, perhaps, to interview one of the more sophisticated, acerbic, polarizing entertainers with whom I've had the pleasure of being obsessed.

Really, few things make my bowels quiver more than the thought of interviewing David Cross. Like Robert Pollard, the leader of my favorite band, Cross seemingly presents several obstacles to rational, calm conversation: (1) I worship his work, almost without exception, and (2) He has demonstrated in the past that he does not suffer fools, turning from friendly and accommodating to sarcastic or dismissive when he realizes the interviewer/fan/random person on the street is a clueless or annoying waste of his time.

Then again, few people have anything to judge Cross by except his TV and film work and his releases on Sub Pop, most of which are as unrelentingly harsh as they are hilarious. The harshness has often earned Cross the "neo–Lenny Bruce" tag. His barbed rants have also been compared to Bill Hicks, Sam Kinison, and Dennis Miller, though Cross would likely bristle at that last one. This helps explain the reputation Cross has with most of my friends, who largely freaked out when I told them I would be traveling to interview him in person. "Man, I love him, but he seems like a real asshole," most of them said. "Good luck with *that*."

Thanks, friends.

Of course, like Robert Pollard (a man whose life I managed to briefly ingratiate myself into via a fanzine I coedited), Cross is just a human being, albeit one who is staggeringly talented in his profession. For all his brilliant, caustic work on *Mr. Show*, Fox's innovative, dearly departed *Arrested Development*, or the dozens of other small to midsized roles he's had in TV, movies, and animated features, I imagined he conducted himself like anyone else, accepting the trappings that come with being a midlevel celebrity and cult hero. That he is worshipped by comedy nerds and a certain swath of cultural critics is often of little use to his mainstream profile, since he is also generally invisible to the people who never miss an episode of *Wheel of Fortune* or who frequent all-you-can-eat buffets and muscle car shows in flea market parking lots.

But the things that place Cross on the margins of popular culture are the same things that have made him a hero to the indie-comedy scene, the first comic to prove to a national audience that his fans would come to see him in droves at underground music venues instead of comedy clubs, undertaking groundbreaking tours in 2001 and 2002 that swiftly influenced dozens of other stand-ups and promoters around the country.

I detected ambivalence when I first began talking with Cross on the phone, trying to confirm an interview date and get him invested in the project. Really, what stand-up would want to be reduced to a term like *indie comedian* or relegated to a single scene that's lousy with hipsters (the most loathsome of all mammals)? Assholes and egomaniacs, that's who. But Cross also understood that for better or worse, he is associated with the indie-music world more than any other stand-up. (Although, as he would later admit, he has pulled himself back from the brink of what he feared could be self-parody, or at least laziness, by no longer constantly hosting and appearing at indie-music events.)

So it was with some trepidation and overall giddiness that I trekked from Denver to Shreveport for a weekend, catchphrases from *Mr. Show* and Cross's not-so-subtly-named CD, *Shut Up, You Fucking Baby!*, dancing in my anxious brain.

I arrived at the Super 8 near the airport on a gray Friday afternoon, intent on going over my notes before the next morning's meeting with Cross. I swiftly realized, however, that I should have sprung for a room at the Hampton Inn next door, as the Super 8 lived up to its reputation as a scary shithole filled with drugs, drug users, and drug users' bodily fluids.

"Are you straight?" an unsteady older man in a baseball cap belched at me in the hallway to my room, which overlooked a car lot and a Foremost Farms dairy distribution center, replete with a giant plastic statue of a cow and her calf ("The Dairy Best!").

"Yeah, I'm cool."

His prompt response of another sonorous belch allowed me to go on my way and stow what little personal effects I'd brought. I next headed out to grab a bite and (I hoped) experience the unmitigated joy that is downtown Shreveport. But other than a few pimply-faced emo kids and stumbling homeless people, the city felt abandoned at 8 PM. Occasionally I'd spot evidence of a film crew, like the half dozen equipment and catering trucks parked outside downtown's Strand Theatre, traffic cones and cops directing the odd vehicle that managed to squeeze by.

It was the kind of place where you find an empty parking lot with a burly old man sitting in a Cadillac taking money. The kind of place where you say, "Five bucks?" and the guy croaks, "That's what it *says* on the *sign*," before wordlessly counting your bills and watching you while you park and amble out of your car. (It didn't help that I fought to untangle the strap of my band-button-laden messenger bag for five minutes while checking my cell phone and lighting a smoke—the likely picture of a douche bag Yankee tourist.)

I stopped in the Blind Tiger restaurant, wondering if maybe I'd catch sight of any of the actors, extras, or crew members from the various productions in town. It was also the kind of place I was expecting, which is to say homey and cute, with "appetigers" like Zydeco cheese fries with bacon, mini crawfish-meat pies, popcorn craw-tails, and desserts like TheDevilMadeMeDoIt (a fudge brownie with French vanilla ice cream, whipped cream, chocolate sauce, and chopped pecans). It's the kind of place where a stuffed-animal tiger in sunglasses sits atop a TV replaying the NASCAR Nationwide series from Atlanta. The kind of place that by 8:30 PM on a Friday was crawling with aging high-school honeys in see-through lace tops and black pushup bras, obese elderly couples, identical T-shirted frat boys, and drawl-heavy gamblers of every age and race. The kind of place where manly-men toss back, without irony, blowjob shots and sing "I Just Called to Say I Love You" in the highest, sweetest voices possible.

It wasn't exactly a historic, stereotypical old-South eating experience, but at least it didn't have that patina of construction dust and forced personality that every T.G.I. Friday's or Applebee's does. And the Budweiser was cheap. And cold.

Returning to the motel, I accidentally kicked over a tallboy of Old English in the hallway, a urine-smelling liquid soaking through the paper bag and onto the carpet as angry young men eyed me quietly while smoking and blocking the path to my room. (I found another route.) I didn't end up getting much sleep that night, either, as around midnight a pair of drunks decided to have it out in the stairwell next to my paper-thin wall.

"Don't judge me! You can't judge me!" a woman screamed repeatedly. "You ain't no *pimp!*"

"Fuck yoooooou!!" her equally besotted male companion replied. This went on and on as I drifted through restless sleep, feverishly imagining a hotel room with walls thicker than cellophane.

David Cross is no stranger to the South, but Shreveport was still a bizarre environment in which to meet him for the first time. He drove his rental car to the Super 8 and picked me up late the next morning, welcoming me with (literally) open arms, wearing a puffy blue jacket, full dark beard, and wide grin in the morning sun. "It's not good, foodwise, around here," he informed me as we listened to hip-hop from Lupe Fiasco on his stereo, hurtling west on Interstate 20. "I mean, really: it's not good."

That would explain why we ended up having breakfast at the Cracker Barrel, a restaurant Cross said he'd never had the pleasure of eating at. (If you can think of a more surreal experience than eating at a Cracker Barrel with David Cross, please tell me.) Our waitress paused to examine Cross's bald head and thick hipster eyeglasses as he sopped up gravy with his biscuits. "You look familiar," she said, stretching out the last few syllables with languid southern inquisitiveness, though she didn't seem to be sure if she really recognized him or not. "Were you on *Just Shoot Me!*?"

He was, but Cross just smiled and shook his head politely as she strolled away.

"Do people generally recognize you around here, or is it more of that 'I *think* I recognize you...?'" I asked.

"Mostly that," he replied.

As I soon learned, there was little to occupy Cross during his two on-and-off months in Shreveport when he wasn't working on *Year One*. He hosted a chili cook-off, read and wrote, played poker at the local casinos, partied with friends from the film, and played with his dog. In fact, as we left the Cracker Barrel, he decided to pick up a couple of toys for his two-year-old Akita/Rottweiler/German shepherd mix, a bright-eyed spaz named Ollie Red Sox in honor of Cross's favorite baseball team.

After breakfast we drove through the sunny, chilly air toward his cabin on the appropriately named Cross Lake, which supplies water for Shreveport and fishing and boating for everyone else. Cross's spacious rental house, situated in a small gated community on a tightly looped street, sported high ceilings and opened out back to a deck on the edge of the lake, where his dog Ollie would romp through the shallow, muddy marsh. As Cross got the battery-operated dog toys from Cracker Barrel up and running (neon-colored plastic balls with fake fur tails that darted alarmingly around the tile floors), we settled into a pair of damp wooden deck chairs, my mini-cassette recorder whirring quietly next to him.

For all the press Cross has gotten over the years, very little of it talks in depth about his origins, or the experiences that inform his wickedly sharp, pissed-off sense of humor. A good starting place is Naomi Odenkirk's episode guide *What Happened?!* But that book only spends a few lines on Cross's upbringing, and I wanted to know more about this man whose sense of humor has had a cometlike impact on mine and so many others'.

Cross was born on April 4, 1964, in Atlanta, a city from which his Jewish family moved away six months later for Florida. His father was constantly getting ejected from jobs, his mother struggling to hold the family together. His family (including younger sisters Juli and Wendy) then moved to New York, where they lived in various places for the next five years. After another move, to Connecticut, the family settled back in Atlanta when Cross was ten years old. Even there, they continued to flit between hotel rooms and apartments, often to prevent themselves from becoming homeless. "My dad either got fired or would quit in an ill-intentioned act of moral outrage over something I'm sure he should have gotten fired for," Cross says of his father, who left the family when Cross was ten and whom Cross has not spoken to since age nineteen. "But I also don't really know the truth, because he was constantly lying and, to the best of my knowledge, never really took blame or fault for anything. I don't know what the real story was, but I know we constantly moved and had no money. Then I found out later we had to move a lot because we were evicted from a couple places."

As a result, Cross frequently played the role of the bespectacled new kid ("the new *Jew* kid," he has said), and always had to prove himself to the natives. His outgoing, comedic persona began forming because of this, with Cross declining to take much of anything seriously —probably his most available defense mechanism. "Like every kid, there were some situations where I would be outgoing or extroverted, and then a situation where I wasn't, often with some of the same people. But I never thought, *Comedy is what I'm really good at. I need to sharpen this skill in order to survive socially.*"

He took guitar, clarinet, and drum lessons in grade school, but they never lasted long, since his family pulled up stakes every eight to twelve months. He found comfort in classic TV comedies and movies, from Abbott and Costello and the Marx Brothers to *Monty Python's Flying Circus, All in the Family, M.A.S.H.,* and *The Carol Burnett Show.* He listened to Dr. Demento's radio show, which featured parodies and novelty songs (the character was later parodied on

Mr. Show), and was thrilled when *Saturday Night Live* premiered (under its current format) just before his thirteenth birthday. While most boys his age were in to baseball and motocross, he—and the handful of like-minded friends he made while moving from place to place—waited impatiently for each new *SNL* or *SCTV* episode.

Unlike his sundry friends, however, Cross was usually the comedy nerd of the group, even if he didn't think of himself that way. "I don't know that I pored over comedy records, but that was definitely a thing that I'd imitate and was really knowledgeable about. One friend was way into prog rock, and one friend was really into punk and new wave. I mean, we were all somewhat into those things, but I was the one who'd say, 'Oh, you gotta check out this thing called Derek and Clive. It's fuckin' awesome.'" Derek and Clive were a cult British duo created by Dudley Moore and Peter Cook, and it's no stretch to think their vulgar 1970s records influenced Cross's profanity-laced sense of humor or his mischievous attitude. He once spray-painted The Who on the door of his apartment building, but sister Wendy painted over it to keep him from getting in trouble. (He would later join in painting The Who across the parking lot of his first high school.)

Music was important to Cross. *The Who by Numbers* was the first album he bought with his own money, when he was ten years old. He attended his first rock show at age fifteen at the Fox Theatre in midtown Atlanta. Cross and another underage friend volunteered to be ushers just to get through the door. "You basically come in with black pants and a little shirt and they give you a vest. It was the easiest scam in the *world*," he says, his eyes sparkling and voice rising to a familiar musical tone. "We took the vests off, changed our shirts, and went into the crowd. Nobody knew who we were. It was stunningly, remarkably simple to do and I would highly recommend it for anybody."

The acts at the Fox that night were The Kinks and John Cougar (pre-Mellencamp), though Cross immediately felt embarrassed by the rednecks in the audience. "I remember somebody hung a big rebel flag from the balcony and then just shouted, 'Kinks, maaaan! Motherfuckin' Kinks!'"

Like any normal teenager, Cross nurtured a strong antiauthoritarian streak and came to despise the double standards and hypocrisy that oozed from institutions and people in power. The music he listened to, including The Clash, The Sex Pistols, Buzzcocks, The Stranglers, The Damned, The Ramones, and various West Coast punk bands, only solidified those feelings.

But by far the biggest influence on Cross's young life was his decision to drop out of Crestwood High School in Roswell, Georgia, in tenth grade. "I absolutely fucking hated it with the passion of ten goths combined," he says. He auditioned for the Northside High School of the Performing Arts in Atlanta—a magnet school of Crestwood, now called North Atlanta High School. "I can't say enough how instrumental to my development in personality and life that was. And going to school closer to the city, as opposed to suburban-rural Roswell, was important culturally, too."

He studied musical theater his sophomore year and switched to drama his junior and senior years, encouraged by teacher Tim Habeger, who still works as producing artistic director for PushPush Theater in Atlanta. Cross appeared in productions like *West Side Story* (as a cigarette-smoking tough), but never considered himself a great actor or singer. For him, the classes were less about developing a skill than turning him on to theater, literature, music, and different ways of thinking. Unsurprisingly, his classmates also named him "most humorous."

In 1982, a few weeks before his eighteenth birthday, he made his first foray into stand-up comedy by playing an open-mic night at The Punchline in Sandy Springs, just south of Roswell. "Not only did I do really, really well, but when I said, 'Oh, the red light's on, I gotta go,' the audience went 'Nooooooo!!' That's *never* happened. And I honestly thought I was the shit, a genius, the greatest. *I clearly am a wunderkind and this is amazing.* And I'd say roughly the next thirteen to fourteen times I was awful. I just ate it."

Killing on his first night—and in a way that would be unbelievable even in a movie—was ironically the worst thing that could have happened for a still-green comic with only five to seven minutes of material. It was the sort of confusing beginner's luck that eventually made Cross quit stand-up for a few years. And although he dismisses his early act, he recognizes it portended a better one. "It was somewhere between Stephen Wright and Andy Kaufman," he says of his style. "I did a lot of weird shit and had musical cues and a lot of meta-comedy. I look back at it and think it's not that funny, but if I saw a seventeen- or eighteen-year-old doing it, I'd say, 'I want to check in with this guy in five or ten years, because I like the way his mind's working.'"

Performing material reminiscent of Andy Kaufman—a big influence on Cross at the time, and one that helped birth his occasionally soft-spoken, faux-innocent delivery—presented a challenge in Georgia in the early eighties. The day after he graduated high school in 1982, Cross's wanderlust led him to New York, where he worked for a lawn care company in Long Island for three months before returning to Atlanta. He stayed there until he was nineteen, then moved to Boston, where he enrolled at Emerson College to study film. He dropped out after only one semester.

Nonetheless, Boston was where Cross grew into something resembling his current self: a hard-partying, unyielding personality who excelled at sketch comedy and loose stand-up, and who relished fucking with audiences he often hated. He eventually met a group of comics and friends he would work with extensively, starting with John Ennis, later of *Mr. Show*.

Cross took an instant liking to Ennis while auditioning for his sketch group *This Is Pathetic* in 1984. The group also included Anthony Clark, Michael Bent, and Laura Kightlinger—who would later appear on *Saturday Night Live* and *The Daily Show* and write for *Will & Grace*—among others. Of the ten people in the group, Ennis came onstage to work with Cross during his audition. The two discovered they had an instant, unspoken ability to riff off each other and soon became good friends. It helped that they took a few road trips to Los Angeles, starting the summer after they met, and spent loads of time bumming around and partying. (Cross has said the biggest influences on him were his peers and their approval of his ideas, more so than any particular comedian or show.)

On one summer trip, Cross and Ennis had been planning to stay with a comedian friend, but when they discovered he was about to leave for the road, they had to find another place to crash. Being summer, a fraternity at UCLA (Cross remembers it as Zeta Psi) was renting out a storage room behind the kitchen in their house. He and Ennis had been sleeping in their friend Paul's car for about a week, so when they saw the flyer for the room, they pounced on it immediately, although they would have to live with a guy named Tiger in the tiny space and put up with the pathetic frat boys who smoked pipes, lamely tossed furniture off the roof, and pompously bossed them around. The nomadic, heavy-drinking LA trips also left Cross and Ennis finding creative ways to get by, like crafting shoddy earrings and selling them on Venice Beach in order to buy cheap whiskey and Fatburgers.

Back in Boston, Cross stuck to sketch comedy for the next few years, honing his chops, but mostly partying and hanging out. When he started doing stand-up again in 1987, the ground was fertile. "Those were the days where you could do stand-up seven nights a week, and there were a million places to do open-mic nights and to do paid gigs, which is not the case anymore," said Janeane Garofalo in *What Happened?!* Garofalo, a senior in college at the time (and just a few months younger than Cross), was part of a rising tide of what would eventually come to be known as alternative comedy.

An ill-defined genre, perhaps, but one that was a direct reaction to the swath of generic, stale stand-ups who came out of the eighties comedy boom. At worst, those "boom" comedians were assholes in blazers and skinny ties, culturally backward and openly homophobic, misogynistic, or racist—the opposite of the edgy, smart stuff Cross liked—but mostly they were just boring, loud, and dumb. The headier, weirder material Cross liked began to coalesce around the Cambridge location of Catch a Rising Star in 1989, where Cross was hosting Tuesday open-mic nights with people such as Garofalo, Kightlinger, Louis C. K. (his roommate for a time), Marc Maron, and Jon Benjamin.

The club rapidly gave Cross more leeway, so he asked to take over the open-mic night and try an entirely new approach. They granted it. He led a loose but serious group of about a dozen writer-performers (including Ennis) through shows that cultivated an off-balance vibe, hybridizing theater, comedy, video, and performance art, elements of which would carry over to *Mr. Show* five years later. "We were maybe three-to-five months into doing the show, but we didn't really have a name for it," Cross remembers. "It would have sort of ruined it, too, because the element of surprise was integral. We'd have like four regular open mic'ers and then a plant, which was a fake comedian that one of us would do. And we'd have plants in the audience. The whole show evolved slowly, but virtually every single time people were confused and didn't understand what was happening. And of course as the show became known and we had a name for it, we sort of lost the element of surprise."

That name, *Cross Comedy*, pointed to Cross's increasing leadership of Boston's progressive comedy scene. Over time the show found an audience (other comedians, hipsters, bike messengers, adventurous cultural types) and garnered scattered press while remaining largely under the radar. The unpredictable, occasionally themed nature of the show prevented many people from knowing what to make of it. It departed radically from the overexposed routines of most stand-ups by offering a variety show of surprising, challenging, and ultimately thought-provoking pieces.

One night *Cross Comedy* staged a telethon to raise money for Seth's brothers, even though no one knew who Seth or his brothers were. The action took place on two stages, with Catch's main stage as the national telethon center and a smaller upper stage twenty feet to the left acting as the local telethon, with which they would check in frequently. Similar setups would reappear in *Mr. Show* sketches like "Evil Genius Telethon" and "The Dewey Awards." "There were definitely some *Mr. Show* elements," Cross says, noting that *Cross Comedy* also incorporated pretaped video pieces that would pick up where a performer's stage exit left off, sometimes in a different part of the city.

Catch's artistic coordinator Robin Hordon felt the show was the future for comedy crowds, the smarter members of which had already tasted the sickly metallic flavor of the comedy boom's crash. *Boston Globe* reporter

John Koch caught one of the *Cross Comedy* shows for a July 1990 article: "The wave of the future, Hordon is convinced, is reconceived comedy combined with music and standup fare...In less than a year, Hordon thinks the standard comedy format will be on the ropes. He sees his early-week showcases and the talents-in-training there as an investment in the future. If Hordon is right, what is now an entertaining assault on the status quo will be familiar fare in the nineties."

It was around this time that Cross picked up his current manager, Tim Sarkes. Early Cross influence, comedy hero, and Emerson College alumnus Steven Wright had seen Cross perform via an introduction by *Cross Comedy* member Lauren Dombrowski, later a head writer and longtime producer for *MadTV*. Wright introduced himself to Cross after a set and, as Cross figures, "I'm guessing he told Tim, who only had three or four clients at the time and was still based out of New York, and he came up to Boston, and the rest is mildly entertaining history!"

But after two years of *Cross Comedy* and nine years of living in Boston, Cross had begun to scrape the walls of his terrarium, especially as *Cross Comedy* reached its capacity limit, moving out of Catch a Rising Star to play five-hundred-seat theaters for several weekends in a row, often with live musical acts.

Garofalo had been urging Cross to come to Los Angeles, where she had moved to work on fledgling Fox sketch comedy *The Ben Stiller Show* with Andy Dick, Bob Odenkirk, Dino Stamatopoulos, and others. The show had jettisoned one of its writers and needed to hire a midseason replacement immediately. "The push to go to LA came directly from Ben Stiller and [writer/executive producer] Judd Apatow via Janeane," Cross says. "I had met with Ben prior to his show, just hanging out informally with him and Janeane at a bar, and we all got along great. But I was very much of the mind-set that what I was doing was pure and had so much integrity that to go to LA and work on television was stupid. I guess maybe I had just reread *Catcher in the Rye* or some shit like that. It felt like it was some version of selling out. Which is retarded."

Cross soon relented and sent a writing submission to the show, which was warmly received and quickly approved. They gave him forty-eight hours to make up his mind.

It wasn't easy: Cross had come to love Boston and his success there. He performed stand-up and sketch comedy full time—or at least enough to quit his day job for a couple years. He played softball three times a week with a group of comedians and musicians, traversed the city on his bicycle, and generally partied like any twenty-eight-year-old would. But Cross had also grown weary of living hand-to-mouth in shitty apartments, so he flew out to LA one late-October weekend in 1991 and started on *The Ben Stiller Show* at once. (He would later return to Boston over Thanksgiving break, pack up his things, and make the 3,000 mile drive back to LA in an impressive three-and-a-half days in his '76 Chevy Malibu.)

There wasn't much of a season left to write for: Cross only contributed to five of the thirteen episodes filmed for *The Ben Stiller Show,* one of which never aired. It also didn't help that he was suddenly thrust into a creative environment starkly different from his previous one, writing bits that included celebrity impersonations and parody—neither of which were his strong points at the time.

On only his second day he relearned what it was like to be the new kid in school when writer Bob Odenkirk passive-aggressively asserted himself. The staff was discussing possibilities for parodies of then-hit film *A Few Good Men* when Cross suggested taking the plot down to the level of Boy Scouts. "Ben liked it and Bob went, 'Great, all right, he's on it. Let's go guys.' He just sort of left me there," Cross says. It was a prove-yourself moment that recalled Steve Martin's early days writing for the *Smothers Brothers Comedy Hour* in the late sixties, when Martin was teamed with staff writer Bob Einstein (the older brother of Albert Brooks), who would more or less bully newcomer Martin. And like Martin and Einstein, Odenkirk and Cross would eventually become friends, even as each pair's respective shows were cancelled—in *The Ben Stiller Show*'s case, because of low ratings, though to be fair it ran opposite *60 Minutes*.

Nonetheless, *The Ben Stiller Show* won an Emmy in 1993 for Outstanding Achievement in Writing in a Variety or Music Program, beating out *Saturday Night Live* and *In Living Color.* Each writer received a statuette, but Cross felt he barely deserved his, since he only wrote a few lines of dialogue for the award-winning episode. (He gave it to his mother, Susie, and it still sits on her mantel.)

Cross had contributed some worthy ideas to *The Ben Stiller Show* and popped up in a few of its sketches—fans particularly adore "The Legend of T. J. O'Pootertoot's," which Cross wrote and briefly appeared in—but the experience was far from ideal. It did, however, introduce him to the next phase of his career with creative partner Bob Odenkirk, one that would come to define him for many people and earn him a permanent spot on the national comedy scene.

After a short nap break—Cross had been up late the night before at a wrap party for a *Year One* cast member—I returned to Cross Lake to finish our interview, Cross dallying on the phone as he worked out the terms of a car he was buying, then marinating chicken breasts (white wine, garlic, sugar, spices) for a meal he was making later for an actress friend.

"I am breaking my rule to never date actresses," he said, lightly shaking the concoction in a clear plastic bag. He didn't offer her name.

I had only a few hours left with Cross and so was more interested in picking up where our discussion left off, which was at *Mr. Show*. However, the storied, jigsaw history of that program has already been chronicled in *What Happened?!*, and if you're reading this book start-to-finish like a normal human being, then you've come across my take on *Mr. Show* and its influence on the indie-comedy world.

It seemed like a good idea, then, to skip past the demise of *Mr. Show* and into the realm of what I had traveled so many miles to talk about. Granted, part of that was the enduring influence of *Mr. Show*'s sensibility and the ways in which its various cast, crew, and fans have retaken parts of the stand-up scene from comedy clubs. *Mr. Show* helped build a national, if cult, following for Cross and his cohorts. Like most of them, Cross went on to do more writing, character acting, and stand-up, just as he had during the production of *Mr. Show*, in 1990s movies such as *The Truth about Cats and Dogs*, *The Cable Guy*, and *Waiting for Guffman*. Cross's appearances on sitcoms during that time, such as *The Drew Carey Show*, *NewsRadio*, and *Just Shoot Me!*, also allow him to live on through syndication.

But I was more interested in Cross's exodus from Los Angeles following *Mr. Show*. After living in that city for nearly nine years, appearing in TV shows, movies, and even his own one-hour HBO special, *The Pride Is Back*, he decided to fulfill a longtime dream of moving to New York—the city in which he still (mostly) lives.

"I always had said I'm moving to LA so I can make enough money to move away from LA. Which means I just wanted to get my career in a place where I could move and not take too much of a hit." Unlike thousands of others in the entertainment industry, Cross did not relish LA's weather, layout, and populace. He didn't hate it, either, he was just bored to tears. "In all honesty, not a day goes by when I'm not conscious at some point of how much I love New York and the [East Village] neighborhood I live in."

There was no real gap in Cross's stand-up performances from LA to New York when he landed there in the spring of 2001. He had done shows before at Luna Lounge, a Lower East Side bar/music venue, but began appearing there more regularly once based in the city. Luna's Monday night *Eating It* show had become a beacon for fans of edgy comedy. Created in 1995 by comedy manager Dave Becky and entertainment publicity agent Michael O'Brien, and later produced by Naomi Steinberg and Jeff Singer, it was originally staged at the Rebar in Chelsea. It moved to Luna and would continue there on a weekly basis until Luna pulled up stakes and moved to Williamsburg, Brooklyn, in 2005 (when the original building was demolished).

The show's "literate laughs," as *New York Magazine* dubbed them, only asked for a seven- or eight-dollar cover, which included one drink. Established comics and emerging names such as Louis C. K., Sarah Silverman, Eugene Mirman, Maria Bamford, Todd Barry, Demetri Martin, Jon Benjamin, and dozens of others graced its tiny, smoky back-room stage. Indie-rock bands Interpol, The Strokes, Nada Surf, The Wrens, and Elliott Smith (who often wrote lyrics there) also played Luna every other night of the week, always for free. The mix of forward-thinking indie music and comedy was not unique to New York or that time period in general, but it offered a reliable and distilled version of either scene's heaviest hitters. "It's where you'll get comedy that may be too ambitious—and sometimes just too weird— to ever make it to the regular clubs," opined *Time Out New York*.

Eating It quickly developed a reputation for show-casing risk-taking material even as some of those risks didn't pay off, as hinted at by the show's name. It provided a safe place for comics to test new jokes, and to see and be seen by agents and bookers. "It indulges us," Marc Maron told Neil Strauss in a 1996 *New York Times* article. "There are people who think differently or lead different lives, and part of the Luna trip is that those people are going to be embraced for that."

Luna wasn't the only alternative comedy venue in New York during the mid- to late nineties. Others included Lower East Side shows like *Collective Unconscious* and *Surf Reality*, and the rapidly expanding Upright Citizens Brigade at the TriBeCa Lab. But for a time, it was the hottest. "I would hang out there anyway because that's where all my friends were, even friends from out of town," Cross says.

A "greedy and disgusting" experience Cross had with the owner of Luna Lounge would eventually inspire him to form his own show across the street. But before that happened, he embarked on a little tour that helped set the template for a new generation of comedians.

Mincing words has never been David Cross's strong suit, so his repeated refusals to take credit for the pioneering tours that would eventually birth his first Sub Pop CD, 2002's *Shut Up, You Fucking Baby!*, and the 2003 road documentary *Let America Laugh*, ring true. His "right time, right place" defense doesn't smack of any false modesty, but the fact is, Cross's reputation and visibility in the indie-music and indie-comedy world are what made those tours such resounding successes.

It started when Nashville natives and childhood friends Shonali Bhowmik and Michelle Dubois, of the Atlanta rock band Ultrababyfat, called Cross in 1999 to play a one-off show at the Earl in East Atlanta. "David became friends with us in Atlanta and I asked him if he wanted to do a show with Ultrababyfat while he was working in Atlanta on his movie," Bhowmik says via e-mail. Cross was shooting the *Mr. Show* spin-off *Run Ronnie Run*, and since he had some free time on his hands, he decided to give it a shot. Nobody had any expectations going into it.

"I got to the club and there was a fucking line around the block, and that was shocking," Cross says. "I had a blast, but it was just one of those things where it never occurred to me to try it again."

"We had such a good time that we started doing more shows," Bhowmik says. "[Like] some one-offs in Savannah, Georgia, during the St. Patrick's Day weekend. Tammy at Velvet Elvis booked, and Cole, who used to book The Echo Lounge in Atlanta, booked the show at the Howling Wolf [in New Orleans]."

Once again the shows sold out, generating excitement in the regional underground community and culminating in standing-room-only concerts. It wasn't a concept that was unique to Ultrababyfat and Cross. He had played with bands before, like his old friend Mark Rivers's band in Boston, The Cave Dogs. But even if it had been tried, and in less-than-ideal environments, Bhowmik and Cross honed the concept by billing the shows specifically as comedy-music pairings. Audiences knew exactly what to expect going in, putting them in the appropriate mood to rock out during Ultrababyfat's sets and to devote the appropriate amount of attention during Cross's stand-up sets.

A few months later, Bhowmik suggested the idea of a mini-tour using her booker, Kevin French, and playing a dozen East Coast and Midwest rock clubs instead of comedy clubs. "It makes nothing but sense when you take comedy out of a comedy club," Cross said at a March 2007 panel at the South by Southwest conference titled *Comedy on the Music Circuit*. "[A comedy club] has a much different energy and vibe and restrictions to it. It's usually in a strip mall somewhere or it's expensive and there's a cover. You can't do all-ages, there's a two-drink minimum. It just felt better and more natural [this way]." Cross later admitted to me that he could have made more money doing a comedy-club tour, but that he preferred being able to perform as long as he wanted (often up to three hours at a time), and to promote it how he wanted, on college radio stations instead of the excruciating "morning zoo crew" shows.

The ensuing mini-tour, which took place in the fall of 2001, again sold out, thanks in part to cheap tickets (around eight dollars per show) and heavy Internet buzz, generating publicity that far outstripped many bigger stand-up shows at comedy clubs and theaters. The demand for this new type of show was beginning to assert itself nationally, and the timing of the phone call Cross was about to receive could not have been more opportune. "Coming back from the Savannah gig, our last show on that first tour, was when I got the call from Sub Pop," Cross explains. "It had never occurred to me to do an album, but I said, 'Sure, that's great.' And then somebody else talked about documenting it. It was all somebody else's idea and I was like, 'Yep, sounds good. Makes sense. Let's do it.' There was never a master plan. Plus, there's a lot of friendships and overlap there."

The phone call came from Tony Kiewel, head of A&R at Seattle-based Sub Pop Records. The label needs little introduction in the indie-music world, best known for releasing Nirvana's *Bleach*, an album that helped kick off the alternative music landslide, and, later, commercially successful records by indie-rock bands The Postal Service, The Shins, and others. But in 2001, Sub Pop remained an unstable enterprise with few hits to show for itself ("Literally inches away from bankruptcy," Kiewel has said). The idea of putting out a comedy record sprang both from fandom and financial practicality.

Prior to moving to Seattle in 2000 to work for Sub Pop, Kiewel had been based in Los Angeles. He and the bands he lived with rabidly consumed comedy, gravitating toward cutting-edge stuff like *Mr. Show*, Patton Oswalt, and Mitch Hedberg. Kiewel would watch Hedberg perform at clubs such as Largo and pass around Hedberg CDs with the same zeal as if they were rare, unreleased recordings from his favorite bands. "We all had copies of his records and felt it was this awesome, secret thing," Kiewel said at the 2007 music-comedy panel at South by Southwest. "I don't really get this very often with music or comedy anymore, because it feels like everything is so available [and] instant. It just felt like that special thing that's yours and your friends'. It's part of this community that you have, and it's this language, and you're quoting jokes to each other."

After he left LA for Seattle, Kiewel made attempts to contact Hedberg about putting out a CD on Sub Pop, troubled that the only way to buy Hedberg's material was through his website. Repeated attempts yielded no response. (Hedberg, of course, later died of a drug overdose, in 2005.) Kiewel was also distressed at the general state of the comedy album, an art form that had languished in the 1990s as cable TV specials negated the need for many people to buy audio-only versions of a stand-up's set. Kiewel had been rediscovering the genius of Richard Pryor, whom he had not listened to since he was a teenager, through a Rhino Records boxed set. He read about how the massive success of Bob Newhart's comedy albums in the 1960s helped build Warner Bros. Records. These albums not only topped sales charts but won Grammy awards. It only strengthened his feelings about the sad state of the comedy album—and the potential benefits Sub Pop might enjoy in attempting to revive it.

Music booker Kevin French of Bigshot Touring Artists, who booked the first Cross-Ultrababyfat mini-tour, eventually suggested Cross to Kiewel as a comedian who seemed ripe for Sub Pop. "I remember reading an interview with David in *Chunklet* and him being a fan of [Sub Pop band] Beachwood Sparks, which blew my mind," Kiewel explained to me. "I was like, 'Wow, he's aware of it!' The idea that there was some intersection between that comedy scene and our music community was surprising to me."

Robin Taylor, who founded New York–based Inland Empire Touring in 1998, had been evangelizing the idea of pairing underground comedians with indie-rock bands before Kiewel thought to contact Cross. Kiewel remembers a show that Taylor booked at Maxwell's in Hoboken, New Jersey, in 2001 with bands Beachwood Sparks and The Shins, and comedians Tim and Eric (now of Adult Swim's *Tim and Eric Awesome Show, Great Job!*). The legendary club, which held around 200 people, was almost ludicrously packed and buzzing with energy.

Taylor, who now books forty-odd indie-rock bands (including Wolf Parade, Modest Mouse, Swearing at Motorists, and Les Savy Fav) and a half-dozen or so comedians (Tim and Eric, Eugene Mirman, Fred Armisen,

Jon Benjamin), sees the shift of comedy toward indie rock as an inevitability, as opposed to anything she helped push. "They were two parallel scenes that were destined to meet eventually," she says. "I book more musical acts than comedians, but I've had Fred Armisen open for bands like Band of Horses or The Shins. Everyone is a fan of each other's, and sometimes it's more fun to put a comedian in the middle than having two opening bands."

Kiewel still looks to her as one of the architects of situating comedy on the indie-music circuit, even as he realizes the movement was starting to happen in other places. "She was one of the first that I encountered that was really pushing for that and making it happen, right around the time David launched his whole rock club tour," he says. "But the New York comedians had been flirting with that for a couple years, that sort of weird crossover format."

For Kiewel, pitching a David Cross comedy album to Sub Pop also made investment sense. The resources required to produce a stand-up album were vastly less than a music album, since bands often required months of expensive studio time with hot-shit producers. Development and tour support costs were negligible to nonexistent, as any comedian fit for Sub Pop would likely already have a manager, booking agent, relationship with venues, and preexisting audience.

But Kiewel wasn't convinced Cross would even go for it. "To me, that seemed way beyond our reach. I mean, just absurdly so. This guy is a star. He was famous as far as I was concerned. So I said [to Kevin French], 'Next time you talk to David, see if he's interested in putting out a record with us.'" Kiewel quickly got everyone at Sub Pop on board with the idea of soliciting Cross. Even if they were unfamiliar with his stand-up sets, their deep, abiding love of

Mr. Show was reason enough. And since the label's biggest bands at the time sold tens of thousands of copies of their albums instead of hundreds of thousands, the marketing potential of having a comedian appear on a show like *Late Night with Conan O'Brien* seemed highly attractive.

"I can't emphasize how different the landscape felt," Kiewel says. "The push to get one of our bands on *Conan* or *Letterman* hadn't been successful for ten years, but a B-level comedian can walk on there anytime. But mostly it was just the idea of David, because we were all fans of his work."

When Cross got the call to join the label, he barely let Kiewel finish his pitch before agreeing to it, being a huge fan of Sub Pop himself. In the late spring and summer of 2002, Cross and Ultrababyfat went out again for a more robust string of dates—albeit equally as bare bones in setup and as whirlwind in scheduling as the mini-tour. Documentary filmmaker and music video director Lance Bangs, who had worked with Nirvana, Sonic Youth, R.E.M., Pavement, and Green Day, tagged along to capture the action with his roving lens. Most of the shows were recorded for a Sub Pop CD, utilizing a five-microphone setup and ADAT recorder.

As with any enterprise that turns over new ground, things occasionally got messy. The result of Bangs's filmmaking, the 2003 Sub Pop DVD *Let America Laugh*, paints vividly the behind-the-scenes antics of the twenty-one-city tour. It intentionally eschews uninterrupted stretches of Cross's act to focus on the uncomfortable and candid moments, like playing to a drunken audience in Little Rock, Arkansas—"A fucking nightmare," as Cross said on the DVD. "It's like babysitting thalidomide-retarded puppies." In an unfortunate bit of venue architecture, the club's stage door led directly to the street. As Cross waits patiently outside to take the stage, a drunken local inadvertently forces Cross to let him into the club for free by preceding Cross through the door, onto the stage, and into the crowd. All Cross could do was watch.

Cross's clash with a stubborn, thin-skinned employee of a Nashville club over table placement and food sales also took on a life of its own. Exit/In operations manager Thomas Weber attempted to sue Cross, then his label and its related companies, two years after Sub Pop released *Let America Laugh* for including Weber's pissy behavior on it. At various points he argues with Cross about what's best for the show, then berates him and attempts to get rid of him after his set as Cross drags out the experience for comedy's sake, slowly stuffing posters and records into his backpack while nursing a bottle of beer. But Weber's case had no legitimacy, since he'd already consented to being filmed. After much wrangling on Weber's part, the suit was dismissed on July 25, 2006, with no damages awarded for using his likeness. (The hate mail Weber received, calling him an opportunistic douche bag, fucking redneck, and whiny little bitch, according to New York comedy website The Apiary, probably didn't help either.)

There's also a good deal of absurdity in *Let America Laugh*. Cross leads clueless interviewers along with fake answers, and closes out one night in Memphis, Tennessee, by accepting an invitation to a "cool" video store called The Black Lodge. As the assembled partiers pass around beers and freshly packed bowls, Cross delights in the freshman dorm–level conversation taking place among the self-important, pseudophilosophical stoners.

Hecklers pop up from time to time, Cross gamely engaging their idiotic outbursts and turning their logic against them. A woman in Portland, Oregon, interrupts the set because she's not "feeling it," though it appears that she is feeling the effects of various psychedelic drugs.

Drunken sorority girls weasel their way backstage to pretend they know Cross and drink his beers. In Vancouver, Cross must play a double-booked venue (disco night!) that forces him to end his set while it's still light outside, disappointing a handful of his devoted fans.

But the tour documentary also reveals Cross's mischievous glee: he buys fireworks in Wisconsin with all the ardor of a sugar-smacked toddler, and dresses up as Ainsley McTree (a "protest singer" from Marietta, Georgia, in a fake beard and checkered shirt, who feels for the plight of the Native Americans). He enjoys giving shit to his millionaire friends in LA, many of whom try to nab free tickets to his show despite their financial status. And, in one of the biggest treats for *Mr. Show* nerds, we briefly get to see Cross interact with alumni of that show at a DVD signing at a Virgin Megastore in LA.

Tellingly, the credits to *Let America Laugh* include camera work from Mac McCaughan (leader of Superchunk and cofounder of Merge Records) and sound recordings from Phil Ek (The Shins, Built to Spill, Modest Mouse) and Chris Walla (Death Cab for Cutie), with indie bands Arlo and The Glands providing much of the DVD's soundtrack. Cross seems reluctant to flaunt it lest he be accused of name-dropping—they never appear onscreen, and he never mentions it in the film—but the fact is, his friends in the indie-music world were never far away, especially around his hometown. "You can't live in Georgia without being one degree away from somebody that knows him," says Henry Owings, editor of *Chunklet* magazine and a friend of Cross.

Bob Mehr had just moved to Seattle in the spring of 2002 to write for Village Voice Media when he heard about the tour. "Being the music guy, I got a package from Ultrababyfat saying they were playing the Showbox. It's a fairly large theater, with 1,500 seats, which in itself was unique," he says. "I don't recall before that, when I was living in Arizona, ever seeing comedians doing rock clubs. I kind of saw this thing happening in front me, and being in the position of music editor, I knew it was something different right away."

With all the credibility and fanfare a respected indie label could muster, Sub Pop released *Shut Up, You Fucking Baby!* on November 5, 2002. The seventeen-track, two-disc package messed with buyers before they even played it: the titles on the back were all put-ons, jokes about how clichéd jokes can be ("Socks and Shoes," "My Daughter's First Date") or silly, offensive toss-offs ("Shaving the Pope's Pussy," "If Baseballs Had AIDS on Them"). The bio was written by literary darling Dave Eggers, and the cover depicted Cross hugging random strangers on the beach at Coney Island. The material, recorded mostly in Portland and Atlanta, approached politics, religion, class divisions, and pop culture like a starved tiger, tearing into raw subjects like 9/11 and faux patriotism, the Catholic Church's priest molestation scandal ("And you know, they're God's representatives, so that means...God fucks little boys."), and even lame restaurant ads (Cosi's Squagle, the square bagel!). It was less a traditional stand-up set than off-the-cuff riffing on news, daily experiences, and general American idiocy. It also, as critics were quick to point out, tended to recall the auto-authority rants of Lenny Bruce and Bill Hicks.

A bit from the album is instructive of Cross's overall ambivalence toward (and frequent hatred of) certain segments of the country: "I had to deal with such stupid people [growing up]. I mean, here's the thing...the South has a certain kind of ignorance that is deeper, and truer, more unwavering and steadfast in ignorance than the rest of the country. And just for lack of a better term, let's call it Southern Baptist...those are some dumb fucking people, man. The shit they believe [is] jaw-dropping."

He also skewers the religious persecution of gays, rejecting the Judeo-Christian/theistic view of sexuality (Cross is an avowed atheist) and asserting that the "gay voice" is genetic, not cultural.

"There's no fucking sixteen-year-old, heterosexual, confused, socially awkward, acne-scarred kid sittin' around in his bedroom going, [in an effeminate voice] 'Guys...everyone hates me. And the girls that I like don't like me, and I don't know what to do. The thought of having sex with another man is physically repellant to me. But you know, maybe it's time I invited even more nonstop harassment into my life. Yeah, THAT'LL be fun. Things have been going so easy, why don't I just introduce the concept of getting the shit kicked out of me for no good reason by a bunch of fucking retards whenever they want?' Yeah. That's good. That's a fun choice to make."

The album received a wide range of reviews, with *All Music Guide*'s Stephen Thomas Erlewine hailing it as the best comedy CD "in years, and one of the best showcases of a genius comic at the top of his game" and "an epic masterpiece." *PopMatters*'s Gary Glauber wrote, "To hear someone take a stand against our national complacency, and to bring it directly to younger rock concert crowds, is reassuring." *Dusted* magazine's Jason Dungan dubbed him "the comic voice of indie rock," joining a chorus of writers articulating what many comedy fans had already been thinking.

But some who were only familiar with Cross through his TV and movie work were unprepared for the slap-in-the-face harshness or the rambling nature of many bits. "They're not what we non-slathering—but still sick and needy—*Mr. Show* disciple-scum expected from this long, long player," wrote William Bowers for influential indie-rock website Pitchfork, assigning the album a 6.5 out of 10. "He's aggressively curmudgeonly, and skirts losing composure as his observations accumulate...I love him, but he sounds defeated. Is the title aimed at his targets or at himself?"

It peaked at number eighteen on the Billboard charts, but *Shut Up* quickly rewarded the risks Tony Kiewel took in signing Cross to Sub Pop. It garnered a Grammy nomination and has since sold more than 100,000 copies, an impressive number for a long, dense comedy album of politically polarizing material. (It didn't hurt that for two months prior to the album's release, Cross traversed the country as part of the *Mr. Show* reunion tour, *Hooray for America!*) It represented Sub Pop's first "intentional comedy album," and went indie platinum, as far as Kiewel was concerned. Of course it lost the 2003 Grammy Award to Weird Al Yankovic's *Poodle Hat*. (Yes, *Poodle Hat*.)

Stand Up! Records, a Minneapolis-based comedy label run by Dan Schlissel, released a limited-edition three-LP vinyl version of the record in (appropriately) red, white, and blue wax, although it sold far more slowly than the CD. "We pressed 500 copies," Schlissel says. "It's still in print, although it's rapidly inching its way out. LPs just don't move the way CDs do."

When the *Let America Laugh* DVD was released in 2003, some longtime fans pounced on it as an example of everything that was right with Cross, a polished window into his unpretentious, play-it-by-ear lifestyle. But many were puzzled or even angered by the choice of footage, expecting full stand-up sets instead of behind-the-scenes bits and painfully awkward moments. Cross says he was "shocked, amazed, confused, and dismayed" by the negative fan reactions. "I purposely didn't include much stand-up because there's two fucking hours of it on audio. Why would I try to charge you for the same thing? I'm not

Dane Cook. I'm not going to charge you twenty dollars for the same thing you can get on CD. That's criminal."

Regardless, the tour helped rekindle an explicit relationship between music and comedy that had largely lain dormant for years, augmenting the format by making comedy the headliner instead of the opener, and warning people in advance of the setup. It also produced nationally distributed CDs and DVDs that intelligently promoted that relationship, to Sub Pop's advantage.

Eugene Mirman, an absurdist New York comedian who would later join Cross on Sub Pop with his 2006 album, *En Garde, Society!*, says the release only justified the original notion behind the tour. "I've always believed that you can do comedy in alternative venues. They've done it in LA and New York for a decade. But with David Cross and Ultrababyfat—that's when it broke it open into a slightly different market." Mirman and fellow New York comedians Demetri Martin and Leo Allen mounted their own tour of rock clubs in the spring of 2003. Dubbed *Underdogs*, it visited seven venues along the East Coast, although it played to significantly smaller crowds. Unsurprisingly, Shonali Bhowmik of Ultrababyfat organized the tour.

"I had asked Eugene if he had ever toured before," Bhowmik says. "He and I had been discussing doing dates together and taking the comedy on the road. We got our friends Leo and Demetri on board, and I started calling clubs that I had played before with Ultrababyfat. Outside of my tour with David, these were the most fun days of comedy and music for me! Comedians were going on the road in the old-school rock 'n' roll way...hitting small clubs and dives where normally only rock bands would play."

Bhowmik and bandmate Russ Dungan provided music under the name The Neverlands as the tour hit clubs such as the Velvet Lounge in Washington, DC, the Kyhber Pass in Philadelphia, the Ottobar in Baltimore, and Maxwells in Hoboken, New Jersey. Or, as Bhowmik says, "All clubs I love to play music in." The next year, she also toured with comedians Mirman, Brendon Small (later of Adult Swim's *Metalocalypse*), and Jon Benjamin.

The tours again illustrated that it only made sense to move a certain kind of show to the right kind of venue. Although, as *Underdogs*'s Mirman soon helped prove, it was also possible to bend unlikely venues to one's will, if one remained persistent. *Invite Them Up*, a weekly comedy show he created with comedian Bobby Tisdale, started in 2002 at an East Village art house film café called Cinema Classics (and later, Rififi). The night began modestly, only drawing a dozen people or so every week, but eventually became one of New York's most respected and loved comedy nights—and one of the worthy successors to Luna Lounge's *Eating It*. It ran for more than five years before they pulled the plug, although in that time it hosted hundreds of stand-ups including Cross, Aziz Ansari, Michael Showalter, Todd Barry, and musicians Craig Wedren (Shudder to Think), Langhorne Slim, and Bhowmik (now of the group Tigers and Monkeys).

The success of the Cross/Ultrababyfat tour and scattered pockets of experimentation on the coasts were inspiring others in Cross and Bhowmik's spiderweb of connections. Cross's relationship with Sub Pop had also quickly gotten the attention of in-the-know music and comedy fans, says Brian Posehn, a *Mr. Show* alumnus and member of the *Comedians of Comedy* tour. "I think we all kind of owe it to [that tour]. David made that connection first with Sub Pop, and Patton [Oswalt] jumped right in and did it with Aimee Mann's label. It's so smart and so obvious, too. We all kind of went, 'Oh yeah, of course. We should be on a music label.'" (Posehn's 2006 album, *Live In: Nerd Rage!*, was released by heavy-metal label Relapse).

When confronted with this quote, Cross repeats his claim that doing the rock-venue tour and releasing an album on an indie-music label would have been safe for anyone to do. "I knew a lot of the bands before I got on Sub Pop, because I'm a fan of that kind of music and I'd gone and seen their shows. When I was on *Mr. Show*, I become approachable to those guys. I was a distinct face in the crowd and they could come up and say 'hi.' You just sort of become friendly."

Writer and prank-call practitioner Andrew Earles says that despite some unintentional side effects, the move Cross made was both positive and inevitable. "I think it's a great thing what he and a few other comedians did by moving good stand-up from comedy clubs into different environments," he says. "I mean, it had to happen. Somebody had to do it. He's one of the more notable of the comedians that could have done it."

Time flies when you're obsessively nit-picking the details of one of your favorite comedian's careers (as that old idiom goes), so it was with mild surprise that I looked up to find darkening skies over Cross Lake, the air spiked with a humid Louisiana chill. I had already talked with Cross about most everything in my tattered notebook, broken biscuits with him at a Cracker Barrel, examined the ballots from his chili cook-off, peeked at his book for Grand Central Publishing (which includes columns he wrote for *Vice* magazine and musings from BobandDavid.com), talked about the music that was exciting him at the moment (Dixie Chicks, Lupe Fiasco,

Wolf Parade, Panda Bear), and watched him play with, make food for, and sing to his dog.

But we had yet to discuss the phase of his career that came just after the first Sub Pop CD and DVD, when the indie rock world declared open season on Cross and began requesting him to appear at seemingly every other indie-music festival in the English-speaking world. During this time (roughly 2002 to the present), his profile rose yet again with a slew of TV and movie appearances—some memorable, some not so much.

A detailed examination of Cross's acting and voice work would require another few chapters (I'll leave that to his biographer), but suffice it to say the man has been busy. He's had forty-seven roles since 2002, out of a total of more than eighty and counting, and his voice has showed up in wildly popular video games (*Grand Theft Auto: San Andreas, Halo 2*) and absurdist Adult Swim cartoons (*Tom Goes to the Mayor* and *Aqua Teen Hunger Force*). He's guest-starred on warped, cutting-edge MTV sketch comedies (*Wonder Showzen, Human Giant*) and various Comedy Central programs (*Crank Yankers, Strangers with Candy*), and even wrote and produced his own cartoon for Comedy Central, called *Freak Show*, with longtime friend Jon Benjamin. That short-lived show employed the talents of pals such as Kristen Schaal, Janeane Garofalo, Fred Armisen, and Will Arnett. Cross's brief appearances in *Scary Movie 2* and other Hollywood pap have netted him a lifetime of "Hey, aren't you that guy from..." But it's in his DIY attitude toward stand-up that he reveals his true personality.

One fateful night at Luna Lounge's *Eating It* show, Cross was unceremoniously stopped at the door and asked to pay the cover, despite the fact that he had performed there, by his estimation, nearly fifty times since the midnineties. "I tried to walk in and Robert [Sacher, the club's owner] was like, 'Where are you going?' I said, 'Oh, upstairs to see the show.' And he wanted to charge me the seven dollars to get in. I was like, 'What?' and he said, 'Yeah, you can't come in unless you're paying.' I thought he was joking." According to Cross, Sacher would also charge people just to be in the bar where *Eating It* was shown on a closed-circuit TV. "I thought that was greedy and disgusting, and the fact that he wanted to charge me was insane. As a comedian, you don't get any money from [performing at] the Luna Lounge, nor should you."

So Cross hatched the idea for *Tinkle*, a Sunday night show he started in January 2003 across Ludlow at the newly opened Pianos. His original, deliciously subversive thought was to host an *Eating It* show, then take the entire audience and march them out of the club and across the street to Pianos. "I was planning on saying, 'Guess what? It's starting right now. Let's get the fuck out of here. Don't ever come back here. My show is cheaper and you don't have to buy a drink and everybody's welcome. And if you can't get in, we're not going to charge you to sit out in the bar." Cross pauses to bite his lip. "I was talked out of that by some of the other guys in *Tinkle* because they thought it was a bit much and it would hurt people that had nothing to do with that policy."

The other guys in *Tinkle* were Jon Benjamin, a comedian whom Cross had known since his Boston days, and Todd Barry, a fixture on the New York comedy scene who has performed with bands The Shins, They Might Be Giants, Jens Lekman, and Yo La Tengo (although Barry does not consider himself an indie or alternative comedian, he was a former drummer, and actually played drums with Yo La Tengo a few times onstage). The trio continued to believe that Luna Lounge was a great place to do shows, but Cross's disagreement with Sacher meant he was never going back. "It still blows my mind that you would charge somebody just to come in and see their friends," Cross adds. "I had performed there for free a zillion times and they used my name as part of their package to entice people to come out. That's what *Tinkle* came out of. It was a 'fuck you' to that guy, and it was fun. I had a blast doing it."

"It was always sold out," adds Shonali Bhowmik, who produced *Tinkle*. "We'd show a live feed of the show upstairs on screen for those that couldn't get into the main stage area."

Tinkle even hosted a booze cruise where, for sixty dollars, you could climb aboard the *Queen of Hearts* at Pier 40 and enjoy comedy from the show's creators and music from indie rockers Les Savy Fav. And, naturally, a four-hour open bar.

"Walking out of [*Tinkle*], I felt like I'd experienced something much hipster-ier and more underground-ier than I would have if I'd stayed home and watched *The Simpsons* and *Boomtown*," commented Mike D. on SlushFactory.com. "Warning: You have to spend a lot of time beforehand lining up for your tickets and being herded around with a lot of other messy-haired trendies. It can be very trying on your patience and put you in a bad mood before the comedy starts. Try to ride it out..."

Wildly varied, informal stand-up and sketch comedy were the norm at *Tinkle*, which hosted comedians such as Fred Armisen, Kristen Schaal, Janeane Garofalo, Demetri Martin, Sarah Silverman, Greg Proops, Jim Gaffigan, and dozens of others. Indie-rock acts Yo La Tengo, Ted Leo, Jim James of My Morning Jacket, and Capitol Years occasionally played short sets, but the core of the show was the anything-goes format its creators encouraged. "They were really mixing it up and messing with the idea of what a show of any kind was," says Sub Pop's Tony Kiewel, noting that authors like Sarah Vowell would stop by to read short stories between comedy sets. "And then other people were doing stuff like *Invite Them Up* at Rififi, and the Largo scene in LA."

Tinkle's quasi-vaudevillian setup worked almost in spite of itself. "Usually you would think a trio of comic hosts would be stepping all over each other trying to carve out the one-liners and it would just be utter chaos. Not the case here," wrote Brooklynite Sam T. on his Samology blog. "Jon and David seemed to have a natural back-and-forth going on, improvising little bits, most of which were actually funny and not just the kind of stultifying emcee material you might be used to. Todd was mostly quiet, in fact, throwing in the occasional cerebral one-liner in his calm, Garrison Keillor earthy monotone."

The media caught on and *Tinkle* began to receive raves in *New York Magazine*, *The New York Post* (which dubbed its comedy "freshly minted"), and other publications. It ran strong for a couple years before slowing down due to its founders' various professional commitments, reuniting for the occasional benefit, like a July 2007 fund-raiser for Gulf Coast hurricane victims, which featured Patton Oswalt and Buffalo Tom as a surprise musical guest.

And anyway, Cross had other projects to keep him busy, including putting out his second Sub Pop CD, *It's Not Funny*. The seventy-plus-minute album, for which Dave Eggers again wrote a tongue-in-cheek bio, was released on May 4, 2004. Even at its hefty running time, it presented a more pared-down set of material than *Shut Up, You Fucking Baby!* Perhaps because of the location (it was recorded over four nights at the Improv in Washington, DC, in January 2004), although more likely due to Cross's political preoccupations, it continued to hammer away at George W. Bush and many people's knee-jerk reactions to 9/11. The bits felt more focused and correct, as in his rebuttal of President Bush's assertion that 9/11 happened because Al Qaeda "hates our freedom."

"I don't think Osama bin Laden sent those planes to attack us because he hated our freedom. I think he did it because of our support for Israel, and our ties with the Saudi family, and all our military bases in Saudi Arabia. You know why I think that? Because that's what he FUCKING said. Are we a nation of six-year-olds? Answer: yes."

Cross's quasi-activism, also apparent his scattered Democratic fund-raising (and other unofficial political events he has played, at festivals and elsewhere, often with punk and indie bands), seemed to have found a more accessible, or at least coherent, tone. *It's Not Funny* worked better overall than *Shut Up*, presenting jokes that invited the audience into the premise instead of occasionally barking it at them, and tunneling to the core of what made Cross's angrily funny perspective so appealing. If *Shut Up* was rambling and short on the satisfyingly taut humor of *Mr. Show*, it's because Cross's jabs tend to hit hardest when aggressively edited. The location of the taping (a mainstream comedy club) may have also nudged Cross toward the conventional setup/punch line structure—ironic, considering his role in dismantling that model three years earlier.

Track titles followed the same sarcastic, borderline nonsensical path as those on *Shut Up!*: "Women, Please Rinse Off Your Vagina and Anus!" "A Rapid Series of Comical Noises!" "My Immigrant Mom Talks Funny!" "I've Taken a Popular Contemporary Pop Song and Changed the Lyrics to Comment on the Proliferation of Starbucks in My Neighborhood!"

You get the idea.

He also steps back from the political subject matter more comfortably on *It's Not Funny*, mocking time-saving conveniences such as electric scissors ("Death quietly and nurturingly takes you by the hand and says it's your time and you're like, 'But I used electric scissors for forty years!' 'Alright, well, you've got three and a half minutes then.'"), reality TV contestants ("Just vile people—awful human beings who get away with everything 'cause they're rich. And the blonde one will blow you, apparently."), and annoying new parents ("About half my friends have kids and, you know, I think that's rude.").

Pitchfork afforded it another 6.5 out of 10, writer Amanda Petrusich calling Cross "an immensely unlikable live performer...The devastating paradox of David Cross's pre-recorded comedy: Is it funny that everything Cross says is nauseatingly smug, yelped out in smarmy, supercilious prose? Or is David Cross just a giant fucking asshole?...Having signed a contract with Sub Pop, liner-note-repped for The Fiery Furnaces, stunt-reviewed for *Rolling Stone* and *Spin*, toured with rock bands, publicly mocked Staind/Evanescence/Scott Stapp, and acquired a perfect pair of black, plastic-framed glasses, David Cross has inadvertently embedded himself in the contemporary indie scene, amassing wads of useless cred and granting hipsters even more reasons to be annoyingly sarcastic over cans of PBR."

But not everyone was dismissive of the album. "He's the enemy of hypocrisy and a voice for all who lament the absence of truth in the world," gushed Zeth Lundy in *PopMatters*. "Onstage, he emits a relaxed magnetism, darts of fierce social commentary shrouded in subversive material delivered as a stream-of-consciousness, verbal steamroller of sorts, as downright hilarious as it is thought provoking." *Paste* magazine's Leila Regan argued that Cross's "fierce intelligence" never crossed into the overbearing snobbery of many social commentators. "Pulling off the 'guy at the bar' mentality with seasoned comedy class, he's a speaker you can relate to, yet look to for insight and answers in today's slightly mad world," she wrote. And comedy bible *The Onion* made familiar but justified comparisons: "A truth teller in the noble tradition of Bill Hicks, Richard Pryor, and Lenny Bruce...as urgent and outraged as a Noam Chomsky lecture, but infinitely more entertaining."

Cross has never fully warmed to the Lenny Bruce comparisons, noting the radically different societal context in which Bruce practiced his stand-up, and the fact that Bruce had even *fewer* punch lines per joke. "I'm probably closer to Bill Hicks, but I'm not nearly as good or articulate or economic with my ideas as he was," he told Simon Guildford of *Drowned in Sound* in 2007. Cross had actually met Hicks before his death in 1994, although he says he was more inspired by Hicks's style than influenced by it.

It's Not Funny went on to sell more than 40,000 copies, according to Sub Pop's Kiewel, less than half of *Shut Up!*, but still a respectable number. Stand Up! Records again released 500 vinyl copies, betting on the demand for an old-school version of the album in a market where even comedy CDs were rare at record stores.

Just before *It's Not Funny*, however, Cross landed a gig that again placed him in front of a national audience on a weekly basis. The Emmy-laden Fox sitcom *Arrested Development*, which ran from 2003 to 2006, offered a calm version of Cross's occasionally vitriolic persona, and one that worked to his strengths. Comedy nerds and Cross fans know the show well, luxuriating in its intricate, intertextual plot lines, clever dialogue, and goofy, irredeemable characters. The show followed Michael Bluth (Jason Bateman), the most responsible of three wildly different brothers in the beleaguered Bluth family. The disgraced, dysfunctional collection of ex-upper-crusters lived in a shoddily constructed model home in coastal Southern California, stepping on each others' toes in a parade of distressing situations. Cross was originally tapped to play blundering man-child Buster Bluth (a role that went to the better-suited Tony Hale) but ended up choosing the character of Tobias Fünke, an ex-psychiatrist unable to confront his homosexuality and naively yearning to break into the acting world.

Cross's facility with the nuanced dialogue made his character's oblivious double entendres endlessly quotable. "Even if it means me taking a chubby, I will suck it up." Or, "I wouldn't mind kissing that man between the cheeks." Or my favorite, "Boy, I sure feel like a Mary without a Peter and a Paul." Quipped guest-starring comedian Dave Attell in one episode, "If this guy's straight, then I'm sober."

Like imprisoned patriarch George Bluth (HBO vet Jeffrey Tambor), the Tobias Fünke role was originally intended to be a small one, but Cross tested so well with the rest of the cast that it swayed creator Mitch Hurwitz, a *Mr. Show* fan, to invite him to appear on every episode.

Universal critical praise and dozens of prestigious awards meant little to Fox as *Arrested Development* suffered chronically low ratings, constantly skirting cancellation even as it built a devoted, if small, audience. Not that it was perfect: producer Ron Howard's smug, uncredited voiceovers and the mildly irritating theme music tended to soften the vicious punch of the sexual and political humor. Plot lines were occasionally convoluted, and by the time it was kicked off the air in 2006, the roving-camera style familiar to fans of *Curb Your Enthusiasm* and *Reno 911!* was becoming old hat (although it must be noted that *Arrested* was tightly scripted, unlike the improvised dialogue in *Curb* and *Reno*).

Still, relative to 99 percent of TV offerings, *Arrested* was that rare, brilliant show that continually reinvented itself and asked the audience to come along with it, offering thick slabs of satire with many layers of meaning.

Better suited for HBO or Showtime, it served viewers more than they could possibly digest in a single viewing. It also welcomed a steady stream of high-profile guest stars, among them Ben Stiller, Julia Louis-Dreyfus, Amy Poehler (whose husband, Will Arnett, played Gob Bluth), Charlize Theron, and *Mr. Show* vets Bob Odenkirk, Jay Johnston, and Jerry Minor. Perhaps most bizarre was the appearance of James Lipton as a prison warden. That bearded bloviater is familiar as host of *Inside the Actors Studio*, a show (and character) Cross mercilessly flayed on the *Mr. Show* sketch "Inside the Actor" some seven years earlier. "If ever a show and a person was right for spoofing and more, it was that show," Cross said in *What Happened?!* "I really have a visceral hatred for that show, and everything it stands for."

In a blatant fuck you to the Fox network, Cross also appears on one of *Arrested*'s DVD outtakes, succinctly condemning the network's stupidity in letting the show slip through the cracks. The off-the-cuff tirade has become an online video favorite, and not just because of Cross's clear and present anger: "I got an idea for what you can do. Why don't you fucking fire your complete marketing team, alright? Get a new one in there that knows how to market a show that won five motherfuckin' Emmys, Golden Globes, SAG awards, WGA awards, DGA awards, Producers Guild awards, critics' top-ten lists. You know, if you can't fucking market that kind of show and get better ratings, then maybe the problem doesn't lie here. Maybe it lies with...*marketing*."

Cross would later say that a "dirty little secret" was that Fox (and, he believed, conservative Fox owner–media mogul Rupert Murdoch) simply didn't like the show, citing its expensive production costs, liberal politics, and the fact that network brass often clashed with the producer.

Take heart, *Arrested* fans: there's always the movie.

★ ☆ ★ ☆ ★

Through the mid- to late 2000s, Cross grew into such a reliable presence on the indie-music circuit that he became virtually inextricable from it. He emceed and performed at showcases—some of which went well, some of which didn't. One of the worst was a 2001 New Year's Eve show with Guided By Voices and The Strokes at the Apollo Theater. "I got peed on and later got in a fight with the guy who peed on me, who was on mushrooms," Cross says. "I still have a scar from it on my leg because I jumped to give him a karate kick or some shit and he blocked it with his boot."

He played music venues from North America to the UK, including a two-week *David Cross and Friends* residency in June 2007 at the 100 Club in London, where the Sex Pistols and The Clash had performed some thirty years earlier. The friends Cross brought were Todd Barry, Kristen Schaal, Eugene Mirman, and Canadian indie-rock supergroup The New Pornographers. He openly talked about his favorite new bands to any interviewer who asked, and reviewed music, usually with a comedic tone, in a few magazines. He set himself at odds with what he felt were shitty comics (Jim Belushi, Larry the Cable Guy) and bands (Creed, Staind), and generally preached to the choir about American political apathy and ignorance.

Anyone with an Internet connection and an irritable finger can locate dozens of other examples of Cross's overlap with the underground and indie-music world, from his ridiculous interpretive dancing onstage during a Spoon show to an inspired *Guitar Hero* head-to-head with Dinosaur Jr.'s J Mascis on comedian Sara Schaefer's AOL video blog *The DL*. Cross and Sub Pop labelmate Eugene Mirman even cracked wise at the New York wedding of A. C. Newman, head of The New Pornographers.

That last example isn't so surprising: Cross had previously appeared in The New Pornographers's "Use It" video and was fast friends with the band. He has also popped up in videos from Superchunk ("Watery Hands"), Yo La Tengo ("Sugarcube"), and The Strokes ("Juicebox"), and directed The Black Keys's video "10 A.M. Automatic." He particularly relished that last experience. "I really liked that video and I hope people can see it," he says. "I got a couple queries about directing one for [...And You Will Know Us By] the Trail of Dead, and the Goo Goo Dolls actually got in touch with me. I came up with three different treatments for their cover of Supertramp's 'Take the Long Way Home,' but they didn't like any of them." Cross also provided the commentary for Tool's *Vicarious* DVD, though he claims it only consisted of him reading from a book of exchanges between a rabbi and psychic Uri Geller. "I can't imagine it was very funny. But I'm friends with those guys so that's why they asked me to do it. [Tool singer] Maynard James Keenan was actually in two episodes of *Mr. Show*, and he used to do the Diamond Club shows in LA before we were ever a TV show. He's a big comedy fan, a huge Bill Hicks fan, and he's a funny motherfucker, too."

Despite all the friendships he had made in the indie-music world over the years, the requests were starting to wear on him. Cross began to feel too intertwined with the scene, even as he realized some of that was his own doing. He started turning down offers to appear at festivals and shows he had played before, such as South by Southwest, Bumbershoot, Sasquatch, and the Plug Awards. "It just seemed gross at a point. Whether this is real or not, it felt like I was being a little needy. It was really cool when I truly came at it as a fan of all those kinds of music, and I *am* friends personally with a lot of the people in those bands, but it was too ubiquitous. You do All Tomorrow's

Parties [a UK festival that Cross appeared at in 2006] and it's great at first because you're introducing bands and getting a backstage pass. They're paying for your flight and putting you up, and you get to hang out with your friends. But the fourteenth one of those you do you just seem like a poser. I'm no better than a DJ flinging Frisbees and lighters out in the audience." Cross says he understands other comedians' ambivalence toward being branded a part of any scene, indie or otherwise. "There's that kind of cool kids corner—or *KKK* for short—that has that feeling that I'm not that comfortable with."

Even with all of his ties to music, and scattered acclaim as an actor and comedian, Cross still occasionally gets tagged as up-and-coming. A 2007 *Esquire* piece named him as the front-runner in the bafflingly titled "Will the Next Dane Cook Please Stand Up?" Granted, it made sense to group him with Patton Oswalt, Aziz Ansari, Demetri Martin, and Flight of the Conchords, but the only thing that Dane Cook's mass-audience humor has in common with Cross's sharpened style is both comedians' intelligent self-promotion. (The article produced a predictable backlash on comedy blogs, with many sarcastically dismissing its premise.)

MSNBC's obliviously titled July 2008 article, "Standup Comedy Didn't Die with Carlin," also noted Cross as a successor to George Carlin's political-minded, truth-telling legacy, quoting comedian Wayne Federman in saying that, "Comedic social commentary has never been more popular. In fact, it's mainstream—delivered by *The Daily Show, Saturday Night Live, South Park, Real Time with Bill Maher,* and *The Colbert Report.*" Of course, the article also cited Dane Cook as an example of stand-up's commercial health, failing to note that Cook has never come close to producing anything as creatively vigorous as either Carlin or Cross.

Cross seems resigned to being vaguely recognized in the mainstream these days, although that doesn't mean he's completely comfortable with it. He penned a piece for *New York Magazine*'s *Urban Etiquette Handbook* called "Where Do I Know You From? How Not to Alienate that Guy from TV." In it he expressed frustration with people who approach him with no frame of reference for his stand-up or sketch work, an understandable but common occurrence in his daily life. "Talking to someone who holds me in no more regard than a guy from the *Real World* who became a celebrity by throwing up on a girl he was trying to date-rape seems a little demeaning to all the actual work I've done," he wrote. "Though I will cut in line if that's cool."

Cross's somewhat unenviable position of being That Guy from TV contrasts with the unrealistically high standards he is held to among hipsters and critics. Case in point: He appeared in the 2007 remake of *Alvin and the Chipmunks* as an unscrupulous record executive, using the money from that role to make a down payment on a cottage in upstate New York. He never made any claims as to the movie's quality, but still found himself defending the choice after various online fans called him a "douche bag" and "dead to me" for even taking the job. A sarcastic response from fellow indie-comedy hero Patton Oswalt about turning the role down was misinterpreted, and Cross found himself crafting a lengthy defense on BobandDavid.com, to which Oswalt wrote his own open letter decrying the whole silly mess. It's no stretch to think that experience made Cross even more wary of his icon status in the idealistic underground music scene. "There will always be one or two people who say, 'Oh, you shouldn't have done that,' or 'Oh, you sold out,'" says Paul Scheer of the MTV sketch comedy *Human Giant*. "But the truth of the matter is that everyone's trying to make a living. I totally agree with David. I think it's awesome that he did *Alvin and the Chipmunks*. It's a family movie, and that's a totally different audience. It didn't make him a different person."

Cross has enjoyed other odd moments in the public eye, as when New York media blog Gawker tracked the every move of a Cross impersonator traipsing around Manhattan in 2005, pretending to be Cross so he could get laid. Even more high-profile was his feud with Larry the Cable Guy of the *Blue Collar Comedy Tour*. Cross took a shot at Larry's "anti-gay, racist" humor in *Rolling Stone*, which prompted Larry (aka Daniel Whitney) to write a chapter in his book, *GIT-R-DONE*, generally criticizing "the PC Left" that had so viciously attacked his salt-of-the-earth fans.

Of course, pegging Cross as PC proved how utterly unfamiliar Whitney was with Cross's act. "Yeah, *I'm* PC," Cross says, laughing toward the sky. "What a thoughtless generalization." Cross's original criticism charged that Whitney was taking advantage of his fans by pretending to be something he was not: a straight-shootin' regular guy from the heartland. In fact, Cross says, Whitney cynically played on people's vague patriotism, anti-intellectual pride, and general homophobia and racism in order to rake in money. (To wit: Larry the Cable Guy's song titles include unironic gems such as "Donny the Retard" and "Titty Bars Christmas." His act has offered lines like "madder than a Keebler Elf gettin' demoted to fudge packer" and "madder than a queer with tonsillitis on Valentine's Day.")

"I take pride in what I do, and when you see somebody doing something that you feel is full of tricks and is easy and fooling people, it makes you speak to that," Cross says. "But the most insane reasons get attached to my [criticisms]. The inane, infuriating response is always like, 'Well, he's just jealous.' That's what [*Blue*

Collar stand-up] Ron White said. 'I'd snap that fucker's neck in two like a twig. He's just jealous.' I'm really not jealous. Not even close. If I wanted a lot of money, I could get a lot of money."

Cross has gone head-to-head with other celebrities, including Jim Belushi, brother of the great John Belushi and star of the sitcom miscarriage *According to Jim*. As the story goes, Cross approached Belushi on the set of a movie they were filming together to sign an autograph for a young, sick fan, to which Belushi replied, "God, I thought you were gonna get me laid and you're giving me this sick kid shit!" That, and Cross's observations of Belushi as "mean, arrogant, and a marginally talented person" set off an intense feud that culminated in Cross and Belushi having it out onstage at the House of Blues on Sunset Boulevard, and Cross crashing a couple shows of Belushi's cover band, The Sacred Hearts. In one instance, Cross found his way onto the stage at a 2006 show at Martha's Vineyard. He was immediately removed, but got up again and giddily danced while clutching a beer, mocking the earnest Belushi as he sang and tried desperately to push Cross offstage. (Cross was eventually kicked out of the club, but a friend videotaped the scene and posted it on YouTube, where it generated 150,000 hits.)

Instances like this may make Cross look petty and childish to people who never liked him in the first place, but they also point to his refusal to compromise his personality or beliefs in the face of what he perceives as idiocy—which only endears him to the rest of us. And by the rest of us, I mean people who find comics like Larry the Cable Guy, shows like *According to Jim*, and bands like Creed to be symptomatic of what ails our culture—the sort of prefab, brain-cell-killing detritus that barely treads water creatively, but that manages to attract millions of dollars and fans.

Then again, a lot of people think David Cross is an angry jerk. *C'est la vie.*

My time with Cross was winding down, the air turning chilly and Cross wanting to give Ollie Red Sox a bath before his date arrived. But after spending a good chunk of time with him, a couple questions still remained: (1) Was his reputation as an asshole deserved, or more a matter of perception-as-reality, a product of his liminal status in an entertainment industry that ruthlessly separates and brands its products and performers? Should we blame Pitchfork, the most widely read indie-rock website and one that may have forever cast Cross as a dick?

Ultimately, I found Cross to be a forthright, friendly guy, and one a little bit puzzled by the jerk reputation he's earned over the years. Maybe it's because Cross knew that everything we talked about had the potential of going into this book, but either way, he treated me with respect and opened himself up to my barrage of questions. As for Pitchfork, that site eventually asked Cross to write a lengthy parody piece for them, in which he cut into Pitchfork's frequently meandering, self-important record reviews.

(2) Was David Cross really responsible for the explosion of comedy on the indie-music circuit or the resurgence of the comedy album?

Again, he demurred, citing other people's ideas and plans as the impetus behind everything that has happened since his tour with Ultrababyfat—itself the brainchild of members Shonali Bhowmik and Michelle Dubois. Certainly, Cross is just one piece of a larger scene that has evolved since the alt-comedy movement of the nineties, and many of his contemporaries have not received credit for the things they've done to keep stand-up vital, relevant, and connected to other cutting-edge art forms. (To note: Michael Showalter, Michael Ian Black, and David Wain, formerly of cult MTV sketch comedy *The State*, rarely get mentioned for their show *Stella*, which ran for seven years at Greenwich Village nightclub Fez starting in 1997, welcoming comedians Cross, Garofalo, Stiller, and countless others in addition to various indie musicians.)

But it's also accurate to say that Cross is responsible for many people's awareness that comedy can take place outside of comedy clubs, using his existing reputation to fill indie-music venues and festivals with his fans, many of whom wouldn't be caught dead at a mainstream comedy club. "He was famous enough from having done *Mr. Show* that he had his own audience he could bring, which is a problem for a lot of comedians who are relying on an audience that is just going to a comedy show," says Jesse Thorn, host of NPR's *The Sound of Young America*. "And it worked. Over a period of time, things have become more and more interwoven, to the point where a comedian like Aziz Ansari, when he's doing stand-up, can make a third of his material about music, and they're the kind of jokes that people would only get if they're Pitchfork enthusiasts."

"David was doing it right off the bat," says Michael Showalter. "He's definitely the Kurt Cobain of alternative comedy."

Cross, however, maintains that it all comes down to where a comedian is performing and how the night feels. "That's really the only difference to me. Certain comedians obviously know that their target audience and demographic would have an interest in this sort of stuff. There's a commonality between a lot of the bands and the comics."

Perhaps Cross is not wholly responsible for the indie-comedy scene, but regarding him as its wayward father isn't much of a stretch. Then again, few people's fathers are as effortlessly funny, cool, smart, and occasionally intimidating as Cross, nor are they friends with nearly every creative person you'd ever want to meet.

"I'm less the father than the fairy godmother," Cross finishes.

As he crouched to hug his dog and wave at me while I snapped a picture of him in the high-ceilinged living room of his rental house, a thought came to mind.

Are you sure I can't stay for dinner, David?

Comedians of Comedy creator Patton Oswalt and his dog
Grumpus stand watch over their home in Los Angeles.
Photo by Seth Olenick

4

FRIENDS WITH BENEFITS:
COMEDIANS OF COMEDY

Don't visit Los Angeles in February. Seriously.

It's gray. It rains. Temperatures flirt with warmth but never seal the deal. Everyone is sick of what-passes-for-winter there, aching to crank up their air conditioners, clean out their pools, and flaunt their new tans and noses. There's nothing more depressing than attempting to fulfill the dutiful tourist role and photograph the famous Hollywood sign only to find it obscured by thick, rolling white fog for hours on end. And did I mention the insane traffic in Hollywood when the city shuts down a couple blocks for the Academy Awards? That's fun, too.

Any self-respecting culture whore or tourist has either made a point to visit LA or actively avoided its luminous, apocalyptic plasticity. At least that's what I believed, never actually having been to the entertainment mecca of the Western world. But in order to conduct face-to-face interviews with comedians like Patton Oswalt, see comedy shows like *Comedy Death-Ray*, and get a general sense of comedy in LA, I would have no choice but to fly there and spend several days exploring it. Not that I was one of those avoiders—I had friends and family in the city, both of whom regularly implored me to come see them and bathe in LA's jolly, delusional milieu.

So I did. It's just that during the late-February week I chose, the weather sucked mountains of ass. Granted, I didn't go there solely to bask in the sunshine, but a little light wouldn't have killed anybody. I was able to stay with my cousin Jerry, who lives in a modest but appropriately hip abode on Sierra Bonita Avenue, just off the busy, boutique-ridden expanse of Melrose. That location afforded me comfortable equidistance from all the restaurants, coffee shops, venues, and painfully trendy bars at which I had planned to meet various people for interviews.

The famed Upright Citizens Brigade Theatre (UCB Theatre) on Franklin Avenue was the first order of business. Nearly every week for the last six years, former *Mr. Show* writers/actors Scott Aukerman and B. J. Porter (aka The Fun Bunch) have presented their *Comedy Death-Ray* show to comedy fans and occasional industry scouts, inviting big and small names to test new jokes and scrape away at older ones. In the great tradition of LA's alternative-comedy scene, it's an off-the-cuff, experimental, generally nurturing environment that can occasionally (and quickly) turn sour. Nearly everyone profiled in this book—and hundreds more—have barked into its hallowed mics. With a long-standing reputation as one of the hottest comedy nights in the country (LA blog Defamer once said it "will have you either soiling your drawers with laughter or from the intimidation of being in such a small space with such big names [or both]"), I would have been a fool to pass it up.

Aukerman and Porter originally staged *Death-Ray* at LA's M Bar on October 1, 2002. They moved it to the UCB Theatre shortly after that improv troupe's Hollywood location opened on July 1, 2005, instantly giving the West Coast another respected outlet for experimental comedy. Like any good punk-rock show, *Comedy Death-Ray*'s Tuesday installments are always all-ages and only cost $5—although you'd better get your tickets early, as they disappear within minutes. (Porter and Aukerman were nice enough to squeeze me in when I noticed the February 19 show was sold out.) No snacks or booze are served, but many in the shallow, black-walled, 100-seat theater enter with discreet brown bags of what can only be delicious Juicy Juice.

A glance at the 2007 two-disc *Comedy Death-Ray* album on Comedy Central Records, or *Death-Ray*'s MySpace profile, reveals candid pictures of the regulars: *Mr. Show* vets David Cross, Bob Odenkirk, Sarah Silverman, Brian Posehn, Paul F. Tompkins, and Mary Lynn Rajskub; *Comedians of Comedy* members Patton Oswalt, Maria Bamford, Zach Galifianakis, Eugene Mirman, and Morgan Murphy; and others such as Neil Hamburger, musical duo Hard 'N' Phirm, Jen Kirkman, Jimmy Pardo, and more. Patton Oswalt has called it "a show that functions like a flight simulator for comedians," and after seeing one, I'm hard pressed to disagree.

I parked my rental car outside the Hollywood Presbyterian Church and hiked a block north to Franklin, where the UCB Theatre sits across from the imposing, impeccably manicured Scientology Celebrity Centre ("See famous weirdoes in person!" *Death-Ray*'s website proclaims. What they don't tell you is that lingering or taking pictures outside the building will draw expressionless, robotlike security guards who demand to know what you're doing). The line to get into *Death-Ray* extended out of the UCB Theatre's door and down the block, composed, or so I gleaned from various conversations, of hipsters, nerds, college students, and industry types in T-shirts, summer dresses, and black-framed eyeglasses. A production assistant walked the line, politely but expediently asking people to sign release forms so they could appear on camera for an Andy Dick VH1 pilot (*You Don't Know Dick*).

People slowly took their seats—I found one on the side of the stage, uncomfortably close to the action—and the show started promptly at 9 PM. Host Eddie Pepitone, of *The Sarah Silverman Program* and *Flight of the Conchords*, came on first, his bowl-shaped frame and brusque New York accent commanding the theater with a "Hey, it's *me* here!" sort of vibe. He poked fun at the nervous-looking girls seated a few feet away and mocked his own portly appearance before setting the show in motion.

A half-dozen comedians each got their ten-to-fifteen-minute shot. A nervous, crack-voiced kid from Austin, Texas, bombed instantly. Alt-comedy hero Blaine Capatch regained the jovial mood, his lanky, goofy gesticulations belying the stinging intelligence of his bits. Notorious substance abuser and *Ben Stiller Show* alum Andy Dick went through an intentionally awkward routine with his son in the audience, multiple video cameras swirling to catch it. Dick's "sponsor" (a morbidly overweight man dressed in black named Robert) appeared unsteadily near the back of the room, heckling Dick while clutching a Heineken. Dick yelled for him to be removed from the theater, but Robert stumbled onstage and began thrashing with Dick. By the time the sponsor disappeared backstage and returned to vomit violently on Dick, I could smell the staged quality of the bit (and the fake vomit), although many audience members seemed genuinely disturbed. Chalk up another win for Andy Kaufman–style confrontational humor.

Tall, pretty, and with a shock of long, curly red hair, deadpan stoner Morgan Murphy joked self-consciously about looking at her body in the mirror, because "this is the best it's ever gonna get." Aziz Ansari, Rob Huebel, and Paul Scheer of MTV's *Human Giant* were slated to headline a few nights at UCB that week, so they took the stage to test a high-energy sketch about red-and-blue-clad fools with T-shirt guns (you know, the kind at arena sporting events), zipping around the theater like meth-addled motivational speakers. They turned on the audience and threatened to rob them of their Urban Outfitters T-shirts, only to double-cross each other, the heist becoming predictably bloody and satisfyingly ridiculous. Martha Kelly offered an appealingly calm set that relied less on histrionic delivery than brutally honest material and occasional injections of harsh, out-of-nowhere profanity. Headliner Brendon Small, the cocreator of Adult Swim's heavy-metal cartoon *Metalocalypse*, performed a short, mildly funny headlining set, a bearded roadie continually attempting to hand him an electric guitar. He finally accepted it and shredded through a technical metal solo before exiting the stage.

Random? Hell yes. The inconsistent tone left me a little flat (particularly as the comics hammered away at themes of self-loathing, depression, and dumb, fat midwesterners), but I could understand why comedy nerds salivated over each new *Death-Ray*, savoring the unpredictability of its lineup and mood. A good night and a bad night at *Death-Ray* are only inches away from each other, although, based on its reputation, most probably lean toward the former.

I considered heading back to my car and returning to my cousin's house for some much-needed sleep when Pepitone announced that *See You Next Tuesday* (*SYNT*), the free after-show, would be starting shortly. I also remembered hearing that Maria Bamford, one of my favorite comics, would be performing at it, so I decided to stick around. Presented by Matt Belknap of popular comedy website ASpecialThing.com, and *Death-Ray*'s Aukerman and

Porter, the show was the alternative-to-the-alternative of *Death-Ray*, a place where up-and-comers could grab valuable time in front of smaller but equally devoted crowds.

"It's easier to do a good show when you're kind of under the radar like that," Belknap would later tell me. "*Death-Ray* is an established brand now in terms of live comedy. The audience sometimes has that attitude of 'Hey, I've heard this is great. Show us what you got. Prove it,' and that affects the comics, too. But *See You Next Tuesday*'s stakes are so low. It's free. It's late at night on a Tuesday. There's lots of experimenting and trying out of material. The crowds are really great because they show up for the right reasons: they want to laugh, and they don't pay to get in. They can leave whenever they want."

I skipped over to a nearby grocery store for some beverages and returned to watch *SYNT*, which only attracted about thirty people. Aukerman and Porter performed a couple sketches they were to unveil at the Vancouver Global ComedyFest the next week, such as a hysterically masculine fight that escalates into a naked slap-match, and a topical spoof of Fidel Castro's security doubles. Avuncular, wide-eyed slab of a man Matt Braunger killed with his perfectly timed bits, presenting an ostensibly tighter set than any on the *Death-Ray* roster an hour before. TV regular Aisha Tyler harped on the inanity of living in LA, while Paul Gilmartin offered a brilliant, dead-on parody of a squeaky-clean Republican politician, taking questions from the crowd and spinning them into improv gold. By the time closers Janice Davidson and Shelagh Ratner came around, my eyelids were leaden and my brain threatening to shut down, so I left to find my car. (Sadly, Maria Bamford never showed up.)

As I walked past the Scientology Celebrity Centre, I divined a pair of footsteps trailing me. They turned corners when I did, crossed when I did. My heart jumped into my throat when I approached my parking spot and found only an empty square of concrete. A street sign informed me it became a tow-away zone after 11 PM (I'd later find out the city towed me at 11:15, two hours before I left the UCB Theatre). I had only been in LA for a half a day and had already managed to strand myself in Hollywood after midnight. Nice.

I turned to confront the footsteps, expecting a couple strung-out addicts eager to jump me for loose change and God knows what else (or perhaps a maniacal Tom Cruise who spotted me from the lofty windows of the Scientology compound). Instead there stood two young, mild-looking guys wearing equally exasperated expressions. "Did you park here, too?" one of them asked, his eyes glinting under the orange street lamp. I nodded. "Well, we parked here because we saw your car and figured it was safe." I shrugged. "Sorry."

We searched street signs and chain-link fences for tow company numbers, eventually calling Hollywood Tow Service and confirming they had our vehicles. One of the dudes lived nearby, so I followed him back to his grubby apartment—probably a foolish thing to do—but the guys turned out to be harmless, talkative types, hungrily devouring fries and burgers from Wendy's while ESPN flickered in the background, their apartment reeking of bong hits and mildew. Just when I was starting to think a cab might have been a better idea, we were ready to leave for the tow company. Two hours and $250 later, I was back at my cousin's house on Sierra Bonita Avenue.

As I drifted off to sleep on the fold-out couch, the *Death-Ray* jokes about dumb midwesterners suddenly didn't seem so off-base.

★ ☆ ★ ☆ ★

My girlfriend, Kathleen, has a thing for plastic surgery.

I don't mean that she wants it for herself, or that she finds it in some way miraculous and just. She just takes delight in the most hideous products of these cosmetic procedures, gawking at them online, whispering quietly to me when we glimpse one of the sad freaks in public, barely restraining herself from staring openly or giggling. It's endearing, and it made me think of her often as I drove around Los Angeles that next morning, my eyes assaulted by the colorful monstrosities that populate the general area in which I was staying.

People streamed in and out of boutiques and trendy cafés in Beverly Hills, iPhones glued to their ears, bags of clothing and jewelry dangling from their impossibly skinny, tanned arms. Remember, this was my first time in LA, so I'd never seen many of these otherworldly places that most people only glimpse on TV and in film, these stores that have arisen to sop up the fat dripping from the entertainment industry, acting as grease traps for the city's ostentatious wealth. The sea of comically large boobs, birdlike noses, tucked tummies, and lifted faces made me feel as if I were adrift in some mixture of John Carpenter's *They Live* and Aphex Twin's "Windowlicker" video.

It was reassuring, then, to arrive at Krust Café and Bakery on Verdugo Avenue in Burbank and find Patton Oswalt looking every bit the normal person. He was seated at a four-top near the counter, flipping through a pile of comic books he had picked up that morning (Wednesday equals comic-book day in Nerd Land). I must have looked the part of the writer, with my black glasses, messy hair, dirty Converse, and overstuffed messenger bag, because the instant he saw me, he rose and said, "John?" I shook his hand, noticing how he looked at once bigger and smaller in person. I'd been vaguely familiar with him for years, occasionally seeing him on the CBS sitcom *The King of Queens*, on which he played star Kevin James's squat, quirky friend Spence Olchin from 1998 to 2007. That role is probably how most everyone else knows him, and Olchin's fastidiousness and comic book/sci-fi obsessions aren't too far from Oswalt's own personality.

But in Burbank, in the sickly gray light of a February morning at this earthy bakery, Oswalt just looked like a regular guy, his sneakers, baggy pants, and loose black T-shirt contrasting with his oversized sunglasses. "Have you been here long?" I asked, hoping he hadn't. "Nah, just got here early," he replied. "I'm so sorry, but I've actually got a thing I have to do at Disney in an hour, so we should probably start."

Ah, yes: Disney. Oswalt had recently starred in the 2007 Pixar feature *Ratatouille* as the voice of Remy the Rat. It was arguably the biggest role of his acting career, and one that would send him to the Oscars four days later, where the movie ended up walking away with the Academy Award for Best Animated Feature Film. Oswalt had already landed himself sixty-odd acting and voice roles over the years, from a video store clerk in a *Seinfeld* episode to appearances on *NewsRadio* and Comedy Central's *Reno 911!* His film credits have usually consisted of brief appearances in movies like *Magnolia* and *Starsky and Hutch*, although he has taken bigger parts in Reno *911!: Miami* and the sports-movie spoof *Balls of Fury*. He's often afforded the everyman role, which is unsurprising considering his calm, rounded face and malleable voice. That last instrument, in particular, is his secret weapon, packing all the satisfying punch of a wet boxing glove filled with concrete.

But I was there to dissect Oswalt's stand-up career, and the way it led to his seminal *Comedians of Comedy* tour and films and, eventually, his Sub Pop CD. Granted, his talents have landed him brief stints on hipster favorites *Mr. Show*, MTV's *Human Giant*, and Adult Swim shows including *Aqua Teen Hunger Force* and *Tim and Eric Awesome Show, Great Job!* But Oswalt is notoriously suspicious of indie cred, even as his career benefits from it. He loves the art of comedy and will perform it whenever he can. And other than David Cross, there's no one else more noted for bringing comedy to the indie-music crowd.

Like Cross, Oswalt is a transplanted southerner. He was born on January 27, 1969, in Portsmouth, Virginia, a waterfront city in the southeastern bend of the state. His dad was a Marine colonel, so the family frequently moved around. At an early age, Oswalt's father exposed him to Jonathan Winters records. He also developed an instant love of horror movies after watching the original silent version of *Nosferatu* at a public library in Tustin Meadows, California, when he was five years old, relishing the way it made the other children scream. Eventually he would appreciate the parallels between horror and comedy—the visceral setup and punch, the mixture of laughter and disbelief at grotesque images and ideas.

His appreciation of stand-up developed along that path. "When I was young, Jonathan Winters and Bill Cosby were really, really big deals for me," he says, leaning across the table as I cradle an enormous cup of green tea. "Especially Jonathan Winters. As I got older it became Steve Martin and Richard Pryor and George Carlin. But it's almost like, you know how in the seventh grade everyone's into The Who for awhile? It just speaks to something, and you kind of always keep that with you. But not every kid has comedic idols like I did, or like most comedians did."

Oswalt became interested in the darkly brilliant writing of Harlan Ellison in seventh grade, starting with the anthology *A Boy and His Dog*. (He now counts the living-legend author among his friends.) Throughout his teenage years, Oswalt envisioned himself becoming a writer, although after he graduated from Broad Run High School in Ashburn, Virginia, in 1987, he was furnished with a more realistic sense of the world. He majored in English while at the College of William and Mary in Williamsburg, Virginia, on a partial scholarship. During his sophomore year he realized that writing alone wasn't going to pay the bills, so he worked a variety of temp jobs, including DJ, paralegal, and reporter for sports papers. He soon came to resent the failed jocks he worked with at the law office. "I couldn't take another liquid lunch at Bennigan's," he told ASpecialThing.com in 2005. "There was an actual Bennigan's on Leesburg Pike Route 7 in the Tyson's Corner area where we would go every Friday, and it was so fuckin' depressing."

Oswalt was a rabid fan of magazines like *National Lampoon* and shows like *Monty Python's Flying Circus*, so he jumped into stand-up while in college, even though he immediately found it difficult and unrewarding. Still, something about the masochistic work-for-it aspect of stand-up subtly appealed to him. His first shot came at Garvin's in Washington, DC, in July 1988. Blaine Capatch was emceeing a radio station–sponsored open-mic contest that included the nineteen-year-old Oswalt and a four-teen-year-old Dave Chappelle. Oswalt took an immediate liking to Capatch and comedian Mark Voyce, who were part of the general DC scene at the time—a scene start-ing to experience the death throes of the eighties comedy boom. He also admired the better touring comedians who would come through town, like Louis C. K., Bobcat Goldthwait, Emo Phillips, and even Jay Leno.

Oswalt played scattered regional gigs in places such as Baltimore and Philadelphia, driving only as far as his dilapidated car could take him, and hosted weekly open-mic nights in DC. He worked the rest of the region when he could, taking stand-up jobs across the Midwest and the South, often subject to last-minute cancellations. He received terrible advice from comedians whose careers were circling the drain—comedians who tried to convince him that being competitive and money-oriented in the stand-up world was the only way to survive.

Oswalt also experienced his political awakening around this time, realizing that the start of the first Gulf War late in 1990 meant some of his friends would be shipped overseas. At one point, he headed down to a commons area at his college to see what sort of protests were going on, only to discover a pair of football frats throwing a prowar rally. "There was a guy dressed as Captain America, there was a guy dressed as Rambo, and there was a dude in a kind of shitty Uncle Sam costume, and a guy wearing a turban with a cardboard scimitar, and Uncle Sam was kicking him and running around in a circle and all this shit," he told IGN.com in April 2006. "I was watching this going, 'These guys are in danger of going to the war, and they're so into this.' Because to them, it's just a big aggressive fight, like it's fun."

Like fellow comedians David Cross and Janeane Garofalo, Oswalt would later become a vocal critic of the George W. Bush administration and its own preemptive 2003 war in Iraq, playing anti-Bush events and lending his material to a *Rock Against Bush* DVD. But in the summer of 1991, Oswalt was mostly thinking about where to live. He had just graduated from college and moved to Baltimore, but Capatch tried to convince him that San Francisco held untold opportunities for the pair. With that in mind, Oswalt moved back in with his parents to save money, eventually heading to San Francisco in the summer of 1992, and making the difficult decision to break it off with his college fiancée.

On the drive out, Oswalt's Volkswagen Jetta blew its water pump in Truckee, California. Fixing it required all the cash he'd saved living with his parents. He was never more desperate for work, and had been sending tapes to clubs in San Francisco before leaving the East Coast. All of them told him the same thing: "Talk to us when you get here." Fortunately, San Francisco's boldly experimental, inclusive .comedy scene immediately heartened Oswalt. The bulging alternative comedy wave had yet to fully wash north from Los Angeles and meet with San Francisco's, but San Francisco already had a scene of its own. Soon, Oswalt's comedic heroes weren't Jonathan Winters and Richard Pryor, but his friends—people like Brian Posehn, Dana Gould, Blaine Capatch, Greg Proops, Bob Rubin, and Jeremy Kramer. Even before alternative comedy became a catchphrase, these comedians forged their own paths in and outside of the traditional stand-up circuit.

"Look at someone like Dana Gould," Oswalt says. "He's very much like the Johnny Cash of this generation. A lot of these so-called alternative comics and newer comics are doing what they do because of stuff they saw Dana do back in the day. He was doing it when most comedians weren't very personal onstage. You had those 'Man, shopping's crazy, isn't it?' people, and he's up there going, 'Man, I tried to *kill* myself the other night.' You're like, 'Wow, what the fuck is this?' And he fuckin' destroyed audiences."

Oswalt marveled at the respect that other stand-ups held for the art of comedy in San Francisco, with comics regularly watching their peers' sets—something Oswalt had never witnessed on the East Coast. Their material and performance styles dripped with surprise and shock, or alternately, thoughtfulness and political material, their sets often presented as cultural events akin to experimental theater rather than mindless nightclub entertainment. These comedians labored to perform each and every night, regardless of the composition of the audience, instead of honing a single set of jokes (although they did that, too). They bared their souls and took humor in whatever direction they pleased. Expectations, in other words, went out the door. Big crowd? Small crowd? Good mood? Bad? It didn't matter.

Bigger touring names such as Dave Attell, Andy Kindler, Laura Kightlinger, Brian Regan, and Janeane Garofalo would stop through, Oswalt giddily soaking up their sensibilities. He gradually overhauled his style, ditching the double-breasted suits and solid but unspectacular subject matter that typified his DC days. He imitated his betters and attempted to get onstage every night of the week at the Phoenix Theater, The Punch Line, and Holy City Zoo. Eventually he found a style all his own, but it would take him seven years and a mini breakdown in early 1995 (when he inexplicably sabotaged his sets onstage) in order to achieve it.

Oswalt had been working toward a direct, conversational style, like that of the guy at a bar relating an amazing story and continuing to drink heartily while doing so. He counted a Washington, DC, sportscaster named Glen Brenner among his influences. Brenner would often reference the artificiality of TV while on camera, pointing out crew members and breaking down the necessarily mediated distance by emphasizing it.

Moving to Los Angeles from San Francisco in 1995 pushed Oswalt into yet another creative realm. He had lived there briefly in 1994 while working with Blaine Capatch on Comedy Central's short-format show *Food for Thought*, in which the pair played pseudophilosophical grocery store clerks, but the timing didn't feel right to establish roots just yet. He returned to San Francisco, then played a short residency with Capatch at Slapstix in Baltimore.

It was a grim sight. The comedy scene in that city—and most every place in the East outside of New York—had been thoroughly decimated by the downturn of the 1980s boom, clubs closing by the dozen and out-of-work comedians littering the streets. Fortunately, the crowds and waitstaff at Slapstix loved Oswalt and Capatch's material, bolstering the pair's sense that moving to San Francisco for the sake of stand-up had been a worthy quest. But the club's owner, Chris Cahill, freaked out when he received a half-dozen negative comment cards about their sets. That, and the owner's refusal to kick out rowdy drunks for fear of alienating them as customers, helped reinforce Oswalt's ideas about the flaws and limitations of the comedy club model. "In the shittier comedy clubs, drunk people are GODS," he asserted in a 2004 Q&A on ASpecialThing.com.

Despite his devotion to touring and playing wherever he could, the experience helped Oswalt realize that his future could only be in Los Angeles. When he arrived, he found a city teeming with "refugees," as he put it, from other scenes around the country: friends and influences like Dana Gould and the darkly brilliant Jeremy Kramer; up-and-comers like Karen Kilgariff, Mary Lynn Rajskub, Laura Milligan, and Greg Behrendt; East Coast– and Midwest-bred comedian-writers like David Cross, Bob Odenkirk, and Paul F. Tompkins. All were coalescing around LA's small, experimental comedy rooms. "The eighties comedy boom was just an intensely genericizing force," says Jesse Thorn of radio's *The Sound of Young America*. "Everybody could get work as long as you weren't too weird, so everybody was working. But once all the jobs disappeared, people were like, 'Well, we want to do the stuff that we like.' So that led to things like the Largo scene and Beth Lapides' Un-Cabaret scene in LA, and then the equivalents in San Francisco and Boston."

Oswalt's idealism would quickly turn on him. He and Capatch were hired as writers for the *MadTV* pilot on Fox, then later as staffers after the network picked up the young sketch comedy. Oswalt watched with envy as his friends on *Mr. Show* aired groundbreaking, inspired sketches, whereas most of the ideas that made it onto *MadTV* seemed creatively retarded by comparison. But as correct as he may have been about *MadTV*'s unchallenging premises and lame recurring characters, Oswalt failed to offer alternatives to the writers on his show. He chose to direct his anger at people in essentially the same boat, like executive producers Adam Small and Fax Bahr. That pair eventually asked Oswalt and Capatch not to return after the second season. By that point, Oswalt pretty much agreed with them.

Oswalt would look back on the situation with some regret, remembering the quality of a writing staff he didn't appreciate at the time, and the fact that a handful of *Mr. Show* regulars actually tried to get on *MadTV*. It wasn't so much a lack of ideas on the show, but the fact that Fox instantly killed most of the good ones for fear of losing viewers who wouldn't get the references. Two years later, Bob Odenkirk and David Cross solicited Oswalt to write for *Mr. Show* in its third season, which Oswalt initially turned down due to a prior writing commitment with MTV. When that inevitably fell through, he returned to Bob and David with a half-dozen hastily written sketches. *Mr. Show*'s staff holes had been filled by then, and Bob and David never used Oswalt's sketches. In the end, Oswalt only appeared as a character actor in a couple *Mr. Show* episodes, and the show's promised fifth season—when he was planning to join as a writer—never happened.

Fortunately, by 1996 Oswalt was a legitimate headliner at clubs. He started to write for and appear on a handful of TV shows, and made his feature film debut in the middling comedy *Down Periscope*. In 1997 he snagged his own *HBO Comedy Half-Hour* special, and two years later, a *Comedy Central Presents* special. Oswalt later pointed to the latter program as an example of how *not* to shoot short-form stand-up, but the material at least showed promise.

Taped in New York, it begins with Oswalt taking the stage in a crisp, dark suit. He talks about ignoring pot laws and treating them like a kid's game, where the rules don't apply because he didn't pay attention when they were laid out. He makes fun of the "Starbucks liberalism" he sees at classic movie houses in LA, listening to audience members complain about the sexism in *The Searchers*, misguidedly attempting to adapt its message to today's politically correct environment. He also drops musical references while talking about the Dolphin coffee shop in Amsterdam, and how Supergrass, Elvis Costello, and the Beastie Boys ("the holy triumvirate") are playing over the loudspeakers while he selects his weed. While enjoying some White Widow from Afghanistan, Queen's "We Are The Champions" rings out, and all he can think about is how he could have been back in LA getting up to work on the crappy sketch show he used to do (*MadTV*).

The special isn't bad, but it pales next to the material Oswalt would later devise, and the organic, inviting way in which he would present it. As he continued to work in the industry, writing for and appearing in shows such as *Dr. Katz, Professional Therapist* and taking small roles in big movies like *Magnolia* and *Man on the Moon*, he befriended other LA comics and musicians, including singer-songwriter Aimee Mann.

A small but vibrant scene had begun to develop around Largo nightclub on Fairfax Avenue in West Hollywood. Mark Flanagan, owner of the artist-friendly venue, and SF Improv and NBC veteran Lisa Leingang went out of their way to book up-and-coming musicians and comedians, helping boost the careers of Mitch Hedberg, Tenacious D, Elliott Smith, Ryan Adams, and others. It wasn't odd to see Elvis Costello, Neil Young, Michael Stipe, or Beck stop by to work out material or collaborate with one of the night's performers, although due to the club's limited capacity (about 100 seats, plus standing room) it almost always sold out. "I have a lot of singer-songwriters who don't write about the happy things in life," Flanagan told the *Los Angeles Times* in 2002. "I mean, there's a sense of humor in there, but you gotta dig deep for it. In Ireland, when I was growing up, a comedian or a magician would often open for an artist. So I thought it would be good to do that at Largo."

Aimee Mann and singer-songwriter husband Michael Penn often played at Largo with friend Jon Brion, whom Mann knew from her days in Boston. Brion's weekly Friday night gigs drew consistent crowds and celebrity musical friends. A producer for Mann, Fiona Apple, The Eels, Rufus Wainwright, and others, Brion went on to score a few movies for Paul Thomas Anderson (such as *Magnolia*, to which Mann contributed the Grammy- and Academy Award–nominated song "Save Me").

Mann, the Berklee-trained singer-guitarist formerly of eighties pop act 'Til Tuesday (remember "Voices Carry"?) had always been a bit wary of stand-up comedy. "I remember when I was in Boston and just the idea of going to a comedy show was like, 'Please, God, no,'" she says. "My idea of a comedian was like Gallagher or something. I thought I would get sprayed with water or the audience would get harassed."

But it was a different story in Los Angeles. One of the first people Mann saw performing stand-up there was Patton Oswalt. She fondly recalls an impromptu "super nerds" bit that Oswalt and Brian Posehn concocted in which they argued about the minutiae of *Star Wars* and *Star Trek*.

They improvised the show-saving routine after a planned reading of the script of Jerry Lewis's infamous, unreleased Holocaust film, *The Day the Clown Cried,* was shut down.

Largo's Monday night comedy showcases helped introduce Mann to the new vanguard of comedy. "I'd already met [*Mr. Show* alumnus] Paul F. Tompkins, and he was a big favorite of mine," Mann says. "But we'd also see Sarah Silverman, Andy Kindler, David Cross, Mary Lynn Rajskub, and people like that at Largo." Oswalt had already opened for several musical acts at Largo, including Jack Black's comedy-metal duo Tenacious D and Men at Work's Colin Hay. "The Largo was a music club. The Diamond Club was a music club," Oswalt said. "The whole thing was that we were taking it out of comedy clubs and doing it anywhere else we could—coffee shops, bookstores, whatever. It was the same thing in New York with the Luna Lounge and the Time Café and all that stuff."

Mann loved the unpredictable artistic fare, intimate mood, and passionate, occasionally boisterous Largo audiences. That eventually led her and Michael Penn to create their Tuesday night Acoustic Vaudeville shows in 1999. As the name implies, the anything-goes format reinforced Largo's already strong mash of cutting-edge comedy and music. Mann and Penn also launched a series of occasional tours starting in 2000 that visited cities across the United States, and eventually England and Ireland. Comedians Oswalt, David Cross, Paul F. Tompkins, Andy Kindler, Janeane Garofalo, and others joined them, with Oswalt logging considerable time on the road. "We just had the idea of involving comedians because we both felt so awkward talking onstage all the time," Mann says. "So the idea was to have a comic, who's a professional talker onstage, to come in and pinch hit. They'd do the heavy lifting of the banter and basically pretend to be us, then we'd step out and take over with the music."

The format worked, and soon critics were heralding its innovative approach—which harkened back to the late-nineteenth- and early-twentieth-century stage format from which it took its name. National publications dubbed the sold-out tours "an intimate cabaret" (*Daily Variety*) and "a new form of entertainment" (*The Boston Globe*), and Largo's designation as "LA's worst-kept secret" (*Q* magazine) only grew. It wasn't the only venue in LA hosting comedy and music, but like New York's Luna Lounge, it was often the hottest.

Mann eventually adopted the format for her annual Christmas variety show, which tours the country with musician friends and features stand-ups Morgan Murphy, Paul F. Tompkins, Fred Armisen, John C. Reilly, and others in a musical-comedy revue. "I really like the ensemble approach," Mann says. "I've always liked that sort of buffet approach to anything."

"She was also very gung-ho about a Presidents' Day show not too long ago," says Paul F. Tompkins. "The more diversity you have onstage, the more interested people remain because they don't know what's going to happen next. For me that's about all I can ask for from a show: to be kept on my toes. The element of surprise is so much fun."

"Aimee Mann is definitely the den mother to a lot of comics," David Cross adds. "Wait, she's the one who directed *Heat*, right?"

Throughout the early 2000s, Patton Oswalt appeared on TV (Adult Swim's *Home Movies*) and in films (Ben Stiller's cult comedy *Zoolander*). *Variety* had already dubbed him one of the "Ten Comedians to Watch" in 1999, and in 2002 *Entertainment Weekly* named him the "It" comedian of the year. He popped up on game shows

(*Hollywood Squares, Pyramid*) and cable TV (*Tough Crowd with Colin Quinn*, VH1's *I Love the '80s*) and as a lifelong comic book nerd, fulfilled a dream by penning DC Comics' one-off *JLA: Welcome to the Working Week* in 2003. Around this time he also started writing "punch-up" for Hollywood movies, a process by which writers attack a preexisting script and add whatever seems to be missing, whether that's pithy dialogue, necessary emotional beats, or, as was often the case with Oswalt, jokes in computer-animated movies.

But Oswalt's love for stand-up remained strong, and in March of 2002 he met someone who opened him to a different side of that world. Oswalt and comedian Brian Posehn were booked for a weekend at The Punchline in Atlanta, where David Cross had performed his first gig twenty years earlier. Atlanta resident Henry Owings, a graphic designer and editor of the unapologetically harsh, hilarious magazine *Chunklet*, knew Posehn through David Cross and wanted to check out the shows. "Brian and Patton were playing Thursday through Saturday and I went out to every single show," Owings recalls. "We just hung out and talked about authors and comics and music. I think Patton was kind of smitten with who I was, as far as the kind of stuff I've done in my life and how I've done it. That weekend I took both of them around to comic book shops and record stores in my ratty old Volkswagen and we just nerded out." .

Owings could immediately sense that Oswalt was unlike most comedians. The way he sought out challenging new audiences and experiences impressed Owings, Oswalt relentlessly honing his set night after night, three shows a night, and eschewing the typical postset dressing room for interaction. "Right after (Patton) got home from that weekend, I got a check in the mail from him for $200 for driving him around, and this is right around the time that I was burglarized," Owings says. "I was just like, 'This guy is a fucking class act.'"

During a *Chunklet* phone interview with Oswalt, Owings asked if he would be interested in playing the magazine's tenth anniversary party at the 40 Watt Club in Athens, Georgia, in March 2003. The 40 Watt had helped kick-start the careers of new wave, post-punk, and indie fixtures Pylon, R.E.M., Indigo Girls, Of Montreal, Drive-By Truckers, and others. And since Oswalt had played music venues before—and gotten along famously with Owings during their first meeting—he agreed to fly out for it. "He absolutely fell in love with the vibe of it and how he was received," Owings says of the show. "He was playing to fans, and not just people that came to see a 'comedy' show. He felt like it was almost opulent to play in front of people that were so appreciative and got what he was doing. I've probably seen him 200 times now and I've never seen him thrive or have as much fun as he has in a rock club. He's a force of nature."

Indeed, Oswalt enjoyed the experience so much that he returned to Athens four months later, although Owings mistakenly booked him in a room that was far too big for Oswalt's draw at the time. "It was this theater with like a 1,000-person capacity, where The Melvins and Queens of the Stone Age would play, and he performed for three hours to forty fucking people," Owings remembers. "He came onstage, and I'll never forget this—he had this kind of wine lipstick ring around his mouth—and he was out-of-his-mind drunk. When he got off stage, he just bear-hugged me and said, 'That was the most fun I've ever had in my life.'" According to Owings, Oswalt even refused payment for the show. "It was very modest, only a couple hundred bucks. He told me, 'It's like getting paid to eat chocolate cake. It's just wrong.'"

The experience, it seemed, threatened to sour Oswalt on the traditional comedy club experience for good. Not that Oswalt hated comedy clubs. His long-standing ethos of performing stand-up for its own sake was (and still is) fully intact. But a bad night at a comedy club was quickly becoming his least favorite experience. In a June 13, 2004, blog entry he opened up about the frustrations of playing to not one, but *two* bachelorette parties, reinforcing every stereotype that existed about the club environment. "I hate bachelorette parties," he wrote. "Not in theory. A woman getting married, surrounded by her supportive friends who want to celebrate someone they love finding a true companion to share this poem called life is a beautiful thing. It's a lullaby sung under moonlight to a child that will grow to bring peace to the world. But a bachelorette party at one of my shows? Like AIDS, rape, and Avril Lavigne at the same time. Take your fake wigs, rubber dildos [wow, you're so dangerous and sassy, waving a big, black rubber cock around in public—guess who else does that? Gay winos] and bullshit *Sex and the City* attitudes to a strip club or a P. J. O'Flannawackery's."

Oswalt savored the rock club environment so much that he returned to the 40 Watt in Athens to record his first stand-up CD, *Feelin' Kinda Patton*. Aimee Mann's United Musicians label released the twenty-eight-track record on June 29, 2004, and Dan Schlissel's Stand Up! Records later issued a limited-edition vinyl version, just as he did with David Cross's albums.

Feelin' Kinda Patton included impassioned and laser-focused attacks on the inanity of America's political leadership and our drooling acceptance of it, but it also employed Oswalt's vibrant vocabulary and nimble, twisted brain to skewer nearly everything else. "There's a bit of David Cross in Oswalt's style, mostly in how effectively both use the F-word, but also in their common ability to weave hilarious cynicism through a jumble of personal experience and mundane pop culture events," wrote Johnny Loftus in *All Music Guide*. "But *Feelin' Kinda Patton* really gets going whenever Oswalt vaults off the usual comic fodder—eighties hair metal, porn, hippies—into bizarre flights of disposable culture surrealism. His recollection of an old Asti Spumante ad becomes an invitation into the twisted sex life of a frustrated midlevel professional; Robert Evans is the anchor for a meta-analysis of 1970s Hollywood Babylon." In a nod toward Oswalt's growing fan base, *Chunklet* later released an unedited version of *Feelin' Kinda Patton* under the title *222*.

Oswalt's reputation in the industry was already on an upswing, thanks in part to his regular presence on *The King of Queens*. His stand-up had found a unique, pointed voice, and releasing a CD necessarily opened him to new audiences. He also appeared in his own one-hour Comedy Central special in 2004, *No Reason to Complain*. In it, he takes on e-mail spam, midgets, food (a favorite topic, including Black Angus's ridiculous ads, and reality TV. He predicts Fox's eventual programming desperation will lead to a program called *World's Most Listless Loiterers*). He expresses deep ambivalence about adulthood: "I'm thirty-five years old now. All my friends are either having babies or getting sober, and they're equally annoying." The camera later cuts to the audience and shows familiar, bearded Anthrax guitarist Scott Ian sitting with a female friend. "If you were into metal in the eighties, guess what?" Oswalt says. "You were gay." The special garnered mostly positive reviews, but despite his growing personal success, Oswalt still felt that the type of comedy he loved would require a brand name of sorts for people to appreciate it fully. Mostly, he just wished he could showcase his talented friends outside of the standard club circuit.

He had seen the comedy-music mixture work on his Acoustic Vaudeville dates, and his early experiences in the alt-comedy scenes of San Francisco and LA had taught him that not every crowd feared guileless, experimental humor. He had also paid keen attention to the success of David Cross's tours with Ultrababyfat, and was quick to remember the negative experiences the comedy club environment could engender, such as the ones that happened at Slapstix. These things ultimately led him to create the winkingly titled *Comedians of Comedy* tour, the next step in stand-up's march away from comedy clubs and onto the indie-music circuit.

The first official *Comedians of Comedy* show took place at the 40 Watt in Athens on April 29, 2004, with Oswalt, comedian Zach Galifianakis, and Superchunk drummer Jon Wurster (one half of the Scharpling and Wurster comedy team). Brian Posehn had been scheduled to perform in place of Galifianakis, but backed out a couple days prior to shoot a commercial. Subsequent shows took place in Chapel Hill (April 30) and Baltimore (May 1, minus Wurster). Henry Owings, always the self-contained unit, managed, booked, and promoted them. "He'd done it for years with bands and had to deal with load-ins and equipment and shipping," Oswalt says. "With comedians it's just us and the microphone, so it's easy."

The setup's simplicity appealed to Owings, who remembered the immense amount of work in schlepping merchandise for the *Mr. Show* live tour, *Hooray for America!*, in 2002. "I come from a very punk-rock, underground, DIY background, a land free of managers and lawyers and publicists," Owings says. "If you wanted to call someone you fucking did it, and I think what I brought to the table was this immediacy. I can manage tours and book shows and design the posters, because I've been fucking doing it my entire adult life. I don't have to go through six or seven hoops and have conference calls about it."

Oswalt realized the potential in conducting his shows the way an indie rock or punk band would, mounting grassroots marketing campaigns on radio stations, in college papers, and at record shop in-stores. "It's not hard to promote yourself, especially for someone like me that is constantly building on my fan base and adding to my website and MySpace page," he says. "And it's especially so if your end goal is to do stand-up comedy. Because it's not like I want to get out of stand-up comedy and just do movies. Everything I do—movies, TV, writing—is so I can keep doing stand-up."

Oswalt introduced the first proper *Comedians of Comedy* tour on September 22, 2004, in Seattle. Filmmaker Michael Blieden and a small crew joined the comedians on the weeklong West Coast jaunt to document their every waking (and sleeping) moment, although manager Owings didn't enjoy the added complication of a film crew on his self-contained tour. Comedian Maria Bamford joined Oswalt, Galifianakis, and Posehn as they played small to midsized rock venues up and down the seaboard. David Cross's 2002 tour with Ultrababyfat provided partial inspiration, but Oswalt intended the *Comedians of Comedy* more as a comic variety show, using his existing notoriety to draw new audiences to artists who lacked that same renown.

"(Cross's tour) was a model I used to put together the travel, logistics, as well as choose the types of venues we'd perform in," Oswalt says. "But the idea came from a lot of different areas—even seeing what *The Original Kings of Comedy* and the *Blue Collar Comedy Tour* did. It was just that whole do-it-yourself idea of promoting it yourself, bringing out your own audience that you like, and not depending on a club." Oswalt says he was particularly struck by a series of shows he did with Cross at Cobb's

Comedy Club in San Francisco a year prior. "The club meant well, but the tickets were way too high, and they weren't advertising in the places that our fans would have seen. That's what really got me thinking, *OK, it's time to put this into my own hands.* I was also coasting on the recognition from *The King of Queens* and realized it was getting easier to fill these clubs. But I was bringing people out that weren't necessarily fans of me. It was just like, 'Oh, that guy's on TV. Let's go see him.' I thought I needed to take a little more control over how I was presenting myself."

Oswalt didn't intentionally create the *Comedians of Comedy* as an antidote to the mainstream club experience, but, like Cross, he sympathized with fans who couldn't afford the high covers, parking costs, and food at those venues. Many of his fans were also too young to satisfy the two-drink minimum at a comedy club. And unlike musicians, comedians rarely had the chance to perform at the sort of small, all-ages shows that drew people in their own age group—or younger. "Comedians start off performing for people that are much older than them," Oswalt explains. "Then you have to either catch up with them or wait until it levels out. I thought that was silly, so I went the other way." At the forefront of Oswalt's mind was the fact that many people still didn't consider stand-up comedy a legitimate art form on par with music or literature. He wanted crowds to feel the same thrill he got from watching his favorite comics, to follow them as they would their favorite bands or writers, watching them experiment, fail, and sometimes triumph with new creative approaches.

But the grind of the road on the first *Comedians of Comedy* tour also paralleled many small bands' experiences. "I've stayed in some pretty shitty places in my 104 years doing stand-up," Oswalt quipped in a September 23, 2004, online tour diary just after the tour's first show, "but nothing could prepare me for the doom-soaked atmosphere of our Seattle residential hotel, which I'm going to call the James Whitmore Hangs Himself In *The Shawshank Redemption* Suites."

Ample evidence of the tour's ups and downs exists on Michael Blieden's 2005 *Comedians of Comedy* documentary, financed by online movie rental company Netflix. It captures Oswalt, Posehn, Bamford, and Galifianakis candidly interacting on and off stage, trading jabs and developing jokes, telling road stories, sitting through interviews at radio stations, and generally marveling at the fact that young people in America were so primed to see stand-up comedy outside of comedy clubs.

Like any tour, the triumphant moments (Oswalt particularly enjoyed an all-ages show in Portland, Oregon, where young fans appeared in droves) mingle with hecklers, breakdowns, clowning, and drunken introspection. In one scene, Oswalt seems acutely aware that what he's doing is simply a step in the evolution of stand-up comedy. "We are the ugly motherfuckers that are setting it up," he tells Michael Blieden after the first-ever *Comedians of Comedy* show. "Someone's gonna spike it and it's not going to be us. I'm setting up the next guy. That's my purpose." The irony of course is that Oswalt *was* the next guy, taking cues from David Cross and others in a tour that helped propel him and his cadre of creative friends into the semi-national consciousness. Not that the movie was general-audience fare. The core quartet in the *Comedians of Comedy* come off alternately as nerds, stoners, smarty-pants, and maladjusted (if mostly likeable) people. "You get to see how antisocial and horrible we kind of are," Oswalt joked on *Jimmy Kimmel Live!* shortly before the film premiered at South by Southwest on March 13, 2005. Indeed, the movie shows the comedians passing time in hotel rooms and tour vans, glued to

their headphones and laptops, their personalities sometimes growing prickly as the tour wears on.

But since it contains only scattered snippets of different stand-up sets, it ultimately fulfills its purpose of
making the viewer want to seek out more of the comedians' material. More to the point, it allows us to get to
know the principals as human beings.

Maria Bamford, the lone woman on the tour, tells
a comedy club horror story of an unruly man getting
tasered by police during a solo set in Boise, Idaho. "He
falls to the ground and starts crawling toward the stage
going, 'I'm having a good time, I wanna watch the rest of
the shoooow!'"

Most of Bamford's negative experiences in clubs,
however, were milder than that. "Some people are like,
'This comedy didn't go with my nachos! I like my comedy
to go with my nachos!'" she tells me. "It's such a bummer
when you have rough shows like that. Somebody will
be like, 'It's my fucking birthday and I didn't want to
see *this!*'"

Bamford's style is significantly different from that
of her counterparts—which is exactly what Oswalt was
going for. Her profanity-free collection of observations
and deeply personal jokes occasionally reference her
battles with depression and obsessive-compulsive dis-
order: "I've never really thought of myself as depressed
as much as paralyzed by hope," she says in 2007's *The
Comedians of Comedy: Live at the Troubadour.* She frequently finds humor in elevating mundane situations to
ridiculous heights. She compares praying to "a bad ven-
triloquism act," turning her hand into a maniacal version
of Señor Wences' Johnny character, who stands in for
God. She also inverts familiar, lazy punch lines: "Your
mama's so fat...she's humiliated and rejected by the very
society that made your mama so fat!"

A travel-hardened comedian through and through, Bamford was born in Port Hueneme, California, on September 3, 1970, the daughter of a Navy doctor. She grew up in Duluth, Minnesota, before leaving for Bates College in Maine, the University of Edinburgh in Scotland, and finally the University of Minnesota, where she graduated with a degree in creative writing. She spent her childhood, as she tells the documentary camera at one point, imitating commercials and doing funny voices around her family, and that flair for impressively distinct voices came to underpin her vignette-driven act. Her normally high, upper-midwestern speaking voice, for example, can mutate into a languid California-cool persona or a Katherine Hepburnesque impression of her mother (a frequent source of inspiration). In one bit, she relates how she ran into a bitchy former high school classmate at Target while visiting Duluth, perfectly affecting that region's coiled accent while skewering the gum-chewing, dismissive provincialism of someone still mired in adolescence.

Bamford had much to gain from the *Comedians of Comedy* tours. She'd been performing stand-up since she was nineteen years old, and had previously appeared on *Late Night with Conan O'Brien*, various Comedy Central specials, and TV shows like *Mystery Science Theater 3000* and *Dharma and Greg*. But her solo touring schedule didn't possess the overall brand appeal and exposure of the *Comedians of Comedy*—a shame, since her vocal mastery and unpredictable nature often provide the highlights of whatever projects she appears in. "Maria's awesome," says David Cross. "She's really unique and talented and I hope other people see that. She's capable of a lot of great stuff that I don't think she gets a lot of opportunity to do."

In one of Bamford's more notable bits, she recounts a story that effectively splits the difference between *Whatever Happened to Baby Jane?* and *Blue Velvet*.

"My mom told me recently, 'Honey, when you don't wear makeup, you look mentally ill.' So now when I go home I'm certain to wear thick green eye shadow and a line of lipstick *around* my lips. [In a shaky voice, eyelids fluttering,] 'Baby look pretty now, Mommy?'"

Bamford's body language reinforces the joke, her thin frame and wide eyes never seeming completely comfortable onstage despite her years of experience. The stance may or may not be intentional. "I like to do shows where nobody's there, where there are only five people, or only other comics," Bamford says. It's the sort of humor-as-therapy approach that attracts many people to stand-up in the first place. (A few of Bamford's bits also involve her therapist.) "Maria's fiercely creative, an absolute font of talent, but I don't think she was meant to go on tour like that," says Henry Owings.

Bamford more or less agrees. "On the *Comedians of Comedy* shows I get more nervous sometimes because a lot of people come to see Patton and Brian," she says, noting that she pretends to know very little about indie rock or metal. "I am a part of the problem! I do love the album covers and I love the T-shirts of the hip bands, though. I asked Brian to teach me about metal, and what's happening in the music, and why they're mad. They're like, 'We're super mad! Everything's happening and it's happening fast!' Of course, I'm not singing fast enough and the drummers are unbelievable on metal. They have a lot of carpal tunnel, which I can relate with because I used to type for a living. But in my brain I think maybe I'm not as hard core as those guys."

Of course, hard core is a relative term. When we visit Brian Posehn's LA home in the *Comedians of Comedy* documentary, we enter a room filled with sci-fi and fantasy action figures, comic books neatly wrapped in protective plastic covers and stacked in boxes, and a vintage *Ms. Pac-Man* machine against the wall. When Bamford says "hard core," it's more likely she's referencing Posehn's reputation as a heavy-metal comedian as opposed to his obvious nerd rep.

Born July 6, 1966, in Sacramento, California, Posehn often suffered the tall, geeky role among his friends and classmates (he's currently a burly, imposing 6' 6"). He took classical piano lessons for eight years, starting when he was twelve, before jumping into stand-up. Moving to San Francisco from Sacramento introduced him to the group of comedians he matured with, including Oswalt, Greg Behrendt, Doug Benson, Laura Milligan, and Blaine Capatch. He met David Cross when Cross traveled to San Francisco to play the Improv, and came to admire his style. He moved to LA in 1993, at the same time as many other comedians, and soon signed with manager Dave Rath (who counted Oswalt, Janeane Garofalo, and others among his clients). *Mr. Show* propelled the dead-pan, potty-mouthed Posehn into appearances on other sitcoms such as *Seinfeld, Friends, Just Shoot Me!,* and *Everybody Loves Raymond.* He also provided voice work for a number of animated shows on Adult Swim (*Tom Goes to the Mayor, Aqua Teen Hunger Force*) and Disney (*Kim Possible*), and currently plays gay stoner Brian Spukowski on *The Sarah Silverman Program.*

But the most undiluted version of Posehn resides on his CD, *Live In: Nerd Rage,* which metal label Relapse released in 2006. It's not his only metal credential: he's also a life-long fan of the genre. "As I started to speak more about who I am onstage it just came out," Posehn says. "I have simple pleasures and simple tastes. I still love the same stuff I loved when I was fifteen, like horror movies, comic books, heavy metal, and video games. So when I decided to talk about that stuff, I tried to be more real." His jokes on the album cover porn, puppies, video games, late-night TV, and the vicissitudes of marriage. His biggest laughs tend to come when he drops all pretense and goes straight for the gross-out, or grafts average-sounding phrases onto bizarre, unfamiliar ones, as when he relates the story of a pickup bar in LA where he's amazed at "how slutty and hot" some of the women were dressed. "And I grew up in the eighties, so I know what sluts look like," he assures us. Then he flips it around, to great effect:

"Guys don't wear outfits that feature the dong. I think we should, though. Start pulling your pants down, show a little bit of neck—little bit of dick neck, a little male cleavage. Just keep it tasteful, like two inches. Classy. That way you let the ladies know that if they play their cards right, later on they can see the other inch. Three-inch cock. Hooray! In summertime out in LA, the girls always wear the half-shirt, you know, showing the bottom tit, which is a sweet look. Fellas, pull up the shorts for a little bottom nut. Tie that in with the dick neck and you're going to be knee-deep in ladies…or dudes."

Between the bathroom humor and adolescent-style sexual observations, Posehn also relates an appropriately indignant bit about feeling betrayed by the *Star Wars* prequels, likening George Lucas to a creepy, molesting uncle. And ever since Posehn and Oswalt became headliners, they can play to audiences who actually get their *Star Wars* and Slayer references, whether it's in a rock club or a comedy club. "I can be pretty sure the majority of my audience is going to know who Slayer is, and they're going to get it because they're close to who I am. We wouldn't have run into that at the Improv when people just went to see whoever, and I'm up there talking about pot and Metallica."

Like stoner-comedian Doug Benson, Posehn also loves his weed. Many of Posehn's jokes are self-deprecating jabs, relating what a screw-up he is when he's high. "He's definitely a bit of a stoner. Or I should say, his motivation is very stonerlike," says Henry Owings.

"I don't mean that negatively, either. It's just how he is."

Posehn's existing notoriety from *Mr. Show* and *Just Shoot Me!* helped draw crowds to the *Comedians of Comedy* tours, attracting cable TV devotees, sitcom fans, and metal nerds alike. (Incidentally, *Mr. Show* alums David Cross, Bob Odenkirk, and Tom Kenny also appeared on *Just Shoot Me!*, the equivalent of Oswalt's *King of Queens* in Posehn's career.)

But the genius of the *Comedians of Comedy* tours wasn't just that they attracted people with tastes similar to their performers', but that the settings tended to ensure even non-metal or indie-rock fans, for example, would get the references. "We knew there was an audience in New York and Los Angeles because that scene has been growing for a number of years," Zach Galifianakis says via e-mail, echoing his peers. "Patton had the clever idea to take it to the rest of the country, and it seemed to catch on. It has been a nice cult following of goth chicks with back acne."

Galifianakis's jokes waver between paunchy awkwardness and javelin-like resolve, appealing to an absurdist wit and contempt for pop-culture inanity. The short, fat, wiry-bearded comedian is the most unhinged of the bunch, sometimes prowling the stage in too-small shirts and a cheap visor, occasionally sitting down to play gentle, Windham Hill–style melodies on his piano while dropping devastating one-liners:

"I wish there was a morning-after pill for Denny's Moons Over My Hammy."

"I think that sign in neighborhoods, Slow Children Playing, is so mean."

"I hate to be gross, but the only time it's good to yell out 'I have diarrhea' is when you're playing Scrabble—because it's worth a shitload of points."

In the 2007 film *The Comedians of Comedy: Live at the Troubadour*, fans even bequeath Galifianakis a homemade pink visor with "Fat Jesus" written on the bill, a makeshift crown of thorns encircling the top. It speaks to Galifianakis's sensitive-yet-harsh persona, which comedy fans have increasingly been gravitating toward as Galifianakis fulfills the role of the tortured genius. Perhaps it's because he comes across as a genuinely complex character, an occasionally depressed, immensely talented humorist with unforced charm and endearing vulnerability (he often buries his face in his hands onstage, as if pushing back a psychotic episode or riding out a nasty cocaine high). He has joked before about being an alcoholic and grappling with losing his mind, genuine fear flickering in his eyes when he says it. "Zach, on the one hand, is a tremendously clearheaded guy," says Henry Owings. "On the other hand, I think he's really coming to grips with what it means to be a celebrity. He's asked me countless questions about Jeff Mangum [the reclusive former leader of Neutral Milk Hotel, who reportedly suffered a nervous breakdown due to the strain of success]. I think he's starting to identify more with that level of seclusion, and being kind of cryptic and not so immediately easy to pigeonhole. Every time he's in Athens he's like, 'Show me where [Jeff] used to live and play shows.' I might be extrapolating where there's no need to, because with Zach at least, he's got a farm in North Carolina that he uses to get away from everything."

Galifianakis counts musicians such as Will Oldham (of Palace Brothers and Bonnie "Prince" Billy—with whom he appeared in a bizarre Kanye West video remake for "Can't Tell Me Nothing," filmed on his farm in North Carolina) and Fiona Apple (another music video buddy for whom he has opened) as friends. But he, like most of his peers, is no indie snob. At least not consciously.

"I don't really think about it," Galifianakis says of the crowds he plays to. "I just show up where there is a stage and a mic and some cheese and crackers. It really has more to do with the affordability of an offensive-smelling rock club versus the high-price comedy clubs. Both work. But both can be horrible, too. I feel it is a bit snobbish to say that only the cool people come to those indie shows. I have a general disdain for all audiences."

Galifianakis was born on October 1, 1969, in Wilkesboro, North Carolina, a Greek Orthodox nephew of former US congressman Nick Galifianakis. After studying film and communications at North Carolina State University, he fled for New York in 1992. "I started performing in the midnineties in the back of a hamburger restaurant in Times Square," he says. "I had moved to New York to act but could not stop giggling in classes because everyone took themselves very seriously, so I ventured into stand-up. It was kind of a last straw thing because I knew I wanted to be onstage but did not know in what capacity. After I got off stage at my first open mic, I knew that's what I was going to do for the next twenty years."

Galifianakis didn't have comedy idols the same way other stand-ups did—at least none that were specific. He listened to records by Bill Cosby, Cheech & Chong, and even Andy Griffith, but mostly he paid attention to his older brother and cousins, "who were so very funny."

He eventually netted random screen roles, appearing in TV shows such as *Boston Common* and *Tru Calling*, and briefly in the movies *Bubble Boy*, *Corky Romano*, and *Heartland*. He even hosted a short-lived VH1 talk show called *Late World with Zach* in 2002, although none of these projects allowed his true humor to shine. "Zach is kind of the merry prankster, the Ken Kesey of comedy," says David Cross, before wryly adding: "He's our generation's Tim Conway."

Henry Owings fell in love with Galifianakis immediately after seeing him at the first *Comedians of Comedy* show, in April 2004. "As a person he's incredible, but as a comedian he's one of the best I've ever seen. He's just a genius. And he's funny the second he wakes up. It's just instinctual, like if you were left-handed. Whereas everything Patton does is poetry—every last fucking word that comes out of his mouth. You think it's totally off the cuff, but it's meticulously written. With Zach, it's the complete opposite. It's like a GG Allin concert. He might take a shit on the crowd, or pass out, or he might not even show up."

The unlikely quartet of Oswalt, Posehn, Bamford, and Galifianakis came to represent the *Comedians of Comedy* to most people, each member complementing the others' strengths and mitigating their weaknesses. Oswalt was the honed, brutally precise wordsmith, spinning elaborate metaphors with a sharp, reference-heavy tone. Posehn was the lumbering stoner giant, as adept in scatological humor and exploring the teenage male psyche as verbal self-immolation. Bamford's vulnerable, randomly devastating, voice-driven characters belied her sophisticated philosophy and impeccable timing. And Galifianakis's surreal, powder keg persona and conceptual jokes made crowds wonder alternately why they hadn't heard of him and whether he was going to walk off the stage halfway through the set.

The quartet showed their solidarity in the *Comedians of Comedy* TV show, a six-episode series filmed during the summer of 2005 and aired that November on Comedy Central. Oswalt pitched the show based on a twenty-two-minute edit of Blieden's documentary, and the TV version attempted to re-create that same spontaneous tone, trailing the quartet as they played venues out East. "Casual fans of funny need not apply," wrote *Entertainment Weekly* in a review. "It's the hard core—those who care how comics write jokes, what inspires them, and whether they play well with others—who'll dig this tour show." (The series has never been released on DVD, and Oswalt doesn't know if it ever will be.)

But the four core members weren't the only *Comedians of Comedy*. Oswalt had originally intended the *Comedians of Comedy* just to be whomever he brought on the tour. When Galifianakis left, Oswalt tapped New York comedian Eugene Mirman to replace him. During the filming of the Comedy Central series, Adult Swim regular and stand-up veteran Jon Benjamin joined. When they toured again in 2006, Oswalt, Posehn, and Mirman adopted LA deadpan comic Morgan Murphy—a favorite of Oswalt and Aimee Mann—who hosts a weekly talk show at LA's Upright Citizens Brigade Theatre with comedian Jen Kirkman. And when *Comedians of Comedy* became the first-ever stand-up showcase invited to perform at the Coachella music festival, Oswalt brought Bay-area comedians Jasper Redd and Brent Weinbach along.

Oswalt envisioned *Comedians of Comedy* as a running showcase of talent that he felt deserved more attention, bolstered by a handful of comedians who'd already gotten some. It was his show, but he played the emcee *and* the headliner, just as David Letterman is the guiding presence on *Late Night*, one whose personality recedes when the guests arrive.

"It's called Boston-style comedy," Oswalt explains. "There's no such thing as, 'Oh, the first guy sucks.' On my shows, everyone's the headliner. It's their show when they're onstage. I just hate that shitty comedy club pecking order, which is like, 'Eh, fighting through all that stuff makes you good.' No it doesn't. It just makes you combative. There's such a thing as seasoning, but there's another such thing as battering someone for no other reason than that's the way they've always done it."

Oswalt likens the power of the Positive Unknown to watching the opening band at a Pixies concert: "It's probably going to be a band that they like, and it's probably going to be something that I like, too. Then I can discover something new. If I bring out unknowns on *Comedians of Comedy*, I guarantee you'll like them at the end of the show. You'll go, 'Wow, who the fuck was that?'"

That approach extended to the two *Comedians of Comedy* concert films. The first, 2006's *Live at the El Rey*, celebrated the end of a tour by bringing Blaine Capatch and Bob Odenkirk onstage at the art deco music venue on Wilshire Boulevard. (Odenkirk is hardly an unknown, but Capatch had probably escaped most people's attention at that point, at least outside of comedy circles.) Odenkirk's set lays the ground rules for the "judging" that will be done during the set, employing the knowingly dubbed Garofalo-Benet Alternative Comic Standards Scale.

"Referring to your notes will get you 3.5 points," he says, looking directly at his notes. "Talking about how you are referring to your notes while you refer to your notes, 5.3 points. And reading directly from your notes, 8.2 points." The scale awards points for references to Hong Kong and French filmmakers, seventies blaxploitation filmmakers, and Michel Gondry (an automatic win). Any mention of deeply ingrained antisocial behavior or an anti-Bush comment will also net points, as would use of the phrase "Who's with me?" in an arch manner. (Self-deprecation had never been so meta.)

But the true tour de force of the *Comedians of Comedy* is 2007's *Live at the Troubadour*. Oswalt pulls out all the stops for the marathon event, inviting the core *Comedians of Comedy* and nearly a dozen others to that storied music venue on Santa Monica Boulevard. Upon taking the stage, Oswalt holds up his fist to his mouth as if choking back a body-racking laugh, a common sight at his shows. (He often begins by saying, "Holy SHIT, you guys. Wow... Look at this!" Whether it's genuine amazement or showmanship, it always seems to set an inclusive tone.) After a few jokes he introduces Dana Gould. "In my opinion, and many people's opinion, alternative comedy would not exist without this next guy," he says. "The Johnny Cash/ Elvis Costello of the alternative-comedy scene—the guy that made me want to be a better comedian."

Gould winds his way through potentially pedestrian topics like kids and marriage, adroitly flipping them over by inserting reactionary, narrative punch lines through the matter-of-fact delivery and "Huh? How's *that* for you?" facial expressions. The crowd seems a little too "on" (likely due to the cameras), but loosens up once Gould begins talking about performing angry oral sex behind a gay bar just to spite a thoughtless comment his father made. He pretends to weep bitterly when he learns that his father has died, all the while pantomiming dispassionate, workman-like blowjobs and handjobs to the invisible customers.

As the camera pans across the audience, we see that everyone seems to be wearing black hoodies and T-shirts, the uniform of choice for scruffy hipsters. Alt-comedy godfather Andy Kindler takes the stage and lays into the premise of the show, testing the hipsters' sense of humor:

"This is fantastic. I hope this whole movement takes off, because I think a lot of people said, 'You know what? Comedy clubs kind of suck. You know what would be good? Let's put comedy in an even more inappropriate venue. How would that be? You know what people would love to do during stand-up acts?' They would like to stand-up themselves. For years they were in a club: 'Why are we stuck here at a table with elbow room and the ability to breathe?'"

Other comedians toy with audience expectations: Sarah Silverman's set begins with random jokes until she spots a portly fellow in the audience and starts mocking him. That fellow is a plant, Silverman's friend Steve Agee, who also appears on *The Sarah Silverman Program*, as Brian Posehn's equally large, bearded lover. Agee takes the stage and dons a guitar, leading Silverman through a number of saccharine, predictably offensive songs.

David Cross offers a truncated set, chiding himself for doing something as pedestrian as getting a dog. "I know that a dog is a cheap, shitty substitute for a kid," he says. "I like my dog but I don't love my dog. They're not better than people. They're better than *shitty* people...but you might as well have a retarded person in the house." He follows with an ingenious, *Mr. Show*esque pretaped piece in which he and friend Jon Benjamin argue in their New York office about heading to the Troubadour for the show. Oswalt had previously announced that Benjamin wasn't showing up, so he plays the video in Benjamin's place. Afterward, Benjamin "unexpectedly" pops onto the Troubadour stage, although Cross has already left by that point. Cross then appears on the video screen, speaking directly to Benjamin onstage, bickering with and cursing at him. Cross starts crying and the video ends, so Benjamin leaves to find him. Then Cross takes the stage again and speaks to Benjamin on the video screen; he's already "gone" looking for Cross.

If it all sounds a bit convoluted it's because it is, but it makes sense visually. The dialogue may be disposable, but the near perfectly timed concept harkens to both *Mr. Show* and *Cross Comedy* bits from the early nineties. In the end, both comedians meet onstage and hug triumphantly while sarcastically singing Bonnie Raitt's "Something to Talk About" to a karaoke backing track. They also pantomime anal and oral sex on an unlucky (but surprisingly good-natured) audience member. When Patton returns to the stage, the only words he can find are "Holy fucking shit."

Jasper Redd, the only comedian of color, talks about growing up black in Tennessee, the birthplace of the Ku Klux Klan. He's surprised, he says, that the state flag isn't a white flag with two eyeholes.

"Don't nobody hate like the KKK. You might think you hate something, but it's actually just a pet peeve. You ain't really hatin'. Like, I can't stand people who snore. I will seriously sneak into your room and hit you with a bag of nickels in your face for snoring. But over that fact, I'm not going to form an organization. You see what I'm saying? I'm not going to get five other motherfuckers who hate snoring and get in costumes and hit the street."

Eugene Mirman's set vacillates between surreal one-liners and longer narratives. "A lot of people think that kids say the darndest things, but so would you if you had no education." Or this bit about a friend who thinks it's okay to call gay people "fags" because she has a gay brother: "That's a terrible excuse—just because you know somebody. For instance, the reason it's okay for *me* to say 'fag' is because I'm full of hate!"

The Troubadour provides the perfect venue for this experimental, boundary-pushing comedy, says booker and historian Brian Smith on the DVD. He notes how the club, founded in 1957, formerly hosted both comedy and music without batting an eye. In the 1970s, for example, people like Tom Waits would perform back-to-back with Albert Brooks. "It's just a big part of the tradition of this place," he tells the camera. "This room really started out as just a place for people to express themselves. My parents saw Lenny Bruce here in '61, and he got arrested here. Smothers Brothers famously performed with John Lennon and Harry Nilsson mucking about. Nina Simone would do three nights, and Richard Pryor, who recorded a record here in 1970, would perform. Cheech & Chong came up here. Steve Martin opened up for an awful band called

Poco." The *Comedians of Comedy*, he says, helped remove the museum aspect of going to see stand-up. "I think Zach Galifianakis and David Cross and Brian Posehn are probably more punk rock than a lot of these bands."

While not widely distributed, the DVD received a handful of loving reviews from the comedy faithful. *The Onion's* Nathan Rabin felt that it flew by, despite its epic 134-minute running time. "For most stand-up DVDs, that would qualify as entirely too much of a good thing, but the scary fact about *Troubadour* is that it could easily be fifteen minutes longer," he wrote. "A lot of great Oswalt material ends up in the special features, especially a scathing dressing-down of a hapless heckler. Oswalt is the rare conceptual mastermind who arguably errs on the side of including too little of his own material in his collaborative projects."

Oswalt agrees, but only to an extent. His intention all along was to showcase his friends and not make the entire project about him. "I never want to be the funniest guy in my time," he says. "I want to be one of many, and that keeps me working harder. I always want the next generation nipping at my heels. I like change and destruction and I see really good things coming out of that."

Oswalt often showcases younger comedians at the Upright Citizens Brigade Theatre when industry types such as writer-producer Frank Smiley of *Late Night with Conan O'Brien* come to LA. When I ask Oswalt to name examples, he nearly runs out of breath: "Where do I begin? Morgan Murphy, Nick Kroll, Ian Edwards, Riley Newton, Nick Thune, Tig Notaro, Kristen Schaal, Anthony Jeselnik, John Mulaney...I'm just hoping that someone in ten or fifteen years goes against what we do and moves it forward. That's the only way the art form stays fresh."

★ ✩ ★ ✩ ★

My hour with Patton Oswalt is almost up, and he's doubled over in laughter, smacking his hand on the table, threatening to upset my wobbly mini-cassette recorder. A few seconds earlier I'd asked him if he thought the *Comedians of Comedy* had inspired other stand-ups to go the nontraditional route, instead of having to "get up in front of the potato skins."

"That's great slang," he says, still laughing. "It's like, 'How's Tig [Notaro]?' 'Oh, she's good, she's just gotta get in front of the potato skins a little more.' I'm stealing that. I'll credit you, but I'm stealing that."

I relate this story not to congratulate myself for accidentally making Patton Oswalt laugh (though I count it among my best unintentional accomplishments, such as shooting my hand with a BB gun or discovering that I love sushi), but rather to illustrate Oswalt's hungry, ever-roaming mind—one that's constantly panning society's verbal detritus for economical nuggets of language. "That bit of slang just got rid of eight paragraphs of explaining in your book," he says. "I'm going to call Greg Fitzsimmons right after this, because we were having that conversation last week. You know, about how people have to get out there more and season themselves? And I've just heard a perfect expression. 'Getting in front of the potato skins.' He's going to fucking lose it."

While creatively valuable (and, often, deliciously salty), seasoning has the potential to suck the moisture out of an artist. Nothing is less appealing than realizing a stand-up grew stale and jaded before (s)he ever hit the big time, having used all the good material on shitty crowds instead of appreciative ones. More heartening are the ones who bring out their most brilliant jokes just as the spotlight begins to crank in their direction.

There's inherent value in paying dues and learning a craft, but there's something to be said for breaking with tradition when it doesn't make sense. As Oswalt had told me earlier, doing something "for no other reason than that's the way they've always done it" often just makes comedians combative.

Fortunately, Oswalt's own years of seasoning had given him a unique voice by the time he launched the *Comedians of Comedy* tours, acquainted as he was with typical club scenes and their politics. Enduring those tours sharpened his perspective and bolstered his already loyal audience. In its January 2006 issue, *Spin* magazine bestowed Oswalt's "Alt-comedy goes rock 'n' roll tours" the Trend of the Year (the article also mentioned the late Mitch Hedberg as an example of comedy-music kinship). With an increasingly public blessing from the hipster-rock media, it became clear that Oswalt's next big step wasn't into the mainstream, but onto a more prestigious record label.

It doesn't take a genius to guess where he landed.

Comedians of Comedy manager Henry Owings more or less acted as Oswalt's A&R rep when he approached Sub Pop Records, pitching him to former publicist Joan Hiller as ideal for that imprint. With the indie-rock friendly *Comedians of Comedy* tours under his belt and an overlap audience with preexisting Sub Pop comedians David Cross and Eugene Mirman, Oswalt seemed like the perfect fit. "Alternative comedians coming up are actually aware of Sub Pop and care about the records we're putting out," says Sub Pop A&R head Tony Kiewel. "That's certainly something that mattered to us. Each community was feeding the other."

Owings wanted to make Oswalt's Sub Pop debut flawless. An obsessive fan of comedy albums (he grew up listening to Bob Newhart, Bill Cosby, and Steve Martin records with a religious fervor), Owings was determined to get the best sound quality possible out of the set, even though Oswalt said he'd be fine with essentially setting up a tape recorder at the edge of the stage. "I spent fucking ages working on that record," Owings says. "It was great to have Patton rely on me and take my judgment calls at their word. I would go, 'Yeah, I think you can do this part better,' or 'I think you need to change this up.' The *Star Wars* bit is a prime example of that: the voice he does for George Lucas is one of the joke voices I do around him. Going into producing the record I just knew his material so thoroughly that I could recite it verbatim. That helped."

Owings recorded the album in December 2006 at the Cap City Comedy Club in Austin, Texas, taking great pains with mic placement and editing. Oswalt's material had never been stronger, thanks in part to an increasingly insider perspective on the entertainment industry (he relates bits about punching-up scripts and performing at a Comedy Central roast for William Shatner) and the relentless test-driving of jokes at previous gigs.

Sub Pop dropped the fruits of that labor, *Werewolves and Lollipops*, on July 9, 2007. A single spin will convince anyone that it's easily the best stand-up album released that year, and one of the overall best of Oswalt's generation. It weathers repeat listens with the strength of a Richard Pryor, Bill Hicks, or David Cross album, with Oswalt's appealingly wet smack of a voice doing much of the heavy lifting. Everything Oswalt had learned—the insanely detailed descriptions, disgusting/hilarious metaphors, and ease of dispatching with hecklers—went into the set.

The album begins with Oswalt's succinct proclamation: "Thank you guys so much for coming out. I'm drunk. Here we go." He launches into "America Has Spoken," a takedown of fast food's top-selling "wet mound of starch that I can eat with a spoon like I'm a death row prisoner on suicide watch," aka KFC's Famous Bowl. The "failure pile in a sadness bowl," as he dubs it, is just the appetizer.

The enduring appeal of character actors, "G-rated filth," racist cell phones, the horrendous *Star Wars* prequels, birth control, ill-advised birthday celebrations, and the death-defying stunts of the Bush White House also come into play. In one of the more memorable bits, "The Miracle of Child Birth," he discusses the moral ambiguity of fertility drugs after reading about a sixty-three-year-old woman who gave birth. "Science," he barks. "We're all about *coulda*, not *shoulda*." His description of a father telling his child about the improbable event is particularly visceral: "You see, when a man loves a woman very much he heaves himself off of his hemorrhoid donut. He takes three Viagra, a beta blocker, and an eyedropper full of blood thinner. Then he lays on top of his beloved like a pile of laundry on top of another pile of laundry. Then his penis, erect in defiance of God's will, enters her vagina like a Chapstick entering the Luray Caverns. Then, nine months later, she gives birth to a beautiful baby, which I will illustrate by pushing this uncooked Cornish game hen through these gray drapes. Now, if you have any questions about the magic of the birthing process..." "Well, Dad, you're going to have to repeat all of that, because I can't hear you over the sound of my DICK SCREAMING."

Werewolves and Lollipops also includes a DVD of Oswalt's October 27, 2006, warm-up set. At one point during it, he breaks down in laughter at the fact that one of his fans has just peed on another. "See, this is where my career starts to go in the wrong direction," he says, thoroughly exasperated. "It's like, 'I can't perform. People just pee on each other at my shows. It's creepy. It wasn't any fun for me, man...' I'm the anti-Gallagher. I get the fans to get each *other* wet." Then later: "This is what a comedy show would be like in *Escape from New York*," he states, before addressing the offended individual. "I'm sorry you got peed on. I never thought I'd have to say this in my showbiz career." Oswalt is making light of the situation, but you can tell he's legitimately exasperated.

Upon its release, critics embraced *Werewolves* as another entry in the growing comedy-album revitalization, an example of classic stand-up loaded with substance and aimed directly at the head. "It tastes like sweet manna from heaven after the five-year reign of the *Blue Collar Comedy* crowd," wrote David Jeffries in the *All Music Guide*. "After so much 'stupid is as stupid does' has flooded the stand-up market, it's good to feel uncompromisingly smart for a change, and even better when the material is honed to perfection."

Pitchfork tossed it an unusually high 8.0 rating, reviewer Jessica Suarez noting its relatable tone. "He never sinks into sneering condescension as David Cross so frequently does. And his careful timing eliminates the non-sequitur flights of fancy that labelmate Eugene Mirman's jokes become...When much alternative comedy consists of clever tricks and YouTube videos, it's a relief just to hear someone tell a joke." Dave Segal of the *Orange County Register* kicked off his review with the assertion that "comedy is the new indie rock," and *Stylus* magazine's Tal Rosenberg said it captured "a seasoned comedian at his prime."

Despite Henry Owings's detail-oriented recording, and the fact that *Werewolves* is more accessible than much of the material on the shock-oriented indie-comedy circuit, the album still flew mostly under the radar. "It's kind of discouraging when you have Patton or Brian putting out really solid records and then you see who's fucking nominated for comedy album of the year on the Grammys," Owings said. "It's George Lopez and Steven Wright and Lisa Lampanelli. They're brick-wall comedians—the people doing the same old shit that Patton and Brian and Zach and Sarah Silverman are trying to fight against."

Nonetheless, *Werewolves* has sold about 40,000 copies (roughly the same as David Cross's second CD, *It's Not Funny*) and remains part of the legitimate creative renaissance of the comedy album. Granted, it's not a mainstream commercial phenomenon. Comedy albums on Sub Pop, Matador, Drag City, Suicide Squeeze, and other indie labels aren't selling by the millions like comedy records did thirty or forty years ago. But the proliferation of quality voices is stunning compared to the relative creative drought of the 1990s. Comedy Central Records has even been releasing discs from stand-ups like Demetri Martin, Todd Barry, and Michael Ian Black that could easily fit on an indie-music label. Dan Schlissel's Minneapolis-based Stand Up! Records also boasts a who's who of alt and indie comedians like Maria Bamford, Greg Proops, Marc Maron, and the Sklar Brothers, as well as cult hero Doug Stanhope and lesser-known stand-ups.

"Dan Schlissel is someone that has done a great job trying to reintroduce some fresh blood into comedy albums," says Owings. "He's even more of a comedy nerd than me, if there is such a thing. He's just completely obsessed with getting, like, original Lenny Bruce vinyl, kind of like how indie-rock nerds are about getting the Halo of Flies single or whatever. If anybody's trying to bring back the idea of comedy albums being something that should be looked at in the same light as a music album, it's him."

Schlissel, who formerly ran the prolific -ismist record label, has released nearly forty records on Stand Up! since 2001. He's generally ambivalent about the idea of indie comedy, and cool to the potential ghettoization such a label spawns. He noted that his imprint, for example, includes a few relatively conservative voices as well as liberal ones. "Jimmy Shubert and Tim Slagel are on the right-leaning side of my label," he says. "To me, diversity of voice is more important than sticking with one thing."

Political material necessarily dates itself, but not every album follows that path. Former *Mr. Show* writer-actor Paul F. Tompkins trades in the sort of delivery style and material that generally steers clear of pop-culture references in favor of righteous indignation, logic, and off-the-cuff crowd interaction. His 2007 album, *Impersonal* (AST Records), is an underappreciated high point in the recent surge of releases. "His stuff is amazing. It's going to be like a really classic Woody Allen album, still great twenty years from now," says *Commercial Appeal* writer Bob Mehr. "I've listened to a lot of comedy albums, and I'm not saying I'm biased toward modern stuff, but some of the albums coming out now are really great. I'm glad the comedy album is important enough that people are releasing them and spending time on them, because they can be excellent representations of these people's work."

By the time they had run their course, the *Comedians of Comedy* tours and films accomplished the things Oswalt had set out to do: shine a light on hidden talent, create opportunities for the performers, and exhibit the array of styles bouncing around the contemporary stand-up underground.

"I remember the first time I did South by Southwest [music festival] was with the *Comedians of Comedy*," says Aziz Ansari of MTV sketch show *Human Giant*. "Very few people in the audience probably knew who I was, but that show was one of the most fun shows I did. Even if they hadn't seen me before, I had that seal of approval from the *Comedians of Comedy* guys, and so [the crowd] was up for it."

The relationships forged between the principal *Comedians of Comedy* also continued, with documentary director Michael Blieden helming Zach Galifianakis's 2006 DVD taping in San Francisco, *Live at the Purple Onion.* That disc paints perhaps the most well-rounded picture of the comedian to date: Galifianakis mixing piano one-liners and uncomfortably awkward (and hilariously mean) audience interaction with what seems like genuinely raw emotion. Galifianakis later took part in a sold-out college tour with Will Ferrell, Nick Swardson, and Demetri Martin in 2007, sponsored by Ferrell's FunnyorDie. com. And starring film roles like 2008's *Visioneers* and TV pilot offers have exploded for the bearded stand-up. "Sometimes explosions have a negative meaning. But my pretentious attitude will assume that you mean that in a good way," Galifianakis says. "I owe a lot to Patton Oswalt, who asked me to be part of that documentary. It has really helped, to be quite honest. It is one of those little films that have a strong word of mouth. Before that I was just sitting around alphabetizing my coat hangers and auditioning for shitcoms."

Maria Bamford's weekly no-cover *What's Up, Tiger Lily?* shows in LA with Melinda Hill have become welcome options for fans of quality stand-up, often hosting many of the same names as the better-known *Comedy Death-Ray.* Her short-form series on the now-defunct SuperDeluxe.com gave her a web presence and an arena in which to exercise her army of characters and voices. Mitch Hurwitz, creator of *Arrested Development,* tapped her to provide the voice of a religious schoolteacher in the cartoon remake of Australia's *Sit Down, Shut Up!* In May 2008, the show was picked up by Fox for a thirteen-episode run, though Bamford was cut from the show after taping three episodes. (The retitled *Class Dismissed* stars *Mr. Show*'s Tom Kenny, *Arrested Development*'s Jason Bateman and Will Arnett, and *Saturday Night Live*'s Will Forte.) Like her peers, Bamford will work in pretty much any environment that wants to have her—it just so happens that she discovered a chunk of her current audience at rock clubs.

"Mainstream shows are great, too. There's great artistry to all types of shows," she says. "I really don't have the opinion that some types of comedy are not good. If someone's getting up there and saying something they've written, that takes a lot of courage, so I feel like all comedy is good. If I don't do well in a particular venue, it doesn't mean that it's a shitty venue, or that comedy clubs are all bad. There's a comic who came and did a show at Tiger Lily [now called Cuba Libre], the little hipster bar that I perform at once a week, and he was kind of more like The Comedy Store and Laugh Factory type, just a different kind of crowd. At Tiger Lily he was like, 'What the fuck's wrong with you people? Why is this going poorly?' It's not anybody's fault, there are just different sensibilities in every place."

His initial goals achieved, Oswalt thinks the *Comedians of Comedy* has run its course. The extended tours, he says, are finished. "The problem with the tours is that you have to deal with all these personalities and it cuts into your creative time. It's like, 'Wait a minute, my job is to be a comedian, not to constantly be a producer and deal with different personalities and egos.' We did eleven tours. We did a TV show. We did a feature film and two concert films. We did Coachella. We did pretty good, and it helped get Zach and Maria and Brian more exposure, which is what I wanted."

At the time, Oswalt wouldn't rule out the occasional music festival or one-nighter, but said the long road jaunts were too burdensome for him at that point in his career, when he and the other *Comedians of Comedy* alumni were in a position to actually turn down roles and focus on the long-term. "It's a young man's game, man. The motivation at the time was my frustration with how people were not using Maria and Zach to their full benefit. I think those guys are truly comedic geniuses, and now they've both really exploded. So I can't call them up and say, 'Hey, yeah, everyone back in the van for five hundred bucks a night. Congrats on the movie, but back in the van.' I have to let people go and do their own thing. And also I'm busy doing shit now."

Indeed, a few months after our interview, Oswalt announced the last-ever *Comedians of Comedy* show, a July 26, 2008, set at Spreckels Theatre in San Diego that included most of the principals and other special guests. But in Burbank on that gray February morning, I could sense that Oswalt was itching to get over to Disney and prepare for whatever evil deed he had to do. On that note, we exchanged pleasantries and handshakes, him assuring me that any follow-up questions would be promptly and happily answered via e-mail.

As I leaned forward and dove into my delicious Krust Klub ($8 worth of smoked turkey, tomato, lettuce, bacon, and Gouda), I laughed to myself as I thought about Oswalt appearing in a Disney movie, then playing club gigs where he says such gentle things as, "Paris Hilton is a cunt who should die of AIDS."

Even Richard Pryor and George Carlin appeared on *Sesame Street*.

Human Giant principals (from left to right) Paul Scheer, Rob Huebel, and Aziz Ansari lather up at the Upright Citizens Brigade Theatre in New York City. *Photo by Seth Olenick*

5

HUMOR IN SMALL DOSES

If talking about music is like dancing about architecture, as Steve Martin once said, then writing about comedy is like tracing those steps on a wet chalkboard. In other words, it's impossible to fully communicate the pleasures of your favorite stand-up, sketch, or improv comedy via the written word, but since much of comedy is verbally based, one can at least get a triangulated sense of it.

Debatably sourced similes aside (Frank Zappa, Elvis Costello, and others have also been credited with the "dancing about architecture" line), it's even more difficult to write about forms of comedy that are inherently visual, as dependent as they are on wordless timing, body language, and a host of other cues working on a near-subconscious level. Just as a good film script provides—but never fleshes out—a movie's visual frame, a written analysis of visual comedy can only attempt to dissect the "how" of its inner workings, to say nothing of the subjective "why" that truth-and-beauty writers have grappled with for ages. Of course, audio-only comedy also presents its analytical challenges, since vocal inflection and subtle pauses can only be described, but never fully reproduced, through writing.

This chapter looks at a pair of TV sketch comedies, and, to a lesser extent, a pair of (for lack of a better term) phone-call duos that illustrate the best examples of the continuing overlap of indie music and a certain smart, surreal, twisted sort of humor, as well as the lineage of the *Mr. Show* influence over the past decade. While my words will never do them justice, I hope these examples will at least get a fair trial at the hands of a relatively sober jury who should feel compelled to seek them out after this civic duty is complete.

We'll begin with the boob tube, since that's where many of us end up after a long day at the salt mines, savoring the passive joy that only the marriage of flickering images, amplified sound, and a cold beverage can provide. MTV's *Human Giant* and Adult Swim's *Tim and Eric Awesome Show, Great Job!*, more so than most sketch comedies of the past decade, share inspirations, sensibilities, and, in some cases, writers and guest stars. Both betray a strong, openly absurdist bent, an unsentimental aesthetic, and an explicit overlap with the indie-music world. Each also offers elements of traditional sketches along the lines of *Saturday Night Live* and *SCTV* while employing surreal, colorful logic more familiar to fans of *Monty Python's Flying Circus*, *Kids in the Hall*, and especially *Mr. Show*. Each also tends toward the dark, disjointed, and comically violent, taking viewers several steps beyond the traditional signposts at which most sketches seem content to rest.

Judging by their late-night scheduling, either show's intended audience falls into roughly the same categories as those of the aforementioned modern classics, as well as of live shows such as *Comedians of Comedy*, LA's

Comedy Death-Ray, and New York's *Tearing the Veil of Maya*. In other words, young, educated, middle-to-upper-middle class/nerd-hipster types with a sick sense of humor, grasp of entertainment clichés, and appreciation for the endless ways in which those can be subverted. *Human Giant* hews closer to the familiar character-based format of most sketch comedies, even as its bits turn in on themselves with a sarcastic self-awareness (such as "Shutterbugs," a child talent agency that pushes its kids to the brink of emotional breakdown; or "Lunartics," a reality spoof that kidnaps innocent people, transports them to the moon, and brutally hunts them down for sport—all sponsored by Quiznos!). That makes *Human Giant* a good place to start, since forward-thinking TV sketch comedies with national, if cultish, audiences have been a relative rarity since the demise of *Mr. Show*.

I met with the cocreators of *Human Giant* at the Upright Citizens Brigade Theatre in Hollywood on a balmy Friday afternoon. The trio was united in LA for a series of *Human Giant* stage shows that would kick off their second season on MTV and their larger national tour in the spring of 2008. (Incidentally, about half of that tour was later cancelled because *Human Giant* principal Paul Scheer nabbed a role on *Year One*, the film David Cross was shooting when I interviewed him in Shreveport.)

Most of my friends are usually surprised to learn that MTV has aired anything even remotely worth watching the past few years, as inundated with pseudoreality soap operas and chirping, shit-headed fleshbots as it is. MTV's scattered history of offbeat sketch comedies (*The State*, *Wonder Showzen*) and cartoons (*Liquid Television*, which helped launch *Beavis and Butt-Head* and *Aeon Flux*, among others) has been obscured as it retreated from music videos in favor of cheaply produced game shows (*Road Rules*), pranks and stunts (*Punk'd*, *Jackass*), and tween-chasing, wealth-as-status programming (*Cribs, Pimp My Ride, The Hills*). Affable *Human Giant* principals Aziz Ansari, Paul Scheer, and Rob Huebel may not possess the muscle to return MTV to its once-respected place in the pop-culture firmament, but they've at least given us a reason to watch it at all. Credit each member's improvisational background and facility with the sketch format for much of that.

The trio first collaborated at New York's Upright Citizens Brigade Theatre in 2005 on the weekly *Crash Test* show, which drew reliably large, devoted crowds to its unpredictable mix of stand-up comedy. Not long after, they began making short films with Jason Woliner, *Human Giant*'s invisible but equally vital fourth member, who directs and edits much of the troupe's output. The films quickly became viral video hits, thanks in part to their impeccable comedic timing, surreal logic, and clean, efficient construction.

Originally screened at the UCB Theatre, *Human Giant* videos such as "Illusionators" mocked the flashy-yet-personality-free brand of magicians who have popped up in recent years, based largely on makeup-smeared *Mindfreak* star/fashion casualty Criss Angel. The hipster-baiting sketch "Other Music," another early hit, scored *Human Giant* a loyal following of online indie-rock fans. That short film is set in the famed NYC record shop of the same name, using it as the wrestling mat to take down elitist record-store clerks—a breed long catalogued but rarely hunted and bagged with any success. In the beginning of the video, the employees (Ansari and Andy Blitz) smugly name-drop Carlos D (of indie-rock band Interpol), Stephen Malkmus (Pavement), and freak-folk songwriter Devendra Banhart to customers with a wide-eyed, dismissive snobbery. The video climaxes with Ansari slapping a woman for not knowing what indie-rock website Pitchfork is, then killing another customer who requests the *Garden State* soundtrack. "It's supposed to be indie-tastic," the hapless, balding schlub says moments before Ansari leads him to the back of the store, produces a handgun, and pops him in the chest.

Human Giant sketches often begin in a familiar place, like a camping trip or city park, with a tone of comforting, buddy-buddy tranquility. But once the gates fly open, they rarely pause long enough for the viewers to catch their breath or untangle the sticky threads of genre parody, making repeated viewings (the hallmark of any viral video) practically mandatory. That, and it gives you a reason to leave your mind-numbing cubicle and lean over Sally Accountant's shoulder while she giggles into her computer screen.

The creative muscles required to pull off sketch comedy are, of course, different from those flexed during stand-up, although a grasp of one tends to strengthen the other. Each performer in *Human Giant* sports a commanding but fresh-faced presence onstage and onscreen, but that has less to do with a background in typical stand-up than with a mastery of improv fundamentals—honed largely at New York's UCB Theatre. It's appropriate, then, that our interview took place at the UCB Theatre in LA, a city in which most of *Human Giant* is now based.

The theater's empty stage looked much smaller than when I'd seen *Comedy Death-Ray* and *See You Next Tuesday* there three nights prior, nudging me toward mild anxiety as I pulled four stools into a semicircle to seat the *Human Giant* guys and myself. In fact, halfway through our interview, UCB principal Matt Walsh dropped by briefly to query *Human Giant* on how their live shows were going that week. I've been interviewing my favorite musicians and comedians long enough not to let stuff like that phase me, but being surrounded by four of the most talented improv/sketch guys in the English-speaking world still made me wonder how I'd weaseled my way into this hallowed space. (Walsh, for better or worse, soon left.)

Fortunately, the guys seemed to have no interest in slapping their dicks on the table and went about making me feel comfortable by asking where I went to college, what my book was about, what I had had for breakfast, etc. By the time we got around to talking about comedy and music, the conversation felt natural. "If you look at the aesthetic of this place, it's basically what a rock club would be if it was a theater," Paul Scheer says, leaning on one arm under the dimmed stage lights. "There are lots of other places that do that, too, but I was doing comedy in New York before UCB came about, and they kind of helped create that aesthetic, doing shows in the back of bars and stuff like that. I really credit them with bringing that out."

Rob Huebel, the square-jawed elder of the troupe, adds that the UCB theaters have become safe places for people who tend to despise safe places. "It kind of created a different delivery mechanism. If a stand-up club is what most people think comedy is, then people don't really know what this is. If they're coming here, or even to New York, they're like, 'Well, what *am* I going to get? What is this show?' Because most people in the country know stand-up, and now people are starting to pick up on, 'Oh, there's this whole other wave of comedy that can be in a different format. It doesn't have to be stand-up. It can be sketch. It can be improv or other bits, weird characters, all that."

Scheer, who performed in the *Chicago City Limits* improv show in New York before joining the UCB, says that UCB has helped dismantle the notion that improv only belonged at one place—or to one theater. "*Chicago City Limits*' mentality was that they were the only sketch/improv in town. And at that point [in the midnineties] there was no UCB. There was nothing. You'd get a similar audience as at a stand-up comedy club, like bachelorette parties and all that. And it was weird because people were just being shuffled in. They weren't comedy fans." He pauses, surveying the 100-or-so empty, darkened seats in the theater. "The difference between that audience and even the very beginning of the UCB audience was gigantic. These were people who sought it out versus people who were literally just dropped off in a bus, or who heard about it from someone passing out flyers in Times Square."

Scheer's gravelly voice and bald, grinning countenance (he sports a David Lettermanesque gap in his front teeth, which he's unafraid of exploiting) tend to belie his versatility as a performer, making him look more like a guy who sells stolen DVDs out of a rapist van than an accomplished comic actor. (Or both, really.) He moved to New York to attend NYU and lived there until relocating to LA in 2006. During his time in New York, he appeared in a number of esteemed improv shows, including the long-running *Chicago City Limits*. In 1998 he joined the Upright Citizens Brigade, where he played in shows such as *Automatic Vaudeville* and the UCB's own short-lived program on Comedy Central.

Rob Huebel had been performing in New York for years, popping up in sketches on *Late Night with Conan O'Brien* and producing for *The Daily Show*, among other projects. (He and Scheer also collaborated in the Respecto Montalban troupe, which included future *Human Giant* regular Rob Riggle.) South Carolina native Aziz Ansari started performing stand-up at alt-comedy venues and clubs while attending business school at New York University, from which he graduated in 2004. When Ansari snagged the weekly *Crash Test* show, he tapped some of his favorite comics to guest host.

"The first thing that we both did together was a version of 'Shutterbugs,'" says Huebel, nodding to Ansari across the semicircle of stools. "We showed little kids' headshots and criticized them, and that gave us the idea to keep that and make it into a short film."

"One week I'd work with Rob and then the next week I'd work with Paul," adds the baby-faced Ansari, scratching his round, dark beard. "Anytime him or Rob were around I'd offer to host because we'd always have a fun time." That mirth extended to the trio's various videos, which generated scattered critical buzz around New York as people began catching on to their warped, web-ready sense of humor.

As the trio cohered, Comedy Central and NBC expressed interest in having *Human Giant* produce content for their digital video sites. The members were skeptical. "That was when YouTube was really, really taking off, and everyone was trying to do their own comedy website and just wanted content," Ansari remembers. "And they're like, 'We'll give you a little bit of money'—like, very little money—'and we own everything. You can't do anything with it.' And we're like, 'Oh, you know what? We'll actually just keep doing them for ourselves and not have a budget for it.'"

"MTV, to their credit, actually came to us," Huebel says. "We didn't pitch them at all. They asked if we wanted to do a pilot and were just kind of laughing. I thought, 'Oh, this'll never get on TV. Aziz is the right age, but me and Paul?' We hadn't ever planned on doing a TV show. We just wanted to make these things for ourselves and our friends."

Nonetheless, *Human Giant*'s distinctive sense of humor and easy professionalism won over a pair of the most influential suits at MTV. The network came calling in the summer of 2006 after *Human Giant* caught the ever-wandering eye of Tony DiSanto, MTV's executive vice president of series development and animation. DiSanto's string of hits (*Total Request Live, Laguna Beach, The Hills*) had put him on track to become a "reality auteur" on par with Mark Burnett, the format's prolific pioneer, according to a 2006 piece in *The New York Times*. "I like to gamble and try things out," DiSanto told reporter Lola Ogunnaike. "I'm almost anti-formula to a degree. If something works, I'm more inclined to take a left turn next time around, to go from a *Laguna* to [MTV2 sketch comedy] *Andy Milonakis*. It makes our jobs more fun."

Rob Huebel says DiSanto, the executive producer of *Human Giant*'s TV incarnation, displays a programming sense that's more savvy than it first seems. "In his mind, there's a lot of value to the press that *Human Giant* gets for being so different from everything else on the network, and the fact that it is, in a way, counter-programming. It's like, 'This is *not* what our channel is about.'"

Brian Graden, president of entertainment for MTV Networks Group, also championed *Human Giant*'s humor, leading the network to offer the troupe a shoestring budget to shoot its eight-episode first season. The rapid-fire sketches, which premiered on April 7, 2007, mocked popular TV shows, websites, and films, with a dizzying narrative spin. They featured comedians familiar to the indie-music set such as Patton Oswalt, Kristen Schaal, Jon Benjamin, Brian Posehn, and Jon Glaser, as well as musicians with stacks of underground cred (Ted Leo, Tapes 'n Tapes, Ghostface Killah). Even the slicing, looping theme music, courtesy of Canadian dance-punk duo Death From Above 1979, set a breakneck pace. The cast and crew had filmed the approximately ninety sketches at an impressive clip of roughly two per day, revisiting early *Human Giant* videos "Illusionators" and

"Shutterbugs" and others—albeit with higher production values and a more considered (yet still laid-back) tone.

The recurring characters in "Space Lords," for example, appropriated the humorless, black vinyl–clad villains of *Superman II* (here renamed Udon, Fay, and Zerg) for mundane settings, forcing them to use their superpowers to cook hot dogs behind the counter at the fictional Weenie King. In a jab at romantic comedies, Ansari, as Udon, falls in love with guest star Mary Lynn Rajskub (of *Mr. Show* and *24*). After she rejects him, Udon's cohorts use their powers to clone her in what evolves into a fractured send-up of sci-fi and soap opera clichés. The first season also features dares gone wrong ("Blood Oath"), twisted dorm-room humor ("Sensitivity Training"), and creepy, frequently hilarious "Product Recall" shorts—the perfect fodder for comic-book nerds and college students. It helped that all had performed on college tours, which reacquainted them with the tone and subject matter of their ostensible target audience.

MTV even allowed *Human Giant* to take over its Times Square studio for twenty-four hours in May 2007. The "Save Our Show" marathon (aka reverse-psychology promotional push) promised to give *Human Giant* a second season if it could score a million hits on its website during the twenty-four-hour period. (It did.) The guys welcomed a handful of indie bands, such as The National, Tegan and Sara, Tapes 'n Tapes, and Ted Leo, and a long list of comedians and actors: Bob Odenkirk, Michael Showalter, Eugene Mirman, Fred Armisen, Tim and Eric, and various *Saturday Night Live* personnel. "We're friends with almost all of those guys, and I think the marathon really helped solidify the idea that there's no competition between us," Scheer says.

Ansari remembers the initial reluctance of the members of metal band Mastodon when they were asked to play the marathon. "They were like, 'We can only play one song, then we gotta go. We're playing a show in Philly.' I'm sure it was just their manager or agent or whatever that didn't want to put them in an awkward position."

"They thought we were just MTV douche bags," Huebel adds. After screening a few *Human Giant* videos for the band, Mastodon decided to stick around and party in the greenroom. For two hours. "We saw them awhile later at the MTV Movie Awards and got drunk with them there," Huebel says. "They're just supercool dudes and they love the show. [Singer/bassist] Troy Sanders was like, 'Man, if you ever want us to do a song for you guys, we would love it.'" A jam-packed, if exhausting experiment, the marathon successfully lent some of *Human Giant*'s credibility to its parent network by inviting a handful of the most cutting-edge comedians and musicians into the belly of a beast that would normally deem them unpalatable.

"You don't get a lot of opportunities to see Mastodon— or Nick Kroll doing Fabrice Fabrice, craft services coordinator for *That's So Raven*—on MTV," says Jesse Thorn, host of *The Sound of Young America*.

Human Giant's deft online promotion, both from the network and the members of the troupe, helped keep the show at the forefront of fans' minds after the first season ended. The members maintained detailed personal blogs, answered questions for popular indie-music site Stereogum, and played music festivals such as Bumbershoot, Coachella, and South by Southwest. Their tours and cheaply priced one-off shows allowed them to test new sketches and generally light the way for anyone looking to gain access to their warped sense of humor. "Even if MTV is not the best network for an audience that would be attracted to us, you can look at our numbers on iTunes," Scheer says. "We were the number one most downloaded cable show when the episodes were still airing. Even if that's how our audience finds us, I still think there's value in that."

Critical kudos rolled in, with *Entertainment Weekly* initially hailing the show's "anarchic surrealism" and later saying it was "everything sketch comedy should be: smart, odd, and surprising." *The Village Voice* called it "a masterpiece of absurd theater" and *Rolling Stone* (never one to hold back on a quote that might grace a DVD cover) dubbed it "brilliant."

The troupe was pleased when MTV decided to pick the show up for a six-episode second season, which premiered on March 11, 2008. The sketches improved incrementally upon Season One by honing their ridiculous premises and characters, displaying an economy, wit, and intelligence that shames most TV sketch comedies. The awkwardly named "Kiditentiary" (just say it out loud) skewered CBS's crap-tacular reality TV experiment *Kid Nation*. "Instead of tasers, they'll disable them with hugs," *Saturday Night Live*'s Andy Samberg explains in the sketch. "Three thousand inmates. Twenty kids. It's the first Kiditentiary!" (At one point, Ansari's "Shutterbugs" character gripes, "They just took our idea for Kidcentration camp and watered it down." Unsurprisingly, the sketch ends with a pile of dead children and inmates.) "Sci-Fi Makeup" features Scheer as an actor who undergoes radical plastic surgery to alleviate his long stints in the makeup chair on the *Star Trek*–like show *Battle Sector 17*. After finding out the show has been cancelled, he goes through a series of depressingly clumsy auditions, trying to get casting directors (including David Cross) to ignore his permanently ludicrous appearance. The continuing balance of goofy and violent (a slow-motion, dramatic beating of a piñata by Scheer leads other angry piñatas to tie him up and hang him from the ceiling. After pummeling and disemboweling Scheer, they gleefully eat his organs) seems to end too soon.

Strong support for *Human Giant* still flowed from select MTV brass, but the network again opted not to devote a great deal of resources to the second season's production budget, forcing them to film many scenes in New York to avoid LA's pricey location-shoot permits. "In New York you can go to a pizza shop and be like, 'We're going to shoot a TV show in here,' and they're like, 'That's awesome,'" Scheer says. "Out here in LA, it's like, 'How much are you going to give me?' Being part of a TV show is not as appealing in LA as it is in New York. So we wrote material for a couple months in LA but we were never able to shoot here because we got screwed with our budget a little bit. We thought, 'Where do we want to put our resources? Do we want to get T-shirts done? Or do we want to go out to New York?' It made more sense in the overall picture, much to the detriment of our friends and loved ones, since we were not at home for months on end."

Production challenges aside, each member's growing success threatens to make Season Two *Human Giant*'s last. NBC, for example, tapped Ansari to star in a spin-off of *The Office*. (Upright Citizens Brigade and *Saturday Night Live* vet Amy Poehler soon joined him on the show.) It's not exactly a starring role in a big-budget popcorn flick, but the allure of steady, higher-profile work is strong—especially if you're not being forced to compromise your sense of humor. "A big misconception is that as soon as you're on TV once or twice, you're a bajillionaire. But that's not the case," Ansari says. "But it's also hard to get your opportunity to do your own show. There are so many good comedians that deserve their own show."

That's probably true, but *Human Giant*'s relentless pinball of logic is a rarity in most sketch offerings, and a big part of what made *Mr. Show* so beloved. "*Human Giant* serves as a vital link between *Mr. Show* and the current generation of web-weaned funnymen who made their names posting homemade videos online instead of working their way through Second City, The Groundlings, or *Saturday Night Live*," wrote Nathan Rabin in *The Onion*. "*Human Giant* may be the only hip rock 'n' roll show left on MTV."

If anything, *Human Giant* suffers from the same unequivocal attitude that indie bands often fall victim to, idealists dismissing them simply for being associated with anything remotely commercial or mainstream. "There's this backlash just because we're on MTV, and people make these assumptions about us," offers Ansari. "When people write about us they always say, 'I can't believe this is on MTV. It makes no sense. I was *not* going to watch this show and then I watched it.' So we have this sort of prebacklash that a lot of underground bands get."

Human Giant's built-in obstacles to finding a larger, more sympathetic audience will probably remain as long as the cultural elite perceives MTV as creatively brain-dead, despite the show's demonstrated commitment to smart, subversive comedy. "Even with *Wonder Showzen*, it was a little bit different version of MTV than what it is now," adds Ansari. And he's right. *Wonder Showzen*'s mock kiddie-show format, hipster cachet, and dark, twisted humor (not to mention the inclusion of guests like Zach Galifianakis, Will Oldham, and David Cross) departed significantly from the majority of MTV's programming during its short run in 2005. "It doesn't necessarily fit with the whole network image, but they still like what it does for the network," Ansari says of *Human Giant*.

Indeed, shortly after our interview, *Human Giant* appeared at the Paley Center for Media in Los Angeles (formerly the Museum of TV and Radio) for a short performance and interview. It was a prestigious gig for any show, let alone one on a network that's been written off as irredeemably trashy. "What other MTV show is going to get a thing like that?" Ansari asks, his elbow resting on his knee and eyebrows perked.

Whether or not *Human Giant* remains a blip in that network's obscenely barren radar, it demonstrates the link between the indie-music and -comedy worlds in a way that few have since *Mr. Show* vanished a decade prior. Bringing indie bands onto their twenty-four-hour marathon and into their sketches, conducting their shows at music festivals, and popping up on Pitchfork along with underground music acts establishes an implicit mental link between *Human Giant* and indie-rock fans.

"One of the things that makes Aziz Ansari's video about [indie-rock band] Tapes 'n Tapes, for example, so great for him and *Human Giant* is that music is something that is a shortcut to people's hearts, something they make an immediate emotional connection to," says radio host Jesse Thorn. "If you connect yourself with that, you can connect to people directly and make fans of them."

At the moment, however, the guys are so in demand that we have to end our interview, but not before they ask me to shoot a promo on Ansari's digital camera. They line up against the back of the UCB stage and, without skipping a beat, practice their lines: "Hi, I'm Paul." "I'm Aziz." "And I'm Rob." "We're from *Human Giant*, and you're watching us on Slide.com." After a few takes, they seem satisfied with their impromptu performance, thanking me for holding the camera, and scattering to their commitments across the city. As I linger in the lobby of the UCB Theatre, gazing at the photos of past/

now-famous performers, it's easy to imagine the easy-going members of *Human Giant* finding a wider audience. As they continue to conduct their careers on their own terms—whether by playing music festivals or inviting their favorite artists to perform with them—that audience will likely be a devoted one.

Or stoned. Either way, they'll be watching.

If you've seen even a single episode of an Adult Swim show since it officially premiered late nights on Cartoon Network in 2001, you know it's pretty fucked up. Not just doing-acid-with-your-grandma fucked up, but rusty-bicycle-without-a-seat fucked up. From 1990s forbearer *Space Ghost Coast to Coast* to more recent shows *The Venture Bros.* and *Fat Guy Stuck in the Internet*, Adult Swim's general sensibility has always tended toward the surreal and absurd. But nothing quite like *Tim and Eric Awesome Show, Great Job!* has ever graced the channel—or American TV in general. I fell desperately in love with it after accidentally catching its premiere on February 11, 2007, my insomnia compelling me to obsessively research its creators after the visual insanity had passed. A fake commercial for B'owl (a ratty, off-putting cross between a bat and an owl, advertised like a Saturday morning cartoon toy) had grabbed my attention, as well as *Mr. Show* cocreator Bob Odenkirk's familiar voice babbling over the screams of young girls and the inexplicably angry stare of a young boy standing against a brick wall.

Of course, it was clear to me even from the opening titles of *Tim and Eric Awesome Show, Great Job!* that this wasn't a typical sketch comedy. The breathlessly fast, synth-driven theme music and incoherent flash of images (confetti-like explosions of cat heads, hot dogs, fax machines, and the cocreators' faces) hinted at the pop-culture dumpster from which Tim Heidecker and Eric Wareheim drew much of their material. The duo formerly created and produced the more lucid but equally bizarre *Tom Goes to the Mayor* animated series on Adult Swim, a project that helped focus their patient, nonsensical approach. Guest stars from *Tom Goes to the Mayor* (including *Mr. Show* vets Tom Kenny and David Cross, and indie-comedy favorites Sarah Silverman and Todd Barry) and the pathetic small-town characters who populated the series only hinted at what was to come for *Awesome Show*. It helped that a few of the characters also carried over to *Awesome Show*, like Channel 5's Jan and Wayne Skylar (The Only Married News Team in the Tri-Country Area); Brian Posehn's diminutive man-freak, Gibbons; and the Cinco Corporation's baffling nonproducts. Both shows operate in Adult Swim's familiar eleven-minute format, although *Tim and Eric Awesome Show, Great Job!* is largely free of narrative constraints, so its limbs swing in every direction.

Like *Mr. Show*, Tim and Eric's sketches are occasionally connected by left-field links, but their aesthetic more often invokes a feverish, confusing dream that melts into a horrendous pixelated nightmare from which there's no escape. In other words, audiovisual trauma with a sinister, strangely appealing edge. "The show is a real working nightmare," says Tim Heidecker, seated comfortably in his second-floor office on North El Centro in Los Angeles. Multicolored Post-it notes with scribbled sketch names line the walls—a familiar sight to obsessive viewers of the show. (The DVD extras on *Tom Goes to the Mayor* and *Awesome Show* often take place in the office, as well as in the high-ceilinged first floor that acts as a green-screen stage.) "It's the way dreams work in general, where things are great and funny and fast and musical, and then all of a sudden something horrible happens."

"It's also like watching a David Lynch movie," Eric Wareheim adds, referring to the director of such iconic films as *Blue Velvet* and *Mulholland Drive*. "You watch it and you're sometimes frustrated, then you think about it the next day and you're like, 'Oh my God,' and pieces start fitting. We don't like handing people the answers. When I watch films, I like struggling to figure out what's happening—and why."

Awesome Show certainly makes good on that comparison. When David Cross appears as a pizza boy in a fake porn video, for example, he sings a tender song about the different ways, other than sex, you can show a woman your love ("Like a walk on the beach or a heart-shaped balloon," he intones sweetly against a seventies-rock backing track, before snatching a crudely animated bird from the air and stuffing it into his mouth). When Maria Bamford or Bob Odenkirk show up in parodies of public-access TV shows, the result is screaming matches and nervous breakdowns, the cohosts or guests squirming in their seats. Zach Galifianakis plays The Snuggler, an overweight superhero in jean shorts who cuddles an injured Tim Heidecker back to health—and teaches him how to kill animals (like Michael J, the friendly fox). The Weird Al Yankovic–hosted "Uncle Muscle's Hour" plays like a telethon gone wrong, the VHS-warped quality of the images adding a level of disturbing realism to kara-oke sing-alongs from disfigured, vest-wearing young-ster Casey Tatum (Heidecker) and his prancing brother (Wareheim). Most sketches end with Tatum vomiting onto the oversensitive microphone. All deftly utilize a green screen and gleefully amateurish graphics.

The show's humor would almost be an acquired taste if it didn't work on such a subconscious level, the sort of funny that occurs to you when you're sleep-deprived and hungover on a road trip, or teetering somewhere between laughter and sobbing. It also flies by in a matter of seconds, creating the sort of giddy "Did I just see that?" confusion that immediately begs another viewing.

Tim and Eric's sensibilities (and grab bag of hilariously awkward, deadpan expressions and costumes) cohered when they began crafting short videos like "Humpers," which consists of a pair of pudgy guys in tight workout clothes humping (what else?) various landmarks around Philadelphia. Much like other comedians chronicled in this book, the pair sharpened their teeth performing at shows with indie-rock bands like The Shins, but Tim and Eric maintain they were never part of any particular movement in comedy. "I feel like we're part of the general alternative-comedy scene, but we're definitely not brothers with anyone else," Eric says. "People have kind of accepted us, though. We found Bob [Odenkirk, *Awesome Show*'s creative consultant] first, and he took us under his wing. He asked David Cross if we could be a part of a *Tinkle* show in New York. That was the first time these guys were like, 'Alright, you guys are good enough to be a part of our awesome, badass nights.' That was really big for us."

"We really didn't come up with any of these guys," Tim says after I ask him why so many *Mr. Show* veterans have guest starred on *Tom Goes to the Mayor* and *Awesome Show*. "People that we're friendly with are people that just work well on our show." The pair's do-it-yourself approach to shooting videos—which they eventually submitted to their favorite New York comedy shows—went a long way toward breaking them into a comedy world where much of the competition was better trained but lesser talented.

"Years ago, before Tim and Eric had their show, me and this other guy were fishing all over for funny short films and would spend hours on the stuff," says *Human Giant*'s Rob Huebel. "It seemed like everyone in the country from every improv club was sending us their short films and so much of it was just crap. Then somehow we found Tim and Eric on the Internet and I was like, 'Oh my God, we *have* to get these guys.' They were doing just the weirdest stuff with cats and weird talent shows...It was so good to find someone that had a similar sensibility."

That sensibility took time to develop, the pair meeting in film school at Temple University in Philadelphia in 1994 then moving to New York City, where they worked a handful of shitty, unfulfilling office jobs. They sent each other instant messages while on the clock and developed ideas, which led them to begin dabbling in more experimental, conceptual strains of comedy. They used the video editing software at Wareheim's commercial videography gig to realize their ever-expanding universe of characters and freeze-frame animated prank calls. "I came up as a teenager in this punk-rock, do-it-yourself hard-core scene where you have no money," Eric continues. "You have to make your own flyers, you have to put those flyers out to get people to come to your shows, and that's a similar sensibility that Tim and I had. We had no money and we had to kind of promote it ourselves. That's just the vibe of the whole indie community—there was no other option. There was no Comedy Store or Laugh Factory. You had to do it yourself, and you're surrounded by those kinds of people."

"It's so isolating when you do stuff on video, because you just make it yourself and then you put it up on your website," Tim adds. "You never really cross paths with other people that are doing it. We had really crossed paths more with rock bands and musicians because the only place where we could show our videos sometimes would be at the Knitting Factory in New York—these clubs where bands would play—and we would show videos to support them."

The duo's break came when they mailed their reel of web videos, including a *Tom Goes to the Mayor* short, to comedic idol and *Mr. Show* cocreator Bob Odenkirk. The package included two glossy headshots and an itemized bill for approximately $50. "It made me laugh because it was so well done and really dry, like everything they do, and it didn't explain itself at all," Odenkirk says. "I put in the episode and watched it and thought there was a really developed voice there, even though there was a lot of work to be done. Having a handle on your own voice is a difficult thing, so we started talking and trying to develop *Tom Goes to the Mayor*."

Part of that development process included Tim and Eric flying to Los Angeles to meet with Odenkirk. He roped in David Cross and together they helped the pair produce another episode that began to dig to the core of Tim and Eric's comedic voice. "He really saw a vision for it," Eric remembers. "And he helped us get Tenacious D for the first Adult Swim episode, which was fucking huge. All the stars were aligned because the show was drastically different from what was going on at Adult Swim at that point, so it helped that we had Jack [Black] behind us."

David Cross says Tim and Eric's down-to-earth personalities and seemingly out-of-nowhere approach helped sell them to other comedians. "There's nothing quite like them," he says. "And they're both super nice guys. Tim's probably a little nicer than Eric by about 7 or 8 percent. But Bob [Odenkirk] was really instrumental in discovering them, as much I dislike the concept of 'discovering' someone. It just applies with Bob going to bat for them, nurturing them, and helping them get *Tom Goes to the Mayor*."

The alluring simplicity of *Tom Goes to the Mayor* is apparent even from its name: Tim, the blond, slightly shorter one of the pair, plays perpetually put-on entrepreneur Tom Peters, who moves to the strip mall hell of Jefferton (aka Anytown, USA) with his nagging, morbidly obese wife, Joy, and her sullen, disfigured stepsons. Peters pitches cheesy, homegrown ideas for civic improvement and commerce to the mayor, played by the tall, bespectacled Eric—usually in a too-tight suit. The inscrutable mayor repeatedly takes advantage of Tom's goodwill, leading to a series of depressing, toxic, spectacularly surreal events. The first Adult Swim episode, which debuted on November 14, 2004, featured Jack Black and Tenacious D partner Kyle Gass as The Bear Trap Brothers, who offer their services to Jefferton in a mangled attempt to increase child safety.

The show's visual aesthetic—a mix of Photoshop-manipulated character stills, intentionally spare animation, and ridiculous logos and products—at first looks simplistic and gratuitously bright, but soon proves itself an apt representation of the deadpan humor. Thanks to the credibility lent by Odenkirk and Cross, and the initial appearance from Jack Black, the show gained momentum and eventually welcomed a gloriously random assortment of guests (Jeff Goldblum, Michael Ian Black, Sarah Silverman, Jeff Garlin, Fred Willard). Adult Swim cancelled it after a two-year, thirty-episode run, which led to the idea of a mostly live-action sketch show that would continue the march of pathetic souls introduced on *Tom Goes to the Mayor.*

"We got a lot of advice and had a lot of time to think about what kind of show it would be," Tim says. "We had been thinking about it for ten years or so in different ways. I remember David Cross said at some point when we were developing it, 'Don't worry about how you're presenting the show. You can do it from the tree house. You can do it from a spaceship. It doesn't matter.' Because everybody in those development meetings, that's all they care about and talk about. Adult Swim was the only place that was really like, 'There's not much to talk about when you're developing it.' We were like, 'Well, we're going to do a show and it's going to be funny. There's no other concept here except just funny, quick, quirky stuff.'"

Odenkirk says the pair's unique sense of humor and relative lack of guile invites polarized reactions because it comes from a wordless place. "They're way more absurd than *Mr. Show* or a lot of the things I've done, but not so absurd that they're not funny. I mean, I love how much absurdity they get away with, but for a lot of people it's a little too disconnected from the world. It comes from their own brains and it isn't that easy to see a connection to the history of comedy. I could talk about what I was doing before I did it, and how it was related to *Monty Python* or *SNL* or numerous things, whereas with them, they just make a show they love and I don't think they would be able to analyze it."

"We weren't trying to be any of those other people," Tim says. "The thing you learn by becoming a student of comedy is that nobody is successful by doing what everybody else does. Everybody that we admire was successful because they went in the other direction."

That path takes them by familiar, easy topics of parody, including commercials, infomercials, talk shows, newscasts, and more. But the approach tends to chip away at the form as much as the content. "I would argue with the people who don't like them and feel like it's silly or absurdity for absurdity's sake. The manner in which they do their show is very much satirizing the form of a lot of media," Odenkirk says.

Some of *Awesome Show*'s regular players would fit perfectly on any cable-access show, such as dead-eyed, inarticulate "ventriloquist" David Liebe Hart (who actually appeared on cable-access shows in the past). Others, such as actor John C. Reilly (*Boogie Nights*, *Walk Hard: The Dewey Cox Story*), expertly mimic the nervous, oblivious manner that's a staple of late-night TV losers, the too-dumb-to-live but too-dumb-to-kill personality that inspires equal amounts of loathing and pity. Reilly plays Dr. Steve Brule, a fool stumbling his way through a series of how-to pieces on the fictitious Channel 5, frequently falling victim to technical glitches and his own idiocy (drinking too much in a segment on wine tasting and becoming unruly, eating rotten fruit, and generally embarrassing himself in everything he does). His mealy-mouthed send-off ("For your health!") has become a catchphrase in fan circles, even though most of his bits are improvised, disjointed, and probably painful outside of a comedic context.

Music plays a central role in the show, reflecting its digitally abused visual aesthetic (courtesy of editor Doug Lussenhop) while perfectly parodying any genre it sets its ears on. Aimee Mann, who contributed a tune to 2008's *Tim and Eric Awesome Record, Great Songs!*, says the music works because it's just plain good—regardless of the comedy. "I tell Tim, 'You know, this song is really great,'" she says. "And he's like, 'Really? It was just kind of a kernel of an idea.' They're like these great lost-band songs."

"We're working on one right now that's called 'I Wanna Be Touched,'" Tim says. "It's about these two divorced dads who are so lonely that they just need to be touched by anybody—they don't care who. So musically we're trying to figure out the reference. We're like, 'Let's make it like "In the Air Tonight" by Phil Collins.' We always use some reference as the starting point for our music."

Many of the hyper-melodic songs have found lives of their own online and in fan circles, offering dead-on impressions of familiar tunes from Boston, Michael McDonald, Spin Doctors, and a plethora of electro-pop acts.

"They're just really catchy and fun," Eric says. "Like, the 'Doo Dah Doo Doo' song was kind of built on 'The Electric Slide,' which kids dance to at bar mitzvahs. I have tapes from when I was a videographer of kids doing it and they're just hilarious. Neither of us are electronic music mega-fans, but some of this hard-hitting techno ['Sports,' 'Beaver Boys,' Awesome Show's theme song] just seem to work with a lot of the visuals. We also work closely with [Tom Goes to the Mayor and Awesome Show composer] Davin Wood—especially Tim—in writing the songs. He's great, and often you can see that it's actually a good song underneath the silliness of it."

The forty-three-track Awesome Record features most of the music from the first two seasons of Awesome Show, plus covers of songs such as "Wipe My Butt" and "Come Over" by indie-rock bands (and rabid Tim and Eric fans) The Shins and Built to Spill, further bridging the gap between the pair's weird humor and a swath of the indie-music world.

You could say it's a mix of Andy Kaufman and Christopher Guest—an absurd, dark, uncomfortable realm with Tex Avery logic and child clowns lurking behind every ratty living room recliner. You could say it's dumb, weird, gross—the kind of show that spends a couple minutes describing a nest of zits around Eric's penis. But it also pushes language and logic onto the train tracks, tapping a part of the brain that was probably dormant since it escaped adolescence. The "Beaver Boys" sketch, for example, not only mocks mindless, club-hopping, beachcombing jocks, it forces them to consume shrimp and white wine until they're vomiting onto their matching white outfits, emphasizing the gross-out factor by putting it on repeat.

The show's jarring editing contributes much of that aesthetic, turning random noises and nonsense words into unexpectedly brilliant beatbox segments, or harmless glances across a room into sinister glares. *Awesome Show*'s loose scripts allow for a great deal of improvisation on the set—like Reilly's Steve Brule segments. It gives the editors a great deal of freedom in crafting the tone and narrative of the segments. "We give a lot of credit to the editors, because they're writers of the show as well," Tim says. "Most of our guys are more in the style of video artists than TV editors. Some of them had no TV experience when they started working with us, just these really young guys with long hair and unicorn T-shirts. It's those kinds of guys that we wanted to work with."

"They're also good at embracing all the horrible things we look at every day," Eric says. "For example, we just finished an episode called 'Jim and Derek,' which is an altered, surreal version of *Tim and Eric*. It looks like Fuel TV—like all these *Access Hollywood* 'extreme' bullshit graphics. We all watched those really fast-edit shows for a week and we're like, 'We're making the most disgusting thing ever.' We use that concept for all of our bits. It's like, 'What's the most awkward transition?' We've always just gravitated toward that stuff."

When the show garnered polarized reactions on Adult Swim message boards and a glowing *A. V. Club* cover story in *The Onion*, Adult Swim knew it had something unique. "It's painful at times, but also the funniest, most original comedy on TV right now," said *The Onion* in a November 15, 2007, interview with the pair (one of the first straight interviews they ever granted). "I don't think you could find a moment of our show that's sincere in any way. It's all meant to be funny," Tim says. "Even our interviews up until maybe six months ago were not sincere," Eric adds. But what prompted that shift? "We respect *The Onion*. A lot."

That paper's Nathan Rabin later wrote, "Though it isn't always apparent, there is a method to the duo's madness, even if that means structuring an entire episode around the little-known profession of gravy robbing and people turning into cats." Adult Swim appreciated that method, however insular and inexplicable it might have been, and approved the show for another thirty episodes over its initial ten-episode run, which led to new characters (Spagett, a balding man with a ponytail who's available for rent to spook out friends at parties) and more TV parodies (an ad for a board game called "It's Not Jackie Chan," in which players need to list something—anything—besides the martial arts film star. The commercial ends with a man bashing the game's irritatingly loud buzzer and slowly turning his face toward the camera as the rest of the players clutch their ears in pain).

Like *Human Giant*, Tim and Eric kept their brand of humor on fans' minds by touring, including a late spring/early summer 2008 jaunt that hit rock venues across the country with a ridiculous stage show, constantly adding dates to keep up with demand. They began hosting an annual AwesomeCon (a play on San Diego's Comic-Con, which attracts comic book, sci-fi, and horror nerds from around the globe). Set in various city parks in Southern California, AwesomeCon featured costume contests, karaoke sing-alongs, and good old-fashioned American junk food. The pair also maintained a regular presence online by appearing in a short-lived SuperDeluxe talk show (*Tim and Eric Nite Live*, which welcomed a rotating cast of amateurs and friends from *Awesome Show*), Absolute vodka ads with Zach Galifianakis (the wigs and bathrobes are brilliantly creepy), and deadpan, unsolicited endorsements of various brands and products (*Shrek the Third*, Papa John's pizza). Finding humor in awkwardness and incoherence, it seems, had paid off. "When these elements appear in a typical television program, they're usually the result of accidents, budgetary restrictions, and bad choices," wrote Dave Itzkoff in a July 27, 2008, *New York Times* article that featured an unusually large photo of Tim and Eric. "When they appear on *Awesome Show*, they're intentional."

"I always think that when you're in the show, you can never be *not* funny," Tim says. "The opposite of that would be *Saturday Night Live*, for example, where you have the blues band that frames the in-and-out of the show, and the titles where you have Horatio Sanz sitting at the bar being like, 'Hi, I'm not being funny right now. I'm going to have a drink and everything's great. We'll be giving you comedy in two minutes.' I want comedy from the very beginning to the very end. Everything about it should be funny, or should be in its own universe."

"I feel like we almost associate with some of the stuff that's going on in England, more so than what's going on here," Eric says. "Like [BBC comedy] *Look Around You*— they go for it in such a way that you don't see out here. I idolize *Mr. Show*, too, because you turn it on and you know what you're watching. Or *Jam* from Chris Morris, which is a British show I've been watching recently. They take it to such a surreal and scary place, and it's still considered comedy. Tim and I push it as far as we can without adhering to comedy rules. We've always gravitated toward that type of thing, even if it's not even funny, even if it's awkward and bizarre. That's the kind of feeling we want to get for our show."

Tim and Eric, however, aren't sure they want to keep doing their *Awesome Show* forever. The dark, David Lynchesque logic that rules their episodes may be inherent to their sense of humor, but the format can only be extended for so long before they move on to something else. And, in fact, they are: the pair is developing game shows, spin-offs, and movies that will likely break them into a wider audience.

Of course, it doesn't really matter if the Nielsen set is watching as long as Tim and Eric's rabid fan base keeps allowing the duo to indulge itself by crafting intentionally dated infomercials, and inviting everyone from Will Forte (a frequent guest) to real-life freaks like James Quall (a talentless impressionist) to share in their pain.

Or is it joy?

It doesn't matter when the line between laughing and screaming has been so thoroughly decimated.

"I think overwhelmingly that the people that we want to get it, get it," Tim says. "Somebody the other day was saying that [*Awesome Show*] appeals to people that are also creative because they can see themselves in a lot of the work. They can see how it might have been something that they could have done, or wanted to do, when they were younger. Whether that's doing a play, making their own little short films, whatever it may be. And now our stuff is sort of referential of itself, but when we were starting out it wasn't like very much anything else. We weren't informed by going to a comedy camp or a school or being around other people who were doing that stuff."

"We don't consider anything precious," Eric finishes. "That's why we don't really care about people loving it or hating it. We're making exactly what we want to make with no compromise and no filter, and that's why we love doing it. It's pretty fucking true to what we want onscreen."

Crafting jokes that avoid the same weary path as every other cultural insect is hard enough without having to make it up as you go along. And when it's audio-only, that challenge is even more daunting, since the performer is necessarily unable to call on props, costumes, and body language for directions.

But the simplicity—and potential for anonymity and improvisation—of phone-call comedy, for lack of a better term, has made it a popular (and essentially free) way to play tricks on random citizens, create elaborate characters, or just pass the time while you're waiting for your pizza, intoxicants, or sobriety to show up. That makes prank calls and phone sketches a lesser-appreciated but equally vital tributary of the comedy stream, and one that has seeped into the same reference-heavy ground that indie-music fans have been trampling.

Andrew Earles and Jeffrey Jensen have for years provided some of the smartest, most inventive prank calls the genre has seen. However, until Matador Records (the home of indie-rock titans Pavement, Liz Phair, Guided By Voices, Yo La Tengo, and dozens of others) reissued their underground-circulated releases as a double-disc set, the larger public was forced to dig fairly deep to pluck their work from the comedy underground. *Just Farr a Laugh, Vol. 1 and 2: The Greatest Prank Phone Calls Ever!* is an album of biblical proportions, collecting nearly sixty classic (and contemporaray) calls from Earles & Jensen, which feature characters familiar to fans of the duo: the short, fat, Big Buford burger–hungry Bleachy; the oblivious, endearingly sleazy Midlife; the jovial Party Doctor; Jazz Jermaine (Ru Paul's personal assistant); Howie Mandell's brother; and other gloriously warm, crackling impressions of has-been musicians and celebs (hint: the disc is named after a certain washed-up *M.A.S.H.* actor).

The real feat? Molesting ordinary citizens, military recruiters, bartenders, nurses, and fast-food employees without resorting to cruelty, caricatured racism and homophobia, or the sort of sickly elitism that makes most prank calls funny only in their cruelty or what-the-fuck randomness. In fact, the joke in an Earles & Jensen call isn't usually on the person who answers the phone, but on everyone, forcing us all to realize how improbably entertaining it is to listen to someone sift through the pop-culture trash bin by bouncing ridiculous phrases off another hapless soul. And to call it juvenile isn't just to miss the point, it's to confuse it. Prank calls are supposed to be juvenile. That's why they're fun.

The *Just Farr a Laugh* release on Matador provides literally hours of breezy, gut-achingly brilliant laughs. "I want to strike a blow against minimalism with this release," asserts Andrew Earles, who formerly produced the fanzine *Cimarron Weekend* (with David Dunlap Jr.) and has scribbled for *Magnet* (his merciless Where's the Street Team column is a highlight of each issue), *Vice*, *Spin*, *The Onion*'s *A. V. Club*, *Paste*, and *Chunklet*. "The decision by Matador to put out this record is probably regarded by some people as completely insane. We're talking about 150 minutes of fairly rough, improvised prank phone calls and a sixty-four-page book of just ridiculous content—drawings, liner notes, what have you. And it's not like we're dealing with a label that's put out five albums. It's one of the top three independent record labels in the world. But I just love the epic overindulgence of it. It probably goes back to my borderline Asperger's syndrome of becoming obsessed with artists that have done really massive, huge, creative statements. I want to be successful for our sake and our label's sake, because Matador took a very big chance on us."

Maybe Matador took a chance from a financial standpoint, but the label's potential to rouse the formerly slumbering prank-call genre is great with *Just Farr a Laugh*, particularly in light of Earles & Jensen's backgrounds and general sensibilities, which place them squarely among the music underground's choice few. Just as Sub Pop helped revitalize the comedy album with discs from David Cross, Patton Oswalt, and Eugene Mirman, and Drag City (and others labels) offering absurdly funny releases from various indie-friendly comedians, Matador's own foray into the niche-comedy world has the potential to broaden the label's focus without watering down its carefully blended, taste-making creative formula.

Prank calls have rarely received the same respect as stand-up and sketch comedy, despite their democratic origins and scattered pop-culture renown over roughly the last half-century. Partly it's because they have never enjoyed the wide distribution or publicity of other comedy releases, mostly getting passed around by musicians, comedians, and industry insiders on cassettes, or popping up on limited-release seven-inch records at college-town music shops and punk-rock shows.

The titans of this DIY genre are well-known to fans. The Jerky Boys, of course, made careers of their prank calling in the 1990s, but their mean, flimsy, repetitive material didn't lend itself to endless listens, nor were they able to sustain their pop-culture profile for long. Thirty years before they made prank calling a commercial phenomenon, tapes of Jerry Lewis's practical phone jokes made the rounds. The guys behind the 1970s-era Tube Bar calls, which became the inspiration for Moe (and the calls he suffered from Bart) on *The Simpsons*, also grew into the stuff of legend among in-the-know types, followed by recent examples such as the Colorado-based genius known only as Longmont Potion Castle (essentially the Jandek of crank calls), *Gregg Turkington's Greatest Prank Calls*, and of course the dozens of wise-ass radio DJs who harass random people as a matter of course on morning drive-time shows.

Comedy Central's *Crank Yankers*, which premiered in 2002, paired crank calls from people such as David Cross, Dave Chappelle, Fred Armisen, Patton Oswalt, Dane Cook, and Sarah Silverman with cartoonish, expressive puppeteering. And despite the rise of potentially call-killing media such as cell phones and Internet voice technology, the prank-call genre continues to evolve in new, unexpected ways.

But the best examples of the current prank-call vanguard are still the work of Earles & Jensen. Few can match the sheer volume and entertainment value of their efforts, bridging decades and subject matter with a parade of lunatic characters, subtle accents, and long-form put-ons. It's no surprise that the book that comes with their CD includes liner notes and drawings from underground royalty Gregg Turkington (aka Neil Hamburger), Gavin McInnes (*Vice*), author Neal Pollack, Matador heavy Gerard Cosloy, and musicians Devendra Banhart, Matt Sweeney (Chavez), and Archer Prewitt (The Sea and Cake), among others. Earles & Jensen's menagerie of distinctly, proudly southern characters and "Z-list celebrities" (as David Dunlap Jr. has dubbed them) practically scream for a smart, twisted audience.

"I've always prank called people," says Earles. "Sixth through eighth grades were big prank-calling years, and that was pre–star 69, so we'd get like five- and six-way calling and literally have an audience on the line while we terrorized our teachers at home, or various businesses around town. Anyone, really, that had proven themselves to be volatile prank-call subjects."

Of course, Earles didn't record any of his calls back then—it's something he only started doing in high school. He and *Cimarron Weekend's* David Dunlap Jr. released some on a seven-inch record and self-distributed tapes. But it was when Earles met New York–based Jeffrey Jensen, a filmmaker and later a *Vice* contributor who played in bands such as Smack Dab, The Closet Case, and The Jewish, through mutual Memphis friends in 2001 that their current renown began to grow. The pair quickly began calling each other late at night to play their respective cache of prank calls for one another, and one hungover Sunday night, created a barrage of improvised calls, the best of which would comprise their first *Just Farr a Laugh* disc (released on Earles's Failed Pilot label, also the title of his densely packed blog).

"When you hear a prank phone call, the first thing that comes to your mind is, 'Oh, I'm listening to some guys fucking around.' And there's an element of that, for sure, especially at the beginning. We had no idea we were going to put out a record, and even when Jeff came to town for two to three weeks one summer there was an element of us just goofing off because he wanted to get away from New York for a bit. But there's a funny backstory to every one of the calls [see the *Just Farr a Laugh* CD book for copious details]. What you hear is usually the first take of that particular call, but most of it was tried on a different person before that. They change and morph into different things throughout an afternoon as you're trying out an idea. Although, I'm applying a lot more conceptual nooks and crannies to the process than are really there. It's pretty much as loose and minimal as it sounds."

Indeed, when Earles calls a tattoo shop to get quotes for facial tats of Warner Bros. Tasmanian Devil and the

Taco Bell dog, it's impossible to imagine how he kept from cracking up while asking: "How much do you think that'll run me, all full color?" His wife (who he says already has tats of a margarita glass with a fake umbrella on her leg), thinks he's lost his sense of adventure with his measly "Primus back plate" tattoo. And on and on.

"Finding a wider audience outside of the music and comedy underground has always been a challenge," Earles says. "I don't know that there's a tight-knit community in terms of prank-call fans. I would imagine that, as with any incredibly obscure genre of art, there are cultists and people obsessed with it. But it seems too loose a genre of comedy to actually have a rabid, weird, Comic-Con-style fan base. The nature of the form is so difficult in a way. It's not stand-up or sketch. It's a weird utilization of technology to prank people."

The pranks, though, are funny without being outright mean, and rapid-fire without being disorientating or forgettable. Or, as *Dusted's* Andy Freivogel said in a review of the Matador release: "Two hours of Earles & Jensen makes everyone a repentant elitist." (Note the word *repentant*.) "These two are a lot more character driven than some of their brethren, and they're eager to poke fun at pop culture and stupidity in general," wrote *The Onion's* Josh Modell in a 2008 piece entitled "I Love Prank Phone Calls."

Earles & Jensen's closest brethren are probably another phone-comedy duo that takes the "prank" element out of the equation but retains the brilliant improvisation and ludicrous characters. "I remember in the nineties, someone played me these tapes of the Superchunk drummer doing these phone [calls]. It was really funny and that, to me, was a bridge between the two art forms," says Fred Armisen, a musician who has also spanned the genre gap.

As noted, Superchunk drummer Jon Wurster is one half of that duo, a mischievous soul with an endless catalogue of rock 'n' roll knowledge and a flair for understated hilarity. His cohort is Tom Scharpling, former editor of the legendary nineties fanzine *18 Wheeler*, writer, and host of the comedy-music radio staple *The Best Show* of WMFU. The Scharpling and Wurster team generally release the fruits of their labor on their Stereolaffs label and on ScharplingandWurster.com, with Wurster playing the call-in characters and Scharpling playing the straight man.

Unlike Earles & Jensen, however, Scharpling and Wurster ply their trade in long-form bits, requiring an initial attention span that most sketch and prank calls would be afraid to approach. But once you're in, you're stuck, welcoming characters such as Philly Boy Roy, The Auteur, Andy from Lake Newbridge, and Timmy von Trimble into the stickiest corners of your brain. It started in 1997 with the character of Ronald Thomas Clontle, the author of the fake *Rock, Rot and Rule*, which placed musical acts into one of those three categories. (Listeners became legitimately indignant and confused when Clontle asserted things like "Madness invented ska.")

"Touring bands seemed to get on board with it first," says Scharpling. "You'd hear nice things from people that had listened to the tapes or CDs nonstop. Then at the same time I was meeting people from the comedy world like Jon Glaser and Jon Benjamin and Todd Barry and all those guys. I'd give them CDs and feel gratified by the feedback I got from like-minded people."

Wurster says that the straight-faced, generally low-key performance aesthetic helps bring the ridiculous material into relief. "What we want is for you to tune in and take awhile to realize that it's not real. It's like doing a prank call without hurting anybody. Actually, the only person that gets hurt is Tom. He gets the death threats, and my character is usually the asshole."

Despite their victimless aim, the calls still impale jocks, narcissistic critics, pretentious filmmakers, computer nerds, hippies, and myriad others. The off-the-cuff nature allows for endless turns and loops. "I like the idea of doing things on the radio where it's not about being flawless," Scharpling adds. "It's looser and more spread out. When I'm doing the show and taking calls or talking, I don't feel like I'm doing a monologue where every word has to be perfect, like what Henry Rollins does."

Scharpling and Wurster first met on the indie-music scene and bonded over a love of programs such as *Get a Life* and *Mr. Show*. They went on to write as a duo for Tim and Eric's *Tom Goes to the Mayor*, although Scharpling's now an experienced TV writer and co-executive producer for USA's award-winning show *Monk*. Despite initial resistance from some listeners, their bits established themselves in the underground music and comedy realms, so far producing an impressive five CDs of material (their most recent Stereolaffs release, *The Art of Slap*, is a three-disc set). It's no exaggeration to say that a dive into their catalogue will provide weeks of entertainment. (It's also unsurprising that Andrew Earles has contributed to Scharpling's *Best Show* on WFMU. A list of other contributors to that show would read like a partial interview list for this book.)

"In the seventies, Led Zeppelin and The Who spent the hours on the road listening to their prized bootleg Derek and Clive tapes," wrote Rob Sheffield in a four-star *Art of the Slap* review in *Rolling Stone*. "These days, Tom Scharpling and Jon Wurster are the traveling rock musician's comedy duo of choice, inspiring a fanatical MP3-trading cult. Like an indie-rock Bob and Ray, they improvise long, absurd dialogues about characters like the Music Scholar [the snob who dismisses The Beatles as ear candy] and Mother 13 [the loser band plugging its gig at the Earthlink/Pringles Summer Slam Jam]. If they remind you of jerks you know, or maybe the jerk you are, that's the point."

"The first people that really liked it were the guys in Guided By Voices, Bob [Pollard] and Doug [Gillard]," says Wurster, referencing a band for which he's drummed. "It just started getting passed around by people like David Bazan [of Pedro the Lion], who was another early guy, and went on from there."

Scharpling says the overlap of subject matter and artists was inevitable. "It's just finding stuff in another medium that appeals to the same people. It never felt like the solution to anything for me. Like, 'Oh, the universe is in order and it's the way it should be that comedy and music have found each other!' It's just fun, and ultimately, the crazy parts of music and musicians have always made me laugh. I thought it was funny when I was eleven and I think it's still funny now. It's just nice to know that there are musicians who are accessible enough that they appreciate those same dopey things."

Zach Galifianakis reigns in his crushing excitement in Brooklyn, New York. *Photo by Seth Olenick*

6

COMEDY WITH AN AMP

If taking comedy out of comedy clubs seemed risky, imagine how stand-ups felt when presented with drunken, sunburned daytime crowds under a giant tent in the middle of a field normally reserved for soybeans or polo. That may sound like a recipe for group beatings behind the portapotty, but more indie-minded music festivals are finding that it's an experiment worth trying.

One of the first contemporary musicfests to welcome comics into its sweaty fold, the Bonnaroo Music & Arts Festival in Manchester, Tennessee, featured Mike Birbiglia, Mark Eddie, and Vic Henley at its inaugural 2002 showing. Comedians have certainly emceed and, no doubt, attended music festivals over the years, but breaking comedy out of the music schedule and giving it a dedicated venue provided palate-cleansing reprieves from the onslaught of melody, noise, and trampled fields that typify most large-scale festivals. Bonnaroo skipped comedy for the next few years but returned with an expanded lineup in 2005 that included college-friendly names Fred Armisen, Charlie Murphy, and Jim Breuer. The roster grew increasingly indie-oriented (adding David Cross, Patton Oswalt, Aziz Ansari, Demetri Martin, and others) until in 2008 it welcomed megawatt stand-up Chris Rock. In a bout of seemingly lunatic scheduling, Rock preceded aging metal act Metallica on the main stage in front of approximately 80,000 screaming fans. The juxtaposition of talent prompted Associated Press writer Jake Coyle to dub it "the rarest of double bills."

Perhaps, but it nodded toward comedy's burgeoning mainstream profile at large-scale music events. Clearly, something about the mixture was working. "Bonnaroo is one of the largest comedy events in the country now," Bonnaroo cocreator Rick Farman told *Billboard* magazine in a 2008 article. "We'll do between 25,000 and 30,000 people in our comedy tents and we're turning away 500 to 1,000 people for every show." Bonnaroo's twenty-four-hour atmosphere, Farman said, allowed fans to hunker down in the comedy tent and break the routine of running from stage to stage to see bands. "It's hard to pull yourself away when there are twenty bands you want to see in one afternoon," he told *Billboard*'s Michael D. Ayers. "That hour to get away with comedy—that dynamic really works in a camping atmosphere."

The trend may have found some footing with Bonnaroo (and, oddly, back when Bonnaroo was a jam-band oriented event), but indie-rockfests such as Bumbershoot, Sasquatch, Coachella, and especially South by Southwest have taken the torch and run with it, offering multiple official and unofficial comedy events in addition to the music, blogging, and late-night circle jerks (i.e., VIP parties). British festivals have tapped the keg, too, with comics such as Phill Jupitus playing Glastonbury and the Latitude Festival in Suffolk, and Julian Barratt and Noel Fielding of the BBC's *The Mighty Boosh* headlining their own outdoor event. After an August 2008 appearance at The Big Chill festival in Herefordshire, in which the Boosh performed a mixture of comedy and music in sparkly spaceman and gorilla costumes, the Culture JamJar blog noted the familiar rock-star similarities: "[Noel Fielding] is a mix between Pete Doherty, Mick Jagger, and a *Hollyoaks* actor/ E4 presenter..."

"Fighting with bands for the audience's attention sharpens you up," wrote Phill Jupitus in *The Times Online*. "If you are going to heckle a comedian in a tent you are either completely off your face on drugs or extremely confident. Probably the former. Ultimately, whether it's bands or comedians it's all about being the centre of attention. We are all fractured egomaniacs."

Nowhere is that potential for egomania more apparent than at the behemoth of North American music conferences, South by Southwest (SXSW)—an overwhelming bitchslap of stimuli that hordes of writers and photographers race to Austin, Texas, each year to absorb. The media is always reliably desperate to squeeze out its words and pictures before the rest of the unlucky bastards (i.e., 99 percent of the nonattending world) grow fatigued by the numbing sameness and overwhelming amount of "I was there! You weren't!" coverage. And certainly, its magnitude—nearly 2,000 bands over the span of a week—justifies that quantity. But few outlets write about anything except the music and the fashion (which find glorious release at the aforementioned VIP parties).

While it's not a huge chunk of the entertainment, comedy sets at SXSW increasingly warrant their own examination. Even as I try to catch bands that have inflamed my musical organs over the preceding months (recently: Land of Talk, Bon Iver, Evangelicals, Helio Sequence, Of Montreal, and The Caribbean), the growing amount of hipster stand-ups, improv types, and sketch comedians excite me far more than most rock shows do these days.

Maybe it's because festival regulars such as Eugene Mirman, Maria Bamford, Brian Posehn, Tim and Eric, Patton Oswalt, and others are filling the same flavor hole that music once did (and still occasionally does), affording me excellent new ways of chewing on the world's absurdities, shredding logical boundaries left and right, and channeling the ethos and energy of punk rock into painfully hilarious truths. Mostly, I just like to laugh when I'm drinking beer for twelve hours a day.

As noted earlier, indie comedy is not the largest or most diverse scene out there. Comedy nerds who weekly devour Adult Swim and online comedy offerings tend to notice the same dozen or so people popping up at these fests. And if you live in New York or Los Angeles, you're also likely to see the same handful of comedians at shows such as LA's *Comedy Death-Ray*, New York's *Tearing the Veil of Maya*, and on labels such as Sub Pop.

But indie-music festivals and scattered awards ceremonies are beginning to play as important a role in people's awareness of indie comedy as rock clubs, websites, and other nontraditional venues, if on a slightly more diffuse (and simultaneously grander) scale. For the last several years, comedians have hosted day parties and showcases at SXSW, using them as branding opportunities and cleverly associating themselves with the storm of hipness surrounding them.

My first chance to see a good chunk of comedy at SXSW was in 2007. My girlfriend, Kathleen, and I wandered into Emo's one afternoon on the corner of Sixth and Red River to catch a handful of stand-ups, including Jon Wurster from Scharpling and Wurster, Aziz Ansari from *Human Giant*, and college/indie-comedy mainstay

Michael Showalter (*The State, Stella*). The noisy crowd afforded little respect to the mild-mannered Wurster, whose characters usually require a more attentive crowd, and Showalter's rambling, tipsy set lost more than a few audience members. But when Aziz Ansari took the stage between the two, his commanding presence made people shut up and listen. (You need a rock attitude, after all, to get a rock crowd's attention—especially if they're not expecting to see comedy, since dozens were loudly streaming through the venue every few minutes on their way to other shows).

More successful that year was the nighttime double-bill at Friends, a long, narrow venue on Sixth Street that hosted back-to-back shows of *Human Giant* and *Tim and Eric Awesome Show, Great Job!* The latter had recently premiered on Cartoon Network's late-night programming block, and the former was set to hit MTV a couple weeks after SXSW. The showcase provided both of them an opportunity to make a visceral connection with their budding audiences, and judging by the energized capacity crowd, it worked. Each set offered an array of stand-up, absurd sketch, and video clips that had the boozy audience practically in tears.

Of course, the centerpiece of SXSW 2007 was the *Comedy on the Music Circuit* panel I'd attended the day before at the Austin Convention Center. Call me cynical, but I harbored mixed feelings even before entering the room. On the one hand, its existence legitimized the article I'd written on indie comedy for *The Denver Post* the year before (which eventually became the seed for this book). In my self-interested, quasi-capitalistic mind I couldn't help think that lending more scrutiny to the scene would only create a bigger market for a potential book. On the other hand, it also felt like someone had taken my idea and articulated it better.

In truth there were (and are) dozens of writers and music-comedy nerds thinking the same thing. (I'm certain I didn't coin the term *indie comedy*. It makes too much sense for any one person to have come up with.) Any critic paying attention to the underground/progressive comedy world over the last five to ten years has likely already thought, *A lot of comedians seem to be showing up on indie record labels and at rock shows. It's a trend. I should write about it.* But I also couldn't help feeling deflated when I saw how excellent and spot-on the festival's description was, reading much like the thesis I'd already formulated: "You could argue that comedy and music have been bedfellows as far back as the ancient Greeks—or at least since Don Rickles opened for Frank Sinatra at The Sands," it said. "But for a new generation of comedians and musicians, that union has become more pronounced in recent years." It was essentially a more concise, historical-minded version of my article's premise, and it went on to note that a few indie musicians had even launched careers as comedy writers and performers, popping up on *Saturday Night Live* (Fred Armisen) and Adult Swim (Scharpling and Wurster).

The panelist roster read like a who's-who of the scene, with a few lesser-known names thrown in for balance and depth. Bob Mehr, a music writer for the respected Memphis, Tennessee, paper *Commercial Appeal* and a veteran of the *Chicago Reader* and *Mojo*, would moderate. Jon Wurster, drummer for seminal indie-rockers Superchunk and skinman-for-hire for Robert Pollard, The Mountain Goats, and The New Pornographers, would represent his partnership with WFMU radio host Tom Scharpling. *Chunklet* magazine publisher Henry Owings was the longtime behind-the-scenes guy, managing the *Comedians of Comedy* tour and helping kick-start the comedy-at-music-festivals trend with his Mess with Texas parties. Writer Andrew Earles (*Magnet, The Onion, Spin*) was representing his and partner Jeff Jensen's *Just Farr A Laugh* CDs, that series of unpredictable, brilliant prank calls that would later be released on Matador Records as that label's first comedy offering. Bearded genius Zach Galifianakis was filling in for *Comedians of Comedy* creator Patton Oswalt, who couldn't be there for some reason or another.

Finally, the two men who were arguably most responsible for the influx of comedians to the indie-music scene would represent themselves: *Mr. Show* cocreator David Cross and Tony Kiewel, head of A&R for Seattle indie label Sub Pop.

And so, on March 16, 2007, I slipped into the conference room in the Austin Convention Center to listen to the assembled experts speak about the subject, savoring the blissfully cool, dark environment and nursing a crushing hangover from the night before.

Bob Mehr kicked it off a little after 12:30 PM, announcing to scattered sighs that Oswalt would be replaced by *Comedians of Comedy* tourmate Galifianakis. Immediately the panel dug to the heart of the gleaming contradiction of the indie-comedy scene: it reinforces indie-rock ideals while deflating them, mocking that genre's social conventions and preoccupations to the same people who create and perpetuate them. And on and on.

As it turned out, the panel was as enlightening as it was entertaining—at least to geeks like myself who had been obsessed with most of its participants for the better part of a decade. Henry Owings later posted an eight-part series of videos (a good chunk, by online standards) of the panel on YouTube and received a predictably varied amount of responses. "Welcome to the most gospel truth ever spoken about indie-rock fucks," user Blissinflux commented. "Wouldn't calling this a hipster panel be more appropriate than calling it a comedy panel?" user yousostupid added. Others responded by praising the wit and brilliance of drummers (as previously noted, Jon Wurster is a drummer, and *Saturday Night Live* cast member Fred Armisen started his comedy career as a drummer by mocking SXSW in his cult video). "They never take themselves as seriously as anyone else, because they will be the first to admit they just hit things," user arollo commented. Some found the footage "boring and pointless." But let's be honest: watching it on a computer screen and sitting in the audience are two different things, even if the earlyish start time tended to ensure that most everyone in the room would be painfully hungover.

Conclusions were few as the panel wrapped up, but the subject matter late in the hour (pandering to indie-rock audiences by using clichéd jokes about rape or abortion, or referencing bands the audience would recognize, etc.) hinted that the cycle had reached a sort of maturity, with entire generations of comedians never having to set foot on a comedy club stage. Tracing the recent history of comedy-music pairings also provided numerous examples of the failure of comedy at music festivals. Galifianakis noted his shaky experience opening for friend Fiona Apple, whose crowd seemed hostile and oversensitive to his humor.

Even when like-minded comedians had appeared at the same festival, the mercurial audience usually dictated how a set would go. Owings related the story of watching David Cross get massacred by a crowd at a UK festival, only to have his own act go over well: "It was...in front of 4,000 people that wanted to see Sleater-Kinney and they would not let him get a sentence out. And the next night I went in front of the same crowd doing a real belligerent, aggro security guard character and I was up there for ten minutes and had them eating out of the palm of my hand. Probably because they thought I was a real security guard."

I suspected the trickle of comedy at SXSW would only grow to a strong, golden stream, especially since the union had been semiprimed at the 2007 comedy-music panel. In 2008, however, comedians were scattered in every mother-lovin' direction, from one-off shows by Michael Showalter, and Matt Besser and Matt Walsh of Upright Citizens Brigade to full-night offerings at long-time comedy club Esther's Follies and Henry Owings's daylong Mess with Texas 2 party at Waterloo Park, which included a dedicated comedy stage.

I stumbled into Esther's late on a Friday just as prank-call duo Earles & Jensen took the stage. Earles's swarthy, sleepy-eyed persona contrasted nicely with Jensen's Mets-cap-and-jacket-clad New Yorker persona. Together they craft some of the funniest, sharpest, oddly uncruel prank calls this side of Neil Hamburger. However, their stage act could have used some polish.

While never botched, the conversational, gently teasing bits merely acted as setups for the inevitable pretaped calls that crackled softly over the speakers. Without the experience to exude authoritative stage presence, they prevented themselves from being a highlight of the evening (although a few of their calls killed, in spite of the crappy sound). New face Reggie Watts, however, projected easy confidence and deft timing during his set, incorporating beatboxing and a synthesizer into his dizzying music-comedy act. (The frizzy-haired Seattle comedian has lately been garnering much-deserved notice on the scene for his act.) New York comedian

Leo Allen, a friendly, self-deprecating hipster who has toured with Comedy Central regular Demetri Martin, also performed, but his set lacked the energy or timing to push it over the "ehh..." mark. I've seen him do better, anyway.

Since many of these cutting-edge comedians are alumni or unabashed devotees of *Mr. Show*, it was unsurprising to see lots of their ilk around. The Fun Bunch, the duo of Scott Aukerman and B. J. Porter, destroyed the Esther's crowd with a verbal argument bit that escalated into a clothes-off fistfight and ended in the two guys kissing, mostly naked, onstage. I'd seen the pair test the bit at *Comedy Death-Ray* in LA three weeks prior, and the lack of variation on their initial experiment proved how laser-honed their original instincts were. *Mr. Show* and VH1's *Best Week Ever* regular Paul F. Tompkins brought his suave, indignant monologues to the table, while metal nerd and *Mr. Show* alum Brian Posehn provided arguably the night's best-received set, cobbling his act from new observations and bits of his stand-up CD, *Live In: Nerd Rage*. His intentionally awkward material, which often mocks his freakish size and appearance, went over well with the drunken (but polite) crowd. Weed jokes never hurt, either.

I failed to make it next door to the Velveeta Room, where more comedians were performing, but did chat at various times with Posehn, Besser, and Earles before and after their sets. Nice dudes they were, although justifiably distracted by the buzzing environment. Posehn, hunched over his notes on a bench in the lobby before his set, could only acknowledge me as I ended sentences, never really adding much (I don't blame him. I would have been annoyed with me, too). Besser and I stood in the back of Esther's main room, him relating how much fun he was having catching so many bands. And Earles and I stood in an open-air center area, smoking endless cigarettes while he cursed himself for what he thought was an underprepared set. "I probably had no business being on that stage," he said, his gravelly voice betraying his fatigue. "But fuck it."

After he left I struck up a conversation with a pair of dudes I'd met at various shows in the preceding days through my friend Bridget. Did they think that comedy at musical festivals was a good idea? "It really seems like they've been pushing it more each year," said Louisiana native Justin Williams. "This year there are lineups of nothing but comedians, and even last year, every time I passed by a venue there was a cheesy comic standing on the corner trying to get people to come in. A good question is whether the comedy's being taken seriously or if it's just becoming a part of the scene. Like, is it just going to become a standard, or do we even want it to be a standard?" His cohort, Jesse Wingard, was more amicable about it: "I think it's a good thing. If it's giving the comedians more exposure and selling more CDs, so be it."

The brunt of that exposure didn't happen at the relatively modest indoor stage at Esther's, but the next day at the Mess with Texas 2 party at Waterloo Park, an all-day fete that took place outside the official festival. The party attempted to condense into a single day and area what previously took place over three days at a much smaller (and virtually impossible to get into) venue, which was not surprising, considering the mix of incredible bands and comedians (Les Savy Fav and David Cross. Need I say more?). My friends and I showed up just as UCB's Matt Walsh was leaving the comedy stage (they thought he sucked—I didn't catch any of his set) and just in time for up-and-comer Jonah Ray. The scruffy, affable stand-up peppered his bits with references to hipster catnip like

Neutral Milk Hotel and the Courtney-killed-Kurt theory, the crowd quickly and hungrily eating out of his hand.

And, Christ, was it hot. The teeming, dust-choked park, nominal sight lines, and quiet sound mix likely prevented more souls from seeing/hearing the comedy in its full glory, especially as larger crowds gathered for marquee acts such as Janeane Garofalo. Her wit and experience were nearly sabotaged by not only the quietness of the speakers, but her omnipresent self-deprecation and nervousness, which found her jumping from subject to subject schizophrenically and barely following through with punch lines. Unsurprising but spot-on political jabs and limited crowd interaction also rounded out her mixed set, which I heard (from various people) wasn't all that different from her set the night before.

Host Matt Braunger, an LA regular who also emceed the previous night at Esther's, provided needed, welcome links between comedians, his slightly tipsy, confident segues translating into cool breezes for the attention-span-challenged. The final comedian I caught was medium-energy master Todd Barry, who uses dry understatement to slip burning slivers of awesomeness into your brain. Barry's material should have been familiar to anyone who caught his then-recent round of talk-show appearances or listened to his Comedy Central CD, *From Heaven*, but it went over surprisingly well among the increasingly antsy, sweat-soaked crowd.

"It was quite a good show and a lot of fun for me," Barry tells me a few months later. "I don't do a lot of outdoor shows, and just to see the faces of the people watching it was great. It was a big crowd and it was such a different environment. Any time I can perform in a venue that's different—in a good way—I will. And they were really into it. Basically, it's about the crowd enjoying it and respecting the performer...I never identify myself as alternative, though, and would never stop working any clubs."

Barry may not consider himself an alt or indie comic, but as noted, he appreciates any crowd who's there to see him. "I've done Bumbershoot six or seven times, and it's just amazing. They have their comedy sets in a theater, and you feel like a star. Every show is packed, and people are walking about taking pictures with you."

Paul F. Tompkins, who performed at SXSW for the first time in 2008, was surprised at how smoothly his sets went, despite his initial (and long-held) misgivings. "I myself am not a big fan of five-hour comedy shows. I think the problem with these festivals, especially if it's Bumbershoot or SXSW, is that they tend to treat the comedy like the rock—and they're not the same thing, as much as people would like to equate them." He says he prefers his comedy shows to be shorter, since the reaction a comedian is trying to get is much tougher during the fourth hour than the first.

"It can be a drag sometimes to go on so late in the show, but I've got to keep my energy up, too," he continues. "I am absolutely opposed to comedy being performed during the day and outdoors with people standing. Either one of those is nightmare enough, but both of them together is terrible. And at the [Mess with Texas] party it was unseasonably warm. That being said, that show was so much better than I thought it was going to be. People were remarkably attentive and respectful given the atmosphere."

It's impressive for any comedian to hold the attention of more than a few dozen people, but when that group is composed of hundreds of drunks who have been on their feet in the sun all day, every day, for nearly a week, it's a feat rivaled only by the more energetic novelty-infused musical acts of the festival like Monotonix or Dark Meat.

It's unsurprising that more festivals around the country have also jumped crotch-first into the comedy tent. That they can still procreate is a bonus.

"Doing comedy at a festival where it's showcase-style and outdoors is tough, but the acts I've seen, like Brian Posehn, Eugene Mirman, Todd Barry, and *Human Giant*, have translated pretty well," says Dan Schlissel of Stand Up! Records.

It helps that the comedians get something out of it, too, watching and hanging out with their favorite bands for free. Any seasoned performer has likely gotten over the wide-eyed, star-fucking awe of mingling with other celebrities (of whatever level), but the mix of genres provides a refreshing change. "We got to hang out at Bumbershoot with the guys from Death Cab for Cutie, so of course it's a cool way to get backstage," says *Human Giant*'s Paul Scheer. "And for them, there's only so much music you can digest."

The challenges of performing comedy at music festivals will probably always remain, since the element of control that's present at theaters and clubs—and even smaller, indoor music venues—is much greater for the performer. "The fourth wall is not friendly at a big festival when there are thousands of people talking," says UCB's Matt Besser. "It's never just completely silent at a concert, no matter who you are. But when you do comedy you pretty much want silence, so you really have to adjust yourself to talk to the audience and interact with them."

Still, the opportunity to plug into new, like-minded crowds has increasingly positioned music festivals as some of the best venues for comedians who don't fit the sitcom, talk-show, or comedy-club mold. "Comedy nerds always seem to be into indie music," Besser continues. "It's just the type of personality of wanting to know what's new and interesting and not mainstream. There are also a lot of people that like music that aren't necessarily into alternative types of comedy, so these festivals are a great way to introduce yourself to them. A lot of festivals have their own tents, the comedians have their own shows, and audiences are starting to realize, 'Oh yeah, there's something funny here now, too.'"

Neil Hamburger: international funnyman, failed husband, poor tipper, and now, country singer. *Photo by Simone Turkington*

7

LEAST LIKELY TO SUCCEED

The cheap title screen and tacky Vegas soundtrack set a playful, off-kilter mood as the comedian fights his way through the red curtains, stumbling onto the stage with an expression of confusion and mild annoyance. His bent right arm supports a ludicrous phalanx of cocktails in clear tumblers. His hair has been combed at a questionable angle over his forehead, so slick with gel it looks like the tentacles of a flattened baby squid, serving only to highlight his receding hairline and unfortunately bulbous skull.

Those glasses aren't doing him any favors, either. The lenses are thick, the frames tall. They arch over his bushy eyebrows like cartoon bridges scrawled with a blunted Sharpie, their curvature so wide they nearly align with his flared nostrils. He's clad in a rumpled black tuxedo, which appears to have seen better days—though likely not with him. The red flower sticking out of the breast pocket fails to impart any class to his appearance. His shoulders melt into what little neck he has, and his head appears as an outgrowth of his chin, instead of the other way around. The squinted eyes allow him to peer at the audience like an angry turtle. He probably smells like the industrial soap at a Greyhound bus station, mixed with stale Fritos.

Then there's the throat clearing. As he fumbles to free the microphone from the stand, he emits a thick, phlegm-soaked growl, a cross between Al Pacino's bowel-emptying "hoo-ahhhh!" from *Scent of a Woman* and the death rattle of a shut-in with tuberculosis. He spits the phlegm into his drink and promptly takes a swig, eliciting groans from the audience. "How's everybody—" he begins, immediately interrupted by the clink of one of his cocktails hitting the ground. "Security..." he barks halfheartedly. "How's everybody doing?" he asks again, coughing, groaning. "Let's get this party started, huh? Bring out some more drinks to the stage, please."

His arms are perpetually unsteady, which allows one of the various drinks to tumble to the stage every few minutes, the crowd vacillating between titters and gasps each time. He has no better luck while trying to sip one of them, the indeterminate liquid finding its way onto his lapel, his pants, the stage.

"My name is Neil Hamburger," he states, his warped inflection like that of a drugged carnie or untreated stroke victim. "Here we go. Let's get this party started." The spilling and throat-clearing go on. And on. And on. Each time you start to wonder where in Christ's name the bit is going he opens his mouth again. "Let's get this party started, huh?" After three or four repetitions it sounds like a taunt, or the mutterings of someone who absconded from a group home, killed an AARP member for his formal wear, eluded the bouncer at the club's entrance, and decided to try his hand at a night of lounge-style stand-up.

"Hey, let's get this party started!" he barks for what seems like the millionth time. You might have stopped paying attention a while ago, except that this pathetic display has started to massage your sense of the absurd. The tape in your mind feels stuck on a loop, each go-round becoming more frayed and insane. A hacking cough. A spilled drink. "Hey, let's get this party started. Whaddya say?" This goes on for nearly five minutes, though it feels like twenty.

By the time he finally spits out a complete, original sentence you feel as if an anvil has been lifted from your ribs. But only momentarily, because the jokes are delivered with a quivering, abused sadness and obvious scorn for the audience that could only have come from years of failing in front of other crowds in dark, lonely, D-list dungeons.

"*Whaddya* call a senior citizen who can't refrain from exposing her genitalia in public?" A few beats pass. "*Madonna*." People laugh politely, scattered claps dotting the back of the room. "*Why* did Madonna feed her infant baby *dog food*?" More beats. "Because she had no choice. That's just what came out of her *breasts*." People begin to laugh more openly, now getting into the spirit of it. More jokes follow this pattern. The introductory "whaddya" and "why" escape from his throat like violent sneezes, the punch lines milked for every last mutated syllable.

It's a similar treatment for Michael Jackson and Paris Hilton, Britney Spears and Kevin Federline, Mick Jagger and Janis Joplin—a relentless string of insults defined by their parallel construction, demented twists, and obsession with tabloid celebrities and dead rock stars. "What did Santa Claus give Paris Hilton for Christmas?" Wait for it... "Well, he *raped* her." Groans and uproarious laughs greet the punch line. The delivery allows the comedian to draw out the sentence-ending words, inflecting them with a shrug that communicates, "Hey, I just tell the jokes here. Don't blame me! These fools set *themselves* up."

The jokes grow more elaborate: "Why did Robert Redford stick his cock in a bottle of Paul Newman's spaghetti sauce?" Three beats. "Well, the two men have been friends for over forty years. Do you think he's going to stick his cock in a *competitor's* product?"

It's awful. The worst thing you've ever seen. A bastardization of what stand-up comedy could and should be.

Or is it? There's professionalism lurking in the delivery, an old-guard, gentlemanly attitude that only wants to entertain the nice people in their pearls and smoking jackets. A glimmer of hope that somehow this might be the gig where he gets his break, instead of being broken, as has been the case so often in the past.

So begins Neil Hamburger's 2006 set at Newtown R. S. L. in Sydney, Australia, chronicled on the Drag City DVD *The World's Funnyman.* The appropriately titled, forty-six-minute *That's Not Gold, That's Dung!* is a textbook example of the Neil Hamburger experience—his screwed-up facial tics and improbable vocal inflection, his audience-baiting demeanor and calculated awfulness, his ridiculously repetitive, tabloid-humping material.

Of course, things won't go well again for Neil Hamburger, because they never do. Not because he's a self-defeating character, although he certainly is that, but because Hamburger is a concept with a predetermined arc, a grimacing cur that laps up laughs, pity, and hatred in equal gulps. And the longer you're in his presence, the more you find yourself loving him, especially if you're into sick humor or tend to listen to indie rock or punk—the audience that Hamburger has thus far cultivated.

As anyone who's witnessed a bad comedy set can tell you, watching someone bomb onstage is almost unbearably awkward. Seeing that carefully constructed joke crumble as the comedian fumbles to regain the audience's goodwill is akin to witnessing a child with Down syndrome drag a dead puppy down the street, only mildly aware that the thing on the end of the leash has expired. (A common sight, I'm sure.) Godspeed to those steel-nerved, masochistic patrons who don't turn away or cringe when an unfortunate soul gets killed instead of killing. It's just awful to watch.

Neil Hamburger is counting on that. The sad-sack comedian intentionally affects a persona based on throat-clearing pauses, copious spilled drinks, and jokes that cultivate as much heckling or silence as laughter, absorbing abuse like a particularly stubborn, fire-haired stepchild. "A deflated nightclub cliché," *The Onion* has called him. "A jab at our sorry fascination with fame, and of the hideous voyeur entertainment industry, in which we derive fetishistic pleasure from watching people we don't know experiencing very public pain and embarrassment," the *Phoenix New Times* wrote.

"I wish everyone would have a great time at my shows, but it's simply not possible," Hamburger tells me over the phone while driving through the desert to a gig, his warbling accent revealing an odd sincerity. "Even the greatest entertainers of all, like Lionel Richie and Kenny Rogers, have people who wouldn't cross the street to see them. Plus, it makes it more entertaining for everyone else who's in the audience. My fans like to listen to some of these Negative Nellies and their running commentaries."

Hamburger invites this ridicule and indifference on himself, cultivating a vibe that verges on a fifth-rate, early-1970s casino entertainer. But his act's subtle brilliance lies in its cringeworthy tenor, indicting hackneyed comedy conventions and easy-target celebs, forcing the audience to be complicit in his failed life. Its stare-into-the-abyss approach proves surprisingly cathartic, provided you have a fucked-up sense of humor. Hamburger's approach also feels distinctly postmodern, situating him among other entertainers this book chronicles by virtue of conceptual kinship. He places deconstruction above (or, often, parallel to) arrowlike punch lines and easy-to-swallow one-liners. Critics have dubbed it anticomedy, but anyone who has seen Hamburger live, watched one of his DVDs, or listened to his releases on Drag City (his renown on that excruciatingly cool imprint is the stuff of legend) and other labels know that the approach is more sublime—and legitimately funny.

Hamburger even released a CD in 2007 that documented his heckle-ridden sets on a twenty-six-date tour opening for metal-comedy duo Tenacious D (*Hot February Night*, recorded at shows in Portland, Vancouver, and Seattle). "Some would say, 'Why would you release a CD that painted such a grim picture of your set, with the booing and yelling?' But you know, why not? We've done a lot of CDs, and this one's something different," he says. "You cannot do the same record over and over again. All these musician creeps do that, but with the comedy records and the very small audience that wants to buy something, you try to do each one with a different angle, sound, and concept."

Sub Pop's Tony Kiewel says his label received hate mail when Hamburger played with one of its bands in the past, the gentle indie-folk group Iron and Wine. "He opened for them in San Francisco and it was weeks before we heard the end of it," Kiewel remembers. "People were like, 'I'm never buying another Sub Pop album again!'

or 'I'm no longer an Iron and Wine fan,' all because Sam [Beam] subjected his fans to Neil Hamburger. It may have had something to do with the abortion jokes. I didn't think he was the most appropriate opener."

Indeed, Hamburger's career confounds expectations. Like others chronicled in this book, he typically eschews comedy clubs for indie-music rooms, theaters, outdoor festival stages, and other nontraditional venues. Legend has it that he started performing on the little-known pizza parlor circuit in the mideighties, bursting out of Culver City, California, to immediately play hundreds of gigs per year. His therapist told him to try stand-up as a means of emotional rehabilitation, so Hamburger packed up his few belongings and hit the road. After meeting Art Huckman (who was rumored to have managed the Ritz Brothers and Rich Little at one point) at a show in Needles, California, Hamburger upped his schedule to a staggering 350 gigs per year, give or take a few.

Since then he has toured with and opened for bands such as Trans Am, Guided By Voices, Pinback, Smog, Tortoise, Fantômas, and Bonnie "Prince" Billy. When he does play a regular club, it's usually out of the way and hostile—sometimes intentionally so, sometimes not. "Generally I like the music crowd," Hamburger says. "They come prepared to laugh, and the stages are nice and dirty. Some of those comedy clubs have vomit on the stage, too, since comedians have problems with their nerves. But music stages have fewer bodily fluids."

A growing number of underground music and comedy fans have come to embrace Hamburger as a kind of Andy Kaufman/G. G. Allin hybrid, a pitiable jerk with confrontational jokes and intentionally public meltdowns. But his profile has enjoyed legitimate bumps from time to time. He has popped up at respected comedy festivals, on *Jimmy Kimmel Live*, Fox's *Red Eye*, Adult

Swim's *Tim and Eric Awesome Show, Great Job!*, the Tenacious D movie *The Pick of Destiny*, and even his own online offering, TomGreen.com's *Poolside Chats with Neil Hamburger.*

"It's probably the most freewheeling talk show I've ever seen," he says of that program, which was on hiatus as of our interview. "It was great to sit by the pool and take the calls from all the degenerates. Most of the people calling were trying to cause trouble. It was a mess, but people loved it. Lots of swearing and drinking and catastrophes and technical problems. Weird people dropped by and invaded the show, like that drug addict Steve-O from *Jackass*." (And, it must be noted, underground music icons King Buzzo of The Melvins and Will Oldham.)

Perhaps the climate has warmed for Hamburger's brand of funny, or maybe he's finally started to perfect his borderline avant-garde act, the jokes getting sharper, the façade more inscrutable. Regardless, it only works if he has something to lament, and it's unthinkable that Hamburger would ever connect with the comedy mainstream the same way giddy, breathless stand-ups Carlos Mencia or Dane Cook would. It takes patience, smarts, and a warped sense of humor to appreciate Hamburger, but his late-2000s uptick of screen and touring activity prove that more people are getting the joke.

In typical fashion, he discounts it: "Sure, high-visibility people might know who you are, but are you getting the good seats at the restaurants? No, you're not even getting into the restaurants because you're not making enough money to eat there."

One more thing: Hamburger isn't real, even though his creator fights admirably to keep him looking that way.

★ ★ ★ ★ ★

Talking about Neil Hamburger to alter ego Gregg Turkington presents certain problems. Turkington never does interviews as himself—only as Hamburger. He fears it will ruin the illusion of the character. And he's probably right. Most publications that interview him play along, treating Hamburger as a legal entity and inviting him to spin entertaining tales of heartache and destitution that feed his growing mythology. "Are you able to keep up with current events?" *Gothamist* asked him in 2006. "Sometimes," he responded. "If you go to these trash cans in the rest areas, you can find some of these *USA Today* papers, and that's where I get a lot of the information."

It's a commendable stance, but few, if any, publications have explored the stark difference between Turkington and his comedic creation. Neil Hamburger is a sloppy mess—a belching, profane, penniless loser who still manages to legitimately endear himself to audiences around the globe. Los Angeles–based Gregg Turkington, on the other hand, is a sharp, normal-looking guy with longish hair, baggy clothes, and baseball cap, a punk-rock devotee who's fiercely protective of the Hamburger persona. The transformation is impressive, to say the least.

Turkington was born in the Northern Territory city of Darwin, Australia, on November 25, 1967, although his parents moved back to the States about six months later. He grew up loving comedy that took its craft seriously, from Albert Brooks records to *National Lampoon* magazine. Brooks, in particular, had a way of taking on showbiz conventions that earned him the early anticomedy tag, echoes of which would show up in a certain stage creation years later.

Turkington's absorption of 1970s comedy hallmarks also paralleled the early days of punk and hard core, and it wasn't long before the California-bred teenager got into bands like Black Flag and San Francisco noise-punk act Flipper. These groups instilled in him the punk scene's anti-career-oriented aesthetic and further sharpened his sense of humor.

It's not surprising that Turkington also went on to play in a string of punk and avant-garde bands, most of them obscure beyond certain circles in San Francisco and Los Angeles. (Ever heard of Hello Kitty on Ice, Bean Church, Zip Code Rapists, The Easy Goings, or Totem Pole of Losers? Didn't think so.) *Breakfast Without Meat*, the fanzine he copublished in the 1980s, championed formerly uncool artists like Jimmy Webb and Tiny Tim. Loving things that most people considered schlock, and without irony, was one of the most punk things you could do in the eighties. In fact, Turkington's favorite singer is Frank Sinatra Jr., for whom he still maintains a fan website.

From 1992 to 2001 he owned and ran San Francisco–based Amarillo Records, which released albums by acts such as U.S. Saucer, Dieselhed, and Harvey Sid Fisher. The widely loved 1996 compilation *You Gan't Boar Like An Eabla When You Work With Turkrys* featured, among others, Sun City Girls, Thinking Fellers Union Local 282, Anton LaVey (founder of the Church of Satan), and a track from none other than Neil Hamburger. Turkington has acted as tour manager for bands (Mr. Bungle, Link Wray), written a book (*Warm Voices Rearranged: Anagram Record Reviews*, with Brandan Kearney), and worked as a contributing editor to the British version of *Maxim* magazine, for which he crafted brilliant, twisted anagrams of rock biography synopses (among other things).

But somewhere along the line, Neil Hamburger was born, and quite by accident. Turkington was an avid prank phone caller, enjoying that time-honored, low-tech tradition of misrepresenting one's self to a random soul on the other end. In 1992, Turkington's friend Becky Wilson decided to tape two consecutive nights of his calls. The genesis of the name occurred during a call in which he pretended to be a loser comedian trying to get a booking in San Francisco, hassling the schlub on the other end with a short audition, heedless of the intimations for him to stop. The completely improvised bit included the off-the-top-of-his-head moniker Neil Hamburger.

At the same time, Turkington found himself on a collecting binge of vanity pressings, those vinyl singles of various genres that people self-finance and release. They were either untalented losers or legitimately talented, unlucky people who somehow got stuck doing it themselves, resorting to cheap, handmade packaging and DIY distribution. Turkington discovered these relics in bargain bins at Goodwill stores, feeding his growing obsession with self-styled entertainers who worked the margins of popular culture.

Becky Wilson, meanwhile, had been circulating the prank-call tapes and was pleased to see they were catching on, so Turkington released them on 1993's *Great Phone Calls* comp on Amarillo, a fifteen-track disc that only included a few Hamburger bits, but otherwise all-original material from Turkington. The *Telephuck You!* single appeared shortly thereafter with an ingenious premise: something so miserable and cheap that listeners would get depressed before even dropping the stylus to vinyl. The conceptual side of Turkington's humor also kicked in, prompting him to litter the same thrift stores he'd formerly combed with his own vanity pressings, heedless of the fact that he wouldn't be around to see the joke come to fruition.

Improbably, distributors who worked with Amarillo Records began asking for more releases in the vein of 1994's *Looking for Laughs* and 1995's *Bartender, the Laugh's on Me.* As these labels grew interested in releasing seven-inches, Drag City came calling for a full-length.

Turkington figured he ought to craft the ultimate Neil Hamburger album for Drag City, employing every hair-brained idea, technical glitch, and parody of comedy tradition he could muster. He hit the road and recorded it in hotel rooms in Albuquerque, Santa Fe, and Modesto, California, adding recorded dive-bar sounds and canned reactions. The result, 1996's *America's Funnyman*, was the culmination of his character up to that point, and it garnered Hamburger wider notice than he had ever imagined possible.

"I remember how confused I was when I heard the first Neil Hamburger album," says David Cross. "I couldn't figure out whether it was real or not, and I didn't care. I was happy either way. But when I found out, 'Oh yeah, it's actually a guy from a band doing a character,' I was both disappointed and even more excited. I was like, 'What a great, fun idea.' He's got some really bad, purposefully corny jokes, but there are some really funny, legitimate jokes that he sprinkles in there that are worthy of anybody."

Turkington continued to release albums and pursue the authenticity of the character, even doing a show in Malaysia that only garnered—I shit you not—a single laugh. (Naturally, he released it as 1999's *Left for Dead in Malaysia*, later re-creating the experience in a black-and-white short film of the same name.) But with four albums under his belt, the larger question of a proper, in-person stand-up show began to gnaw at him. He doubted he would even be able to re-create the bleak, defeated vibe that made the records work, worried that hipsters would show up and ruin the delicate atmosphere. And what's more, Turkington didn't look much like the pathetic drawings of Hamburger that adorned the album covers. An offer from his birthplace changed all that.

In 1999, Turkington received an invitation to fly to Australia to perform a few shows as Hamburger, opening for the popular punk band Frenzal Rhomb. Their manager, Chris Moses, had initially met with Turkington in San Francisco (where Turkington lived at the time) and convinced him to do the dozen dates down under. Turkington figured that if the shows went poorly, no one in the States would be any wiser, and anyway, the airfare was paid for. He bought a tux, experimented with hair gel, and found a pair of oversized Coke-bottle eyeglasses, quickly realizing he could make himself look more like the cover drawings than he had imagined. The first-ever gig took place at the University of Sydney in September 1999. By the sixth show he was playing to a crowd of 30,000 people at an outdoor music festival.

It wasn't quite like the records, and Turkington had never considered Hamburger to be anything but an audio-only act, but he found that he could develop the character in a way that worked on its own terms. He spent a good amount of time in Australia, appearing on TV and radio, and even in a video with Frenzal Rhomb, which was banned from TV after a single showing, due to the graphic, blood-soaked "Ball Chef," which featured Hamburger cutting off Frenzal Rhomb's testicles and feeding them to the band.

After more gigs in Australia (Turkington lived there on and off from 1999 to 2003), he returned to the States and started booking dates to satisfy the growing US audience, who had learned about Neil Hamburger primarily through his recorded output. A tour with Chicago instrumental rockers Trans Am and other bands was followed by several solo dates, none of which took place at comedy clubs.

Turkington couldn't stand the places. He had trouble relating to people who possessed an all-encompassing love for the *Seinfeld*-style, blazer-and-tie guys peddling intelligence-insulting, false-premise jokes that dripped with implicit misogyny and xenophobia. He hated people who wanted to laugh in the mindless, convulsive way that audiences on television did, people who treated comedy like background music or fast food, who showed up simply because the stand-ups had been on *Letterman* or *Leno*, and not because they had any familiarity with their act.

The more he played music clubs, the easier it became to return, whether it was California or Texas, Illinois or Florida. Hamburger has appeared at the legendary indie club Emo's in Austin, Texas, for example, every year since 2000. People were starting to grasp the joke, to understand that Hamburger's creator really *feels* for the pathetic souls of which Hamburger is an amalgam, those downtrodden entertainers who work hard, often for nothing, simply to follow their dreams. But the ratio of unhappiness and horror to *American Idol*–style stage glory is higher than most people realize.

There's no single inspiration for the character, but those things still helped create Hamburger: the hacks at open-mic nights, the depressing no-cover entertainment in casino side rooms, the oblivious jerks on the street strumming a terrible song for pocket change. In that way, Hamburger is also a logical mesh of Turkington's own impulses. He may not have sought it, but his punk-rock credibility is impeccable, even as he admires hokey pop artists of yesteryear. He's intelligent, with flashes of intense vulgarity; absurd, yet sports an inner sense of how to time (or rather, how *not* to time) his jokes. It's a conceptual, almost abstract put-on, but it's one that has managed to go farther than Turkington ever imagined. Over the course of fifteen years, he went from making prank phone calls and creating fake, sad pizza-parlor circuits on record to playing Madison Square Garden with Tenacious D or Caesar's Palace with friends Tim and Eric of *Tim and Eric Awesome Show, Great Job!* (on which he has also appeared as Neil Hamburger, the taxi cab driver. As you might guess, he's not much of a driver).

"*Whaddya* get when you cross Sir Elton John with a *saber-toothed tiger*?" he asked the crowd at the Big Day Out festival at Gold Coast Parklands, Queensland, in January 2003. The thousands of Australian kids in the audience greeted him with indifferent noise and a few boos. "I don't know, but you better keep it away from your *ass!*" Scattered laughter, more boos, and middle fingers followed. When a Ronald McDonald look-alike came onstage to toss hamburgers into the audience, the crowd hurled them back, although Hamburger seemed unperturbed, engaging in a mock gang-style beating of McDonald with a few band members.

That Hamburger has been given stage time at such high-profile gigs speaks to his renown in music and underground comedy circles. Whether people listen or not is almost beside the point; just getting in front of that many souls is a coup. And though the act has changed over time, Turkington has managed to sustain it without acquiring an agent or schmoozing with corporate executives. He respects those loose-nut comedians like Andrew Dice Clay, and contemporaries like Patton Oswalt and Doug Stanhope, who do it for the same authentic reasons, using whatever TV and movie notoriety they achieve to further their stand-up careers, and not the other way around.

Unlike them, however, Hamburger is so down-on-his-luck that he makes Elliott Smith look like a Cirque du Soleil acrobat.

The opening acts for Hamburger's November 9, 2007, show at Denver's Larimer Lounge could not have been more appropriate: local deadpan comic Ben Kronberg, a founding member of Denver's Wrist Deep Productions, wore his signature white, little-girl cowboy boots, hunched over a keyboard and drum machine, and punctuated jokes with bursts of cheesy synthesizer and percussion. (Sample: "I like my coffee like I like my slaves: free," plus assorted rape and abortion material.) Denver madman Magic Cyclops, a Hamburgeresque, bandana-clad hipster with a fake UK accent who occasionally sells locks of his hair online (by popular demand, mind you), followed with another array of keyboard-driven songs that served to highlight his clueless, anachronistic, frequently laugh-out-loud persona.

Hamburger's tourmates, the Seattle duo Pleaseeasaur, presented a low-tech, oddly effective grab bag of parodies that employed Tim and Eric–style costumes and video backdrops. Led by singer J. P. Hasson, the group set its sights on evening news anchors, exercise videos, child-safety jingles, and other familiar targets that ended up being far funnier than they had any right to. (The props and perfectly timed visuals, courtesy of behind-the-scenes member Thomas Hurley III, went a long way toward selling the humor.)

As expected, Hamburger's set that night was flecked with hysterical disdain and defensiveness, taking trite comedic conventions down a notch by exposing their flimsy premises, mean-spirited cores, and ultimately pointless execution. Unsurprisingly, a couple audience members at the dimly lit rock club heckled the shit out of him. (Perhaps the pair of raging egos in baseball caps didn't realize Hamburger was not above hurling drinks at people during his sets. We got it, bros—you don't think it's funny. They eventually grew bored and left for whatever frat kegger was calling them.)

"But *thaaaaaat's* my life!" Hamburger occasionally said, employing a catchphrase that references both his Rodney Dangerfield–style victimization and hapless, helpless personality.

"Since I stopped doing the second-string comedy circuit, the pizza-parlor and Indian-casino scene has dried up," Hamburger told me a few days before the Larimer Lounge set. "I began working almost exclusively at the music clubs. And the clubs first said, 'Neil, I don't think this is going to work,' but honestly the attendance has been much better at the music clubs, and a lot more comedians are touring exclusively at the music clubs. These kids are all eager to see something else. See, my records had been released on the Drag City label, so we thought, 'Let's take it to these clubs.' A lot of these people buying my records have never set foot in a comedy club in their lives."

The space between laughing and rocking out is a short one for indie-music crowds, says Drag City's sales manager Rian Murphy, who staged the Chicago indie-comedy night *People Under the Stares*. "A lot of the punk rock in the eighties was hilarity based, and then there were things like Butthole Surfers with a humor quotient. All of this was formative and inspirational, though a distinction was always made between these and certain other types of comedy-rock that seemed more obvious, like Frank Zappa or Ween. There's a subtle difference...but there's always been room for that, going back through classic rock all the way to 'They're Coming to Take Me Away, Ha-Ha' in the early sixties and The Treniers in the fifties and before that even, too!"

Despite the indie-music connection, Hamburger does not wish to remain accessible to only a few people. He won't change his act to do it, but if bigger crowds start flocking to his shows, so be it. As radio host Tom Scharpling wrote in 2007's *The Best of LCD: The Art and Writing of WFMU-FM 91.1 FM*: "That's not to say Neil Hamburger lives in the ghetto of Outsider Art—he is not 'the Jad Fair of comedy.' While the Elite dig Mr. Fair's intentions, you'd be hard-pressed to get Joe Lunchpail to put on *Music to Strip By* after a hard day in the factory. Neil doesn't play to a specific scene. While his records are released by indie-rock record labels, his goal is to have his comedy heard by all people. Like the title of his most recent album states, he does indeed strive to be America's funnyman."

With all of Turkington's musical associations and experience, it's not surprising that Hamburger eventually made his own proper foray into music, 2008's *Neil Hamburger Sings Country Winners*. The album finds him backed by a group composed of Atom Ellis (Dieselhed, Link Ray), Prairie Prince (The Tubes), Rachel Haden (The Rentals), and others on songs like "Please Ask that Clown to Stop Crying," "Zipper Lips Rides Again," and "The Recycle Bin." That last song features the delicate opening lines, "Not everything goes into the recycle bin, you stupid pricks. You can't recycle Styrofoam, or a potted plant, or artichoke waste. You *cocksucker*. Fucker! *Motherfucker!!* Stop tainting the waste stream with pieces of wood and old underwear. What are you going to recycle those into, huh, assholes?" Of course, it's all set to pleasantly loping drums, acoustic guitar, and feathery female backing vocals—music that plays the straight man to Hamburger's indignant, profane babbling.

The Onion was none too kind to the disc, dismissing it with a C-minus rating in its April 29, 2008, edition. "Anti-comedian Neil Hamburger is adept at finding new ways to be horrible. Unfortunately, those ways are often designed more to be annoying than exciting," wrote *A. V. Club* reviewer David Wolinsky. "The only conceivable way the audience-baiting, obnoxiously throat-clearing Hamburger can alienate his audience further is with a straight-faced country album—and terrible singing. He dons a Texas toupee and bolo tie, but the shtick is essentially the same. Though it succeeds at being boring, unbearable, and cookie-cutter Music Row fare, there are scattered moments that make the bumpy ride worthwhile."

The acquired-taste nature of Hamburger allowed for a predictably wide spectrum of responses. "[*Country Winners*] goes far beyond anything the man's cult could hope for and is arguably the best disturbing country album from a failed and faux lounge comedian that you'll ever find," wrote David Jeffries on AllMusic.com.

Love him or leave him, Hamburger constantly meets his goal of crafting a unique record each time out. For a character who started as an impromptu joke, it's remarkable how far he has traveled, especially in spite of (or, perhaps, because of) abrasive humor like, "Why did God, in his *infinite* wisdom...create Domino's Pizza? Well, to punish humanity in their complacency for letting the Holocaust happen." Or this sensitive zinger: "Why did the chicken cross the road? To take a photograph of Princess Diana dead in her car."

As Hamburger continues to play, as he has put it, "Three hundred ninety-nine shows to a total of three hundred ninety-nine people per year," we can only watch him grow darker, weirder, and, improbably, more popular. The number of people who get the joke is ballooning, hinting that stale comedy conventions have themselves become the punch line for a self-aware crowd who views earnest stand-ups as relics of the past, and who take pleasure in increasingly distilled shots of awkwardness. Comics have been separating the mechanics of comedy from the content for decades, but as Hamburger shows, it's now an approach you can employ almost exclusively.

"It's definitely a part of the so-called alternative comedy world. It's not the only part, but it's a part," says Jesse Thorn, host of public radio's *The Sound of Young America*. "You see Andy Kindler, whose act is essentially him complaining about his act. He'll tell a joke, and that joke is often a very good joke, but sometimes the biggest laughs come from the five minutes of him talking about the audience's reaction to the joke, or talking about why he should never have told that joke. Neil Hamburger is very much in that specific tradition."

Another frequent Hamburger comparison that Turkington has resisted is Tony Clifton, the Vegas-style nightclub entertainer character that legendary anticomic Andy Kaufman created. He usually took the stage in a fake hairpiece, mustache, and sunglasses, berating audience members, dumping pitchers of water on their heads, and generally testing their tolerance for in-your-face performance art. "Clifton was a menace—Kaufman's corrosive satire of the sadomasochistic underbelly of show business," wrote Richard Zoglin in *Comedy at the Edge*. "At one concert in San Francisco, where Clifton was booked as the opening act for Rodney Dangerfield, the crowd reportedly got so angry that they began throwing beer bottles at the stage. Clifton fled behind the curtain for safety—and sang three more numbers from there."

Though he denies any direct inspirational link to Clifton, it's tempting to see Hamburger as an evolution of the concept. Still, Hamburger's ability to transform initial reactions of revulsion and apathy into sympathy and laughter (not the so-good-it's-bad kind, but honest, unselfconscious laughter) and the consistency of his performances shield him from easy comparisons. And anyway, sad-sack, put-upon stage performers have long been a stock character in entertainment history, from the one-liners of old-school practitioner Jackie Vernon to the perpetually emasculated material of Rodney Dangerfield. "He spoofs those Borscht Belt sixties, seventies, and eighties comics, plus older Tin Pan Alley or Vegas comedians," says writer Andrew Earles, one half of the Earles & Jensen prank-call duo.

Hamburger's act simply proves that increasing numbers of people understand the character as a depressing by-product of the entertainment machine—all without Turkington having to compromise any of Hamburger's defeated, prickly tenor or wink at the crowd from time to time.

Then again, he'll still probably never leave that cardboard box he calls home.

"Despite giving so much, Neil, like Christ before him, is morally and emotionally bankrupt," opined an Australian documentary about Hamburger's time there. "And yet, like Christ before him, Neil is perpetually on the verge of redemption and success."

Amen.

Members of comedy collective Wrist Deep Productions (from left to right) Greg Baumhauer, Jim Hickox, and Adam Cayton-Holland outside Orange Cat Studios in Denver.
Photo by Cyrus McCrimmon, courtesy of The Denver Post

COMEDY THAT GETS ITS HANDS DIRTY

As you've probably guessed by now, comedy nerds are a special breed, those prickly souls who get the same thrill from a well-told joke that others enjoy from stellar ski runs, gourmet meals, or ear-rending concerts. They do not settle at candlelit tables to hear jokes from a random stand-up. They instead follow comedians around like bands, devouring their every release and obsessively seeking out new material, mentally tattooing catchphrases on their gray matter until their vocabulary resembles a Wikiquote page.

But wither the Denver comedy nerd? The city I've lived in for nearly a decade is a far cry from Los Angeles, New York, Chicago, or San Francisco. Save for the occasional theater or rock-club show, we don't consistently get the national indie-comedy names who have made the coasts such furnaces of creativity. Where's our David Cross, the king of East Village sarcasm? Our Sarah Silverman, the Hollywood baby-face who drops laugh-out-loud bombs about AIDS and rape? Our Louis C. K. or Patton Oswalt? Our Tim and Eric?

In dive bars and art galleries, as it turns out.

A collective of stand-ups known as Wrist Deep Productions has been providing the comedy-nerd thrill for a growing number of Denverites, putting on shows at nontraditional venues and drawing audiences that rarely, if ever, set foot in mainstream clubs like Denver's Comedy Works or The Improv. They're part of the movement that takes inspiration from other DIY artists, building creative homes on their own land instead of sending away for the prefab stuff or renting squares of someone else's property. These enterprising souls craft the scenes they'd like to see for themselves, eschewing the allure of the Big Two coastal cities (which, let's face it, are still the fastest, most practical places to jump-start an entertainment career).

Not that they're the most prolific breed in the world. "There's no one else doing their style of comedy in Denver," says Donna Ayers, webmaster of MileHiComedy. com. "They've really tapped into something, and they're making huge strides with it. Between [Denverite] Josh Blue winning *Last Comic Standing* and what they're doing, they're helping put Denver on the map."

Wrist Deep's harsh, hilarious perspective on such familiar shy-away topics as AIDS, abortion, genocide, religion, and politics doesn't preclude them from using their wits in absurdist time-travel sketches or self-aware puns that operate on multiple levels. In other words, smart, aggressive comedy that shatters expectations without spinning off into abstractions. The result is an injection of the punk-rock ethos into an art form that, at least in the middle of the country, is still largely the province of talk-show regulars and comedy-club road dogs.

Wrist Deep principals Greg Baumhauer, Adam Cayton-Holland, Ben Roy, and Jim Hickox form the core of the collective, four young, slightly moppy, self-aware guys whose mellow demeanors belie their busy schedules and hard-partying habits. Wrist Deep holds a long-running open-mic night at Denver's divey Squire Lounge every Tuesday, and it's always a shoulder-to-shoulder affair. (Beware of using the bathroom when it's crowded. Trust me.) Their monthly *Los Comicos Super Hilariosos* shows at the Orange Cat Studios are regularly packed. In 2008 they took over Thursday night's *Monsters on the Mic* comedy show in Boulder in addition to various others, like the occasional mountain gig in Breckenridge or Aspen, or the even more infrequent but equally hilarious *You Suck! Get Off the Stage* gong show at Denver's historic Oriental Theater (which features, I shit you not, the original gong from the 1970s show).

"All of comedy is about control, and you can't control a place like Comedy Works," says Ben Roy, leaning over a half-eaten pizza at City, O' City café and bar on Denver's Capitol Hill. "Which is great—we all perform there and love the regular checks. That's [owner] Wende Curtis's place. But you can't control who's performing with you or what the night feels like."

Sound familiar?

Like countless DIY artists, Wrist Deep is fashioning a universe with its own rules and tone. More importantly, their stand-up takes legitimate chances with subject matter and context, which sometimes means having a gun pulled on you during a set. Ben Kronberg, a founding member of Wrist Deep, held his farewell show at one of the Squire's open-mic nights in November 2007. In the course of his routine, he thanked a variety of the bar's patrons for the jokes. "He was like, 'I want to thank the drunks, the faggots, the bitches, the Spics, and the Chinks,'" says Greg Baumhauer. "And then he thanked 'the niggers.' And there was a gentleman who took some offense to that."

"Someone was like, 'There's a gun outside!'" cofounder Adam Cayton-Holland remembers. "So Kronberg jumps off the stage, lies down on the floor, and continues performing while lying on his back, still telling abortion jokes. It was fucking great. And the funniest thing is, he said if he had been shot that night he would be bigger than he could ever be as a live comic. The Legend of Kronberg would have been huge." The bar's bouncer, a burly Iraq-war veteran, defused the situation before it escalated any further (and reports of an actual gun are fuzzy to verify), but none of the Wrist Deep guys will forget the potential for violence that lies in misinterpretation.

Then again, anyone who has seen Kronberg knows (1) that he is not a racist man, and (2) that his humor is about as far from politically correct or delicate as it gets (if golden showers mean anything to you, cheers). Now based in Los Angeles—where there is, as of this writing, no official Wrist Deep outpost—Kronberg says he certainly wasn't inviting the situation at the Squire. "I am one of the first to fucking run away if I think somebody has a gun," he says, a tinge of incredulity lingering in his voice.

The Squire's open-mic contest typically draws 100 people to the cramped space, making it the bar's busiest night—and it doesn't even start until 11:15 PM, about two hours before bars close in the Mile High City. The kind of visceral energy that Wrist Deep engenders is unique in a city with only a handful of underground comedy offerings, all of which pale in quality, experience, and force compared to Wrist Deep's.

Sure, Denver's comedy scene has grown over the years: we're the launchpad of Roseanne Barr and the late, troubled genius Don Becker, and rising indie comedians Kristen Schaal and Tig Notaro. In addition to marquee venues such as Comedy Works and the Improv, smaller joints like Wits Ends Comedy Club regularly welcome national acts. The Oriental, an aging art-deco theater in Denver's Highlands neighborhood, welcomes indie-friendly comedians Todd Barry, Paul F. Tompkins, and Doug Stanhope. Laughing Bean Café and There Coffee Bar & Lounge host Denver-specific stand-ups, and improv and sketch thrives at Bovine Metropolis Theater, Impulse Theater, and elsewhere. Even beer-stained rock venues like the Larimer Lounge and Bender's Tavern host the occasional comedy show. But if you're jonesing for creative, envelope-shredding humor that doesn't fear the occasional face-plant, the Wrist Deep crew is it.

"Wrist Deep originally started with Ben Kronberg and me," says Baumhauer, a loose-limbed guy who works weekends as a drag waitress at Bump & Grind Café. "It wasn't really meant to be anything, just something to put on top of a flyer. I just felt we should have some sort of umbrella for all the stuff we were doing."

The members originally cohered in early 2004 while performing at open-mic nights at the tiny, dingy Colfax Avenue club the Lion's Lair, a venue seemingly more suited for bar fights, barfing, and gutter punk than stand-up comedy. Each had varying levels of experience but shared an aggressive, intelligent sensibility.

"Part of it is that they don't care if you like them or not," says MileHiComedy.com's Ayers. "They know they're funny, and this is what they're going to say.

You're either on the train, or you're not. I don't know that there's another term to describe what they're doing other than indie rock. They certainly take a chance with mainstream audiences, and they're winning them over. And it's smart comedy. It's not watered down to the lowest common denominator. You have to be well-read and informed of what's going on."

A refusal to pander further codified the group, which at one point included expatriate Andrew Orvedahl. "I think what we all have in common is that we've tried to create a platform for ourselves and our friends to do exactly what they want," says Cayton-Holland, a writer who pens the weekly *What's So Funny?* column for local alternative newsweekly *Westword*. His humor is frequently harsh, and Wrist Deep's material is generally R-rated, but it never crosses into exploitation or malice. "We can offend the paint off of a wall, but there's thought behind it," Cayton-Holland adds. "They're all intelligent jokes. We're not just swearing to make our mothers mad."

In the end, it's all in service of the laugh, but also attempts to bend the rules for what's funny by turning the audience in on itself. The monthly *Los Comicos Super Hilariosos*, for example, takes place at Orange Cat Studios, a ragged art gallery in the gradually gentrifying warehouse district just down the street from Denver's Larimer Lounge. The cracked walls and naked stage seem more suited to avant-garde art than stand-up. "It's the beautiful informality of people walking up onstage during our sets to get to the bathroom," says Baumhauer, who once allowed someone to punch him in the face repeatedly at Denver's Comedy Works just to get the stage time. "On the day I got out of the hospital after breaking both my hands, that night I did *Los Comicos*," he continues. "They pushed me out onstage in a wheelchair while I was smoking a cigarette with this big old hospital jug full of beer. I was so fucked up. I was in so much pain. I was howling."

The Orange Cat only holds about 125 people, but *Los Comicos* crowds don't seem to mind standing two-to three-deep in the back when the seats are filled. The audience consists of everyone from hipsters to college instructors and construction workers, diverse in ethnicity and gender (although all looking like they'd be right at home at an indie-rock or punk concert). *Los Comics* has even attracted a few groupies who follow the principals around, helping them write material and pull off sketches.

The disregard for convention extends to the show's format. Stand-up forms the foundation, but the show always includes a few local luminaries (Troy Baxley, Chuck Roy) and touring comedians (*The Sarah Silverman Program*'s Tig Notaro, Michelle Miracle, Louis Katz, etc.), as well as sketches and short videos. "We like to look at it like we're one of the best comedy shows in the country," says Jim Hickox, the affable Wrist Deep stand-up who helms their multimedia offerings.

That's no idle chatter. Former regular Ben Kronberg has performed at some of the most prestigious comedy gigs around since moving to LA, including *Comedy Death-Ray* and *What's Up, Tiger Lily?* His well-received appearances at HBO's US Comedy Arts Festival in Aspen, and later on *Jimmy Kimmel Live,* earned him agents and meetings with Comedy Central, Spike TV, and HBO. In early 2008, Cayton-Holland nabbed a spot in *Tearing the Veil of Maya* in Park Slope, Brooklyn, playing next to indie-comedy heavies Zach Galifianakis and show cohost Eugene Mirman, among others. "After four years of doing standup, I don't get all that nervous anymore," Cayton-Holland wrote in *Westword* after the experience. "But as I rubbed elbows [translation: slammed Stellas] with my idols, I started to feel some nerves, enough so that I removed my show shirt to avoid pit stains."

Big deal, right? Hundreds of comics have shuffled through TV shows and hot comedy nights over the years. What Cayton-Holland found, however, was that Denver and its insular scene had done a fine job training him for an ostensibly more sophisticated, experienced audience—especially one presided over by comedy veterans. After his set at *Tearing the Veil of Maya*, in New York, Cayton-Holland was offered gigs for the following weeks. Which, of course, he had to turn down. "There was this subdued, literate, hipster crowd in Park Slope, and as I came out telling my jokes I noticed my performance. I was like, 'Goddamn, I'm really aggressive,'" he says, eyeing his Wrist Deep cohorts. "That's really a product of Denver, because we're all kind of aggressive. Not like, 'I'm going to punch you in the face.' But more this sort of urgency. I think it's because we don't have anyone offering us contracts. People assume we're a cowtown so we're like, 'Oh, you don't think I'm funny? Well fuck this. I can show you how funny I am.' And I'm probably even less aggressive than some of these guys."

Wrist Deep's Ben Roy, easily the most aggressive of the group, likens it to the first day of school for a dirty, awkward kid from an alcoholic family: "You're not very threatening and you get the shit kicked out of you every day. So when you're finally out among normal people and someone does one little thing, you just fucking stab him—like it's way overaggressive and uncalled for. It's just because we sit here and brew in our own thing."

"What surprises me is that New York guys that come through at the Squire are shocked," adds Greg Baumhauer. "They can't believe they're hearing abortion and AIDS shit.

And I'm like, 'You're from *New York*, dude.' One of the things that allows us to be like that is that the glass ceiling here is a lot lower, so we don't have to worry about offending anybody. There's not going to be some fucking network guy in the audience. It's just a bunch of drunks, so we can say whatever the fuck we want to say."

The rise of Wrist Deep and its crown jewel, *Los Comicos*, parallels the larger indie-comedy movement, taking cues from scenes in bigger cities with far more comedians and venues. Wrist Deep formerly staged *Los Comicos* at Old Curtis Street Bar, a venue where punk, indie, metal, and folk bands regularly mingled. Moving it to the Orange Cat gave them even greater control over the environment. And since *Los Comicos* began getting attention outside of a select group of friends and comedy fans, the members have turned away modest sponsorship and documentary offers in favor of creative rule. The scene they have built did not come fast or easy.

They paid their dues at nearly every comedy club, bar, and music venue around town. After nine months of poor turnout, the weekly open-mic nights at the eminently dumpy Squire finally clicked and began drawing larger crowds. None of the members takes that for granted. "We could go to LA or New York, and it probably wouldn't be too long before we were on *Live at Gotham* or *Premium Blend*," Baumhauer says. "But you know what? If I move to LA, I'm just another guy telling dick jokes. Here we've started our own movement."

None of the members begrudge former principal Ben Kronberg his move to LA, but their persistence in Denver is part of why indie comedy is starting to reach into the interior of the country. "That's what all of us have in common," Cayton-Holland says. "Every DIY scene has tried to create a platform for themselves and their friends to do exactly what they want. If that manifests itself as profanity here and dirtiness here—and probably hipster surfer jokes in Southern California or whatever—it's just having that platform."

Kronberg says that as much as Wrist Deep may be part of a larger movement, it maintains a distinctive vibe. "I still haven't encountered a room that's like the Squire. There's a uniqueness that's created by both the performers and the audience and the particular night. Fucking trudging through the snow on a December night—nobody has to do that in LA...I came here to have opportunities that I wouldn't have otherwise. But I'm not even 100 percent sure it's a direction I want to go in. I'm sucking it up by working at Starbucks. But would I rather not suck it up just to do something closer to what I want to really do?"

Outside the Orange Cat on a freezing night in November, the Wrist Deep principals stand smoking cigarettes and poring over notes for that evening's installment of *Los Comicos*. Their relative nervousness never rears its head onstage, however, as they seem to embrace technical difficulties and awkward moments as just another part of the act. Save for an impromptu stand-up show in your parents' basement, it's comedy at its underground finest, even if you sometimes have trouble hearing punch lines through the noisy heater that hangs from the ceiling, turning on and off randomly, or the chattering of your own teeth as frigid air wafts in from the street. All part of the charm. This is my first time at the show, although

I've been meaning to check it out for a while, having heard nothing but good things about it.

The group's MySpace page says it all: "Wrist Deep is the type of production company that believes comedy is best served with cheap beer and lots of friends." Indeed, the crowd at times feels insidery, calling out performers' names or getting name-checked from the stage. (Wrist Deep also has a saying that not-so-subtly nods to the fist-fucking origins of its name: "Comedy that's not afraid to get its hands dirty.") Fortunately, it never translates into a sense of exclusivity. You don't have to be friends with the guys to appreciate their skewed take on the news (think *SNL*'s "Weekend Update," but punchier and more unpredictable), the video sketch in which they react to the Two Girls, One Cup Internet poo-porn video (I find myself laughing so hard I can't breathe), or their pointedly offensive humor in general.

The self-consciousness is apparent at times, as when Adam Cayton-Holland notes the number of anal rape jokes vs. little people jokes that have been told throughout the night ("for those keeping score"). And really, the guys do lean on a number of perennially uncomfortable, predictably shocking topics like abortion, masturbation, race, and religion.

But the notes they hit are uniquely satisfying, making you wonder why America ever dug crap like Dane Cook or Larry the Cable Guy to begin with, and why more people aren't putting on shows like this. The entire night is solid, but closer Ben Roy presents perhaps the most compelling set. His unhinged, drunken persona is gloriously erratic, mixing Louis Black's quivering indignation with Bill Hicks's vitriol and David Cross's unapologetic misanthropy. He even starts his set by noting the environs, which he refers to as "The set from *Schindler's List* and *Saving Private Ryan*" before moving on to topics such as upper-decking (if you've heard of it, you can imagine how he used the folding chair to pantomime shitting into a toilet's water tank), pregnancy tests, and interacting with his mom while stoned. In the end, it feels just like a sweaty rock show, albeit with less standing around and sweating and a lot more good-natured profanity and cheap beer.

Comedian Tig Notaro and her Crackpot Comedy Tour want to come to your house. Seriously. *Photo by Seth Olenick*

8

SUPPORTIVE UNDERGARMENTS

Unlike most indie-rock shows, the larger world of comedy sometimes feels more showbiz-related than the scruffy small-club sets that hipsters hold dear, thwarting attempts to draw exact parallels between them. And why should we? They're two different things. But that doesn't change the fact that the scattered, ever-increasing examples of indie comedy that have sprouted outside of bigger cities like New York, Los Angeles, San Francisco, Chicago, and Seattle tend to use indie-music shows as models for their own, dismissing audience expectations and allowing a loose, anything-goes vibe to reign in the name of stripped-down art. "There's not a lot of stand-up shows at rock 'n' roll house parties, but I think the way it gets people excited is comparable, in that it's like, 'Wow, there's this whole scene of creativity and these people who are amazing that I've never heard of,'" says musician Neil Cleary, who in addition to his solo work has filled in as a drummer for a host of touring indie bands (Ladybug Transistor, The Essex Green, Annie Hayden). "That's the way this scene has hit me. It was definitely the most exciting thing *since* indie rock. And since I'm of that era, it was the only thing I had to compare it to. I'd wager it wasn't all that different from the way activism and grassroots politics struck young people in the sixties, to drag out a hackneyed, overused comparison."

The mutual fascination that cutting-edge comedians and musicians share for each other also has something to do with their recent but inexorable mingling. "There's a kind of awe and overly undue amount of respect given to the other person, whereas for me, doing what I do is second nature," says David Cross. "People are like, 'Man, I can't believe you get up just by yourself and talk for an hour and a half.' But I'm like, 'I wouldn't know how to get up and play an instrument for an hour.' I think it's pretty clear there's more opportunity to be uncomfortable with stand-up. With music you can just crank it up to ten, and you usually have more people to share the blame. But with stand-up, any silence is your silence."

As each genre poaches the other's turf, the comedy-anywhere-we-want ethos only expands. Comedians Tig Notaro and Martha Kelly took it one step further, creating the improbably informal Crackpot Comedy tour. Anyone can apply to book a show, according to the tour's MySpace page, which offers a 1950s-style instructional video outlining the five easy steps. Notaro says there wasn't a grand plan behind the idea, other than it just seemed like fun. "We'll set up in garages, basements, rooftops, lofts, living rooms, backyards—they just have to promote it and get people out there," she says. The show encourages $10 to $20 donations, but doesn't require any advance booking fee or guarantee of turnout. And lest you think this is some desperate attempt to stage shows when nowhere else would take them, the tour features professional, talented comedians with film and TV credits (the founders, plus Steve Agee, Tom Sharpe, and others) and big-name surprise guests (Zach Galifianakis, Sarah Silverman). These aren't C-list comedians with nowhere else to go; they just happen to enjoy the novelty of playing one-bedroom ranch homes.

"One of the big enabling factors of the past five to ten years is the proliferation of channels, and I don't just mean on television," says *The Sound of Young America*'s Jesse Thorn. "It means that there's more value placed on something that inspires passion than ever before. So as with Adult Swim shows, for example, you can be really, really weird and exclusive. You can produce shows that have a 10-out-of-10 on a scale of having unique voices. It's the same young audience that supports college rock, really. And the Internet has played a huge role in uniting them, just as it has with knitting or flower arranging groups. You can build a community around an idea rather than a physical space, which couldn't have happened pre-Internet. It existed around college radio and fanzines and music, but it certainly didn't exist before in comedy."

The next step, however, isn't to have David Cross open for Radiohead, but for more places like New York and LA's Upright Citizens Brigade theatres, to open in smaller cities, becoming regional hubs for experimental humor. In other words, places that are not traditional comedy clubs—places where people are either going to see a specific performer or a weekly show, or where they're opening themselves up to an unpredictable mix of sketch and stand-up.

As the relationship between comedy and indie rock continues to develop, however, some think it's an uncomfortable one, at best. "Tastemaker underground rock is one of the biggest offenders when it comes to lacking a sense of humor," says Andrew Earles. "And that, for whatever reason, is the style of music that comedy has recently latched onto."

The potential to alienate audiences is another pitfall of many current music-comedy pairings, says Dan Schlissel of Stand-Up! Records. "Once it becomes an end unto itself it's a bit problematic for the fan. If it all of a sudden becomes a big inside joke, it's not accessible to the greater population. That can be creatively damaging. If you actively want to be part of any scene, you can become kind of precious. I don't like going to a record store and asking where the Mötley Crüe stuff is and being sneered at."

Nerds of any genre, of course, have always been that way, and comedy nerds are no different. "They're a vocal minority that doesn't seem to understand they have an extreme interest in something," says Todd Barry. "The vast majority of people are not seeing comedy six times a week."

Still, as long as musicians and comedians tend to admire each others' output, there will remain a link between them—even when it's not explicitly stated. Ross Flournoy, guitarist/singer for Merge Records band The Broken West, echoes his peers when he considers the challenges of an art he respects but doesn't fully understand. "It scares the shit out of me just to go see stand-up comedy. It looks so fucking hard. At every moment there's this potential for complete humiliation." He counts LA comedians Matt Braunger and Matt Dwyer among his friends, and used to see comedians like Marc Maron and Mary Lynn Rajskub at the (now-defunct) record store Sea Level in Echo Park. "It seems so difficult and scary, and strangely enough, I think that's reciprocated by [the comedians]."

The true achievement of indie comedy is that it's moved stand-up out of the all-or-nothing club format.

And not just to indie-music clubs, bookstores, and festivals, but everywhere.

"Two to three years ago, digital video cameras became really affordable, and editing on a computer is affordable and easier. So now everyone's making videos, and videos are in everybody's sketch shows," says UCB's Matt Besser. "Sketch comedy and comedy in general has caught up to indie music in the last couple years. You can finally not have to sell your idea to a network, whether it's Comedy Central or some sitcom idea. You don't have to wait for that moment to come along. You're getting your own stuff out there."

"Whether you're a band or a comedian, you're [always looking] around for a process to make your statement in a way that gets it out there, has potential to make money, and is comfortable for you [i.e., as few people telling you what to do as possible]," says Drag City's Rian Murphy. "This road does seem to lead back to indie-mindedness. The space between laughing and rocking is a reasonably short distance for us."

But what really unites all the comedians in this book, beyond their shared love of and experience with *Mr. Show* and other groundbreaking sketch comedies? Is it their appreciation of independent music, nontraditional venues, and booze? Their hipster cachet? Their mutual distaste for lame stand-ups like Dane Cook and stupid, evil politicians? Their deft self-promotion and increasing profiles in the entertainment world?

Did I just answer my own question?

"Everybody feels like, 'Well, I don't want to label a scene as this or that,' but it's a real thing," says *Commercial Appeal* writer Bob Mehr. "Almost every indie label has their comedy thing. You look at any small to midsized music club in any big city in America and every month there's something related to comedy happening. That's different than what was happening five or six years ago."

Jesse Thorn has interviewed nearly every comedian profiled in this book. He says the scene, as it were, exists almost out of necessity. "The reason that all these people have connections is not just because they all became friends and started performing this kind of comedy. It's because all these comedians want to do the kind of comedy that they love, and they go to the places where they can perform it, which is relatively difficult. All these comedians share these values and they tend toward the places that will support them."

Whether it's digital or analog, DIY or corporate, that supportive underground is starting to push through to the most visible levels of everyday culture. Indie comedians may currently be the stand-up equivalent of Guided By Voices's *Bee Thousand*—a relatively obscure breed appreciated mostly by nerds and critics for its subcultural currency, gleeful oddity, and groundbreaking qualities—but many music geeks also consider *Bee Thousand* to be one of the finest indie-rock albums ever released. Or they hate it. Either way, it got their attention, and it went on to influence other bands that far outstripped the commercial success of the original.

It's impossible to predict how the people profiled in this book will fit into the larger history of comedy, but over the last few years, they have comprised the most visible part of the movement away from traditional comedy clubs, helping make that format seem like the phase it may one day become, instead of an inexorable reality of stand-up. "The reason I see comedy clubs as a thing of the late seventies and eighties is because there used to be sort of cabaret clubs and theater clubs, and that's where most comedy happened," says Eugene Mirman. "If what's happening now continues for fifteen more years, it will seem like comedy clubs were just an odd moment in time."

More than that, comedy is coming around again as a relevant art form on par with its 1970s renaissance, speaking to young minds turned off by the homogenized messages of most mainstream comedy clubs. It's not the bastard child sitting in the corner, but the bastard onstage with a microphone, berating or gleefully befuddling anyone within earshot. Indie-comedy audiences are able to conceptualize comedy differently because comedians are thinking about *themselves* differently, no longer shackled by the imperative of a one-size-fits-all sensibility, blissfully free to explore their creative muses in whatever way they choose. For more and more people, comedy has added to (and in some cases supplanted) the overall appreciation and excitement of other once-dominant independent art forms. Comparing a kick-ass comedy show to your average rock concert these days often leaves the latter looking anemic.

And as weird, offensive, divisive, and obscure as the material can be, it's no stretch to think that a handful of these comedians will someday achieve the same exposure as respected contemporary stand-ups such as Chris Rock, Lewis Black, and the late, great Bernie Mac. Popularity doesn't preclude quality, and certain comics richly deserve a spot in the limelight (as well as a bit of financial stability). But moving an art form forward doesn't always coincide with success, and the experimental underground is justifiably reluctant to compromise its ideals in order to tap mass audiences.

Whether or not comedians continue to actively court the underground music set, good comedy will survive. If I learned anything darting around the country to interview people and catch shows, it's that the scattered pockets of fandom for smart, twisted, risk-taking humor have simultaneously proliferated and increasingly merged. Places like the Upright Citizens Brigade Theatre have become clubhouses and boot camps for comedy nerds, a fact that I chewed over as I sat on the venue's empty stage in LA, scanning the darkened seats and nondescript, multipurpose room.

I could have been anywhere, really, and that's the point: stand-up and sketch comedy are no longer chained to a handful of TV shows and clubs, once again free to roam and take whatever forms they please. For those of us who once feared the faceless beasts of the mainstream comedy world, that's a glorious mutation.

Author John Wenzel. *Photo by Mat Luschek*

John Wenzel

John Wenzel grew up in Dayton, Ohio, where he spent far too much time being obsessed with Guided By Voices. He has written for websites and magazines such as *Rockpile*, *Shredding Paper*, and Aversion.com, and from 1997 to 2005 coedited and published *Sponic* fanzine. He currently writes about music, comedy, and new media for *The Denver Post* and lives in Denver's Capitol Hill neighborhood.

A NOTE ON SOURCES: All quotes in this book were obtained during interviews in person or via phone or e-mail exchanges, unless otherwise noted. Every effort was made to independently verify all facts and figures used from outside sources. Thanks to *The Denver Post* for allowing me to use portions of previously published articles, and extra special thanks to Matt Besser, Andrew Earles, Henry Owings, and Jesse Thorn for their excellent recommendations. They know far more about comedy than any sane person should.

SOURCES

Aaronson, Lauren. *New York Magazine: Bar Guide*. Luna Lounge capsule. nymag.com/listings/bar/luna_lounge.

AdultSwim.com. Various online videos.

Anderman, Joan. "Spontaneous Combustion." *The Boston Globe*, August 13, 2000.

Ankeny, Jason. Review of *Gimme Indie Rock!*, by Sebadoh. AllMusic.com. www.allmusic.com/cg/amg.dll?p=amg&sql=10:fbfpxq9jldte.

Aqua Teen Hunger Force: Volume One. 2-disc DVD. Turner Home Entertainment, 2003.

Arrested Development: The Complete Series. 8-disc DVD. 20th Century Fox, 2006.

ASpecialThing.com. Various Patton Oswalt interview/user-generated Q&A threads. 2003–present.

Austin Comedy Panel with David Cross & Zach Galifianakis. Multipart YouTube video series from South by Southwest Music and Media Conference and Festival, Austin, TX, 2007. Originally posted July 3, 2007. www.youtube.com/watch?v=_xzWQuTzGfM&feature=related.

Ayers, Michael D. "Indie Comedy Finds Footing at Music Festivals." *Billboard Magazine*, April 12, 2008.

Bamford, Maria. *The Burning Bridges Tour*. CD. Stand Up! Records, 2003.

———. *How to Win!* CD. Stand Up! Records, 2007.

Barry, Todd. *Falling Off the Bone*. 2-disc CD / DVD. Comedy Central Records, 2004.

———. *Medium Energy*. CD. Comedy Central Records, 2005.

——. *From Heaven.* CD. Comedy Central Records, 2008.

Benson, Doug. *Professional Humoredian.* CD. AST Records, 2008.

Bienstock, Hal. "Does 'LOL' = 'RIP'?" *Paste Magazine*, May 2008.

Black, Michael Ian. *I'm a Wonderful Man.* CD. Comedy Central Records, 2007.

Bowers, William. Review of *Shut Up, You Fucking Baby!* by David Cross. PitchforkMedia, December 4, 2002. www.pitchforkmedia. com/article/record_review/16385-shut-up-you-fucking-baby.

Carr, David. "Son of a Gun, Hollywood Has Big Fun on the Bayou." *The New York Times*, May 20, 2008.

Cayton-Holland, Adam. "*What's So Funny?* Missionary Position." *Westword*, April 10, 2008.

——. "*What's So Funny?* Baby Steps." *Westword*, May 29, 2008.

——. "Curtain Call: Denver Mourns the Loss of Its Favorite Bipolar, One-Armed Comic/Poet/Playwright." *Westword*, June 19, 2008.

C. K., Louis. *Shameless.* DVD. HBO Home Video, 2007.

Comedy Death-Ray. 2-disc CD. Comedy Central Records, 2007.

Coyle, Jake. "Bonnaroo Fest Opens with Metallica, Chris Rock." *The Associated Press*, June 14, 2008.

Cross, David. *The Pride Is Back.* Directed by Troy Miller. HBO, 1999.

——. *Shut Up, You Fucking Baby!* 2-disc CD. Sub Pop Records, 2002.

——. *Let American Laugh.* DVD. Sub Pop Records, 2003.

——. *It's Not Funny.* CD. Sub Pop Records, 2004.

——. "Where Do I Know You From? How Not to Alienate that Guy from TV." *New York Magazine: The Urban Etiquette Handbook.* nymag.com/guides/ etiquette/17332/index2.html.

——. "Guest List: Albums to Listen to While Reading Overwrought Pitchfork Reviews." Guest column. PitchforkMedia, May 17, 2005.

Dangerfield, Rodney. *Rodney Dangerfield: No Respect.* 3-disc DVD. R2 Entertainment, 2004.
Dr. Katz: Professional Therapist: The Complete Series. 13-disc DVD. Paramount, 2007.

Dungan, Jason. "Fusing Politics with Dick Jokes." Review of *Shut Up, You Fucking Baby!* by David Cross. *Dusted*, November 18, 2002. www. dustedmagazine.com/reviews/478.

Earles & Jensen. *Just Farr a Laugh, Vol. 1 and 2: The Greatest Prank Phone Calls Ever!* 2-disc CD. Matador Records, 2008.

Edwards, Gavin. "Larry the Cable Guy Bared." *Rolling Stone*, April 26, 2005.

Electric Apricot: The Quest for Festeroo. DVD. Hart Sharp Video, 2008.

Erlewine, Stephen Thomas. Review of *Shut Up, You Fucking Baby!* AllMusic.com. www.allmusic.com/cg/amg. dll?p=amg&sql=10:w9frxq9aldje.

Flight of the Conchords. *The Distant Future.* CD EP. Sub Pop Records, 2007.

———. *Flight of the Conchords: The Complete First Season.* 2-disc DVD. HBO Home Video, 2007.

———. *Flight of the Conchords.* CD. Sub Pop Records, 2008.

Flynn, Gillian. "Skit Parade." *Entertainment Weekly,* March 28, 2008.

Freak Show. Created by H. Jon Benjamin and David Cross, Comedy Central, 2006.

Fred Armisen's Guide to Music and SXSW '98. Short introduction and video, posted March 12, 2008, at stereogum.com/archives/video/ fred-armisens-infamous-guide-to-music-and-sxsw-98_008389.html.

Freivogel, Andy. Review of *Just Farr a Laugh Vol. 1 and 2,* by Earles & Jensen. *Dusted,* May 8, 2008. www. dustedmagazine.com/reviews/4249.

Galifianakis, Zach. *Live at the Purple Onion.* DVD. Shout Factory, 2007.

Glauber, Gary. Review of *Shut Up, You Fucking Baby!* PopMatters, January 15, 2003. www.popmatters.com/music/ reviews/c/crossdavid-shut.shtml.

Goodman, Dean. "Flight of the Conchords Soar on U.S. charts." *Reuters/Nielsen,* April 30, 2008.

Guildford, Simon. "David Cross: Off Rupert Murdoch's Christmas Card List." Drowned in Sound, June 26, 2007. www.drownedinsound. com/articles/2129634.

Hamburger, Neil. *America's Funnyman.* CD. Drag City, 1996.

———. *Left for Dead in Malaysia.* CD. Drag City, 1999.

———. *Inside Neil Hamburger.* CD/EP. Drag City, 2000.

———. *Great Phone Calls Featuring Neil Hamburger.* CD. Ipecac Recordings, 2002.

———. *Laugh Out Lord.* CD. Drag City, 2002.

———. *Great Moments at Di Presa's Pizza House.* CD. Drag City, 2005.

———. *The World's Funnyman.* DVD. Drag City, 2006.

———. *Neil Hamburger Sings Country Winners.* CD. Drag City, 2008.

Hedburg, Mitch. *Mitch All Together.* CD/DVD. Comedy Central Records, 2003.

———. *Strategic Grill Locations.* CD. Comedy Central Records, 2003.

Hicks, Bill. *Rant in E-Minor.* CD. Rykodisc, 1997.

————. *Love, Laughter, and Truth.* CD. Rykodisc, 2002.

————. *Sane Man.* DVD. Rykodisc, 2005.

Hitchens, Christopher. "Why Women Aren't Funny." *Vanity Fair*, January 2007.

Human Giant: Season One. 2-disc DVD. MTV/Paramount, 2008.

Hyman, Peter. "Alt Comedy Goes Rock and Roll." *Spin Magazine*, December 2005.

I Am Trying to Break Your Heart: A Film About Wilco. 2-disc DVD. Plexifilm, 2003.

Internet Movie Database. Various filmographies. www.imdb.com.

Invite Them Up. 3-disc CD/DVD. Comedy Central Records, 2005.

Itzkoff, Dave. "The Bizarre Brains of Nightmare TV." *The New York Times*, July 27, 2008.

Jay, Chris. "Film Reel." *(Shreveport) CityLife*, March 6, 2008.

Jeffries, David. Review of *Werewolves and Lollipops*, by Patton Oswalt. AllMusic.com. www.allmusic.com/cg/amg. dll?p=amg&sql=10:dnfwxz95ldfe.

————. Review of "Neil Hamburger Sings Country Winners, by Neil Hamburger. www.allmusic.com/cg/amg. dll?p=amg&sql=10:3xfqxzejldfe.

Jens Hannemann: Complicated Drumming Technique. DVD. Presented by Fred Armisen, Drag City, 2007.

Jupitus, Phill. "Comedy is the New Rock 'n' Roll (Again)." *The (London) Times Online.* June 2, 2008.

Just Shoot Me!: Seasons One and Two. 4-disc DVD. Sony Pictures, 2004.

Karakh, Ben. "Neil Hamburger, Comedian." *Gothamist*, August 18, 2006. gothamist.com/2006/08/18/ neil_hamburger.php.

Koch, John. "Catch the Future at Catch a Rising Star." *The Boston Globe*, July 22, 1990.

Lanham, Robert. *The Hipster Handbook.* New York: Anchor Books, 2003.

Larry the Cable Guy. *Git-R-Done.* New York: Three Rivers Press/Crown, 2005.

Loftus, Jonny. Review of *Feelin' Kinda Patton*, by Patton Oswalt. AllMusic.com. www.allmusic.com/cg/amg. dll?p=amg&sql=10:hjfrxqyaldke.

Lundy, Zeth. Review of *It's Not Funny*, by David Cross. PopMatters, May 24, 2004. www. popmatters.com/pm/review/15137/ crossdavid-itsnotfunny.

Lynch, Stephen. *The Craig Machine.* CD. What Are? Records, 2005.

Magnolia. 2-disc DVD. New Line Home Video, 2007.

Martin, Demetri. *These Are Jokes*. 2-disc CD/DVD. Comedy Central Records, 2006.

Metalocalypse: Season One. 2-disc DVD. Turner Home Entertainment, 2007.

Miller, Jeff. "Will the Next Dane Cook Please Stand Up?" *Esquire*, July 2, 2007.

Mirman, Eugene. *The Absurd Nightclub Comedy of Eugene Mirman*. 2-disc CD/DVD. Suicide Squeeze, 2004.

———. *En Garde, Society!* 2-disc CD/DVD. Sub Pop Records, 2006.

Modell, Josh. "Best Albums of 2004: Comedy: Still the New Punk Rock." *The Onion A. V. Club*, December 8, 2004.

———. "I Love Prank Phone Calls." *The Onion A. V. Club*, Aug. 12, 2008. www.avclub.com/content/blog/i_love_prank_phone_calls.

———. "Interview: Tim and Eric." *The Onion A. V. Club*, November 15, 2007.

Mr. Show: The Complete Collection. 6-disc DVD. HBO Home Video, 2006.

Mr. Warmth: The Don Rickles Project. DVD. Salient Media, 2007.

Nelson, Sean. "Mr. Cross: Half the Brains Behind *Mr. Show* and *Run Ronnie Run* Tours with a Rock Band." *The Stranger*, May 30, 2002.

NewsRadio: The Complete First and Second Seasons. 3-disc DVD. Sony Pictures, 2005.

Nichols, Natalie. "Forget the Velvet Rope." *The Los Angeles Times*, January 17, 2002.

Odenkirk, Naomi. *Mr. Show: What Happened?!: The Complete Story and Episode Guide*. Los Angeles: Squaresville Productions, 2002.

Ogunnaike, Lola. "MTV's Man Behind the Series." *The New York Times*, March 13, 2006.

Onion, The. "Does Music Belong in Humor?" *The Onion A. V. Club*, May 29, 2008.

Oswalt, Patton. *Feelin' Kinda Patton*. CD. United Musicians, 2004.

Oswalt, Patton. Guest appearance on *Jimmy Kimmel Live!* ABC, March 7, 2005.

———. *No Reason to Complain (Uncensored)*. DVD. Comedy Central, 2006.

———. *Werewolves and Lollipops*. 2-disc CD / DVD. Sub Pop Records, 2007.

P., Ken. "An Interview with Patton Oswalt." IGN.com, April 5, 2006. movies.ign.com/articles/700/700224p1.html.

Petrusich, Amanda. Review of *It's Not Funny*, by David Cross. PitchforkMedia, May 14, 2004. www.pitchforkmedia.com/article/record_review/16386-david-cross-its-not-funny.

Posehn, Brian. *Live In: Nerd Rage.* CD. Relapse Records, 2006.

Rabin, Nathan. "Interview: Neil Hamburger." *The Onion A. V. Club*, March 24, 1999.

———. Review of *The Comedians of Comedy: Live at the Troubadour*. *The Onion A. V. Club*, October 25, 2007.

———. Review of *Human Giant: Season One*. *The Onion A. V. Club*, March 5, 2008.

———. Review of *Great Job: Tim and Eric Straddle Funny-Strange and Funny-Ha-Ha*. *The Onion A. V. Club*, May 8, 2008.

Regan, Leila. Review of *It's Not Funny*, by David Cross. *Paste Magazine*, June 9, 2004.

Reno 911!: Miami. DVD. 20th Century Fox, 2007.

Rock Against Bush: Vol. 2. 2-disc CD/DVD. Fat Wreck Chords, 2004.

Rosenberg, Tal. Review of *Werewolves and Lollipops*, by Oswalt Patton." *Stylus Magazine*, July 23, 2007. www.stylusmagazine. com/reviews/patton-oswalt/ werewolves-and-lollipops.htm.

Run Ronnie Run. DVD. New Line Home Video, 2002.

Samology.com. *Tinkle* blog post, 2003. www.samology. com/archives/2003/03/.

Scharpling, Tom. "Laughs, Love and Live with Neil Hamburger," in *The Best of LCD: The Art and Writing of WFMU-FM 91.1 FM*, ed. Jim Jarmusch, 164–169. New York: Princeton Architectural Press, 2007.

Scharpling and Wurster. *The Art of the Slap: The Best of Scharpling and Wurster on the Best Show on WFMU Vol. 4*. 2-disc CD. Stereolaffs, 2007.

Schletter, Eban. *Eban Schletter's Witching Hour*. CD. Oglio Entertainment Group, 2008.

Sebadoh. *Gimme Indie Rock!* 7-inch single. Homestead, 1991.

Segal, Dave. Review of *Werewolves and Lollipops*, by Oswalt Patton. *The Orange County Register*, July 12, 2007.

Sellers, John. *Perfect From Now On: How Indie Rock Saved My Life*. New York: Simon & Schuster, 2007.

Sheffield, Rob. Review of *The Art of the Slap*, by Scharpling and Wurster. *Rolling Stone*, May 2007.

Showalter, Michael. *Sandwiches & Cats*. CD. JDub Records, 2007.

Shydner, Ritch, and Mark Schiff. *I Killed: True Stories of the Road from America's Top Comics*. New York: Three Rivers Press, 2006.

Silverman, Sarah. *Jesus Is Magic*. DVD. Interscope Records, 2005.

———. *The Sarah Silverman Program: Season One*. DVD. Comedy Central, 2007.

SlushFactory.com. *Tinkle* fan forum, 2003. www.slushfactory.com/forums/archive/index.php?t-676.html

Stanley, Alessandra. "Who Says Women Aren't Funny?" *Vanity Fair*, April 2008.

Strauss, Neil. "Take the New Comedy. Please." *The New York Times*, May 31, 1996.

Stella: Season One. 2-disc DVD. Paramount, 2006.

Suarez, Jessica. Review of *Werewolves and Lollipops*, by Oswalt Patton. PitchforkMedia, August 2, 2007. www.pitchforkmedia.com/article/record_review/44557-werewolves-and-lollipops.

Super High Me. DVD, B-Side/Red Envelope/Screen Media Films, 2008.

Superchunk. *Crowding Up Your Visual Field.* DVD. Merge Records, 2004.

SuperDeluxe.com. Various online videos. www.superdeluxe.com.

Sweet, Jeffrey. *Something Wonderful Right Away: An Oral History of The Second City & The Compass Players.* New York: Proscenium Publishers, 1978.

Tenacious D in the Pick of Destiny. DVD. New Line Home Video, 2006.

Tenacious D: The Complete Masterworks. 2-disc DVD. Sony, 2003.

Tepper, Steven J. and Bill Ivey. *Engaging Art: The Next Great Transformation of America's Cultural Life.* New York: Routledge (Taylor & Francis Group), 2008.

The Apiary. "Whatever Happened To...That Lawsuit Against David Cross?" August 18, 2006. www.theapiary.org/archives/2006/08/what_ever_happe_1.html.

The Ben Stiller Show. 2-disc DVD. Warner Home Video, 2003.

The Best of Comedy Central Presents. DVD. Comedy Central, 2008.

The Best of Comedy Central Presents II. DVD. Comedy Central, 2008.

"The Boosh at The Big Chill Festival 2008." Online review, Culture JamJar, August 6, 2008. culturejamjar.wordpress.com/2008/08/06/the-boosh.

The Colbert Report. "Rock and Awe: Countdown to Guitarmageddon." Comedy Central, December 20, 2006.

The Colbert Report. Apples in Stereo performance. Comedy Central, August 4, 2008.

The Comedians of Comedy: The Movie/Live at the El Rey. DVD. Starz/Anchor Bay, 2007.

The Comedians of Comedy: Live at the Troubadour. DVD, directed by Michael Blieden. Image Entertainment, 2007.

"The Gig Venue: Largo."
Q Magazine. www.
largo-la.com/articlesreviews/q.html.

*The King of Queens: The
Complete Series*. 27-disc
DVD. Sony Pictures, 2007.

The Musical Comedians of Comedy.
Various videos and text. www.
musicalcomedians.com/gallery.php.

Thunderant. Various videos and
text, Carrie Brownstein and Fred
Armisen. www.thunderant.com.

*Tim and Eric Awesome Show,
Great Job! Season One*. DVD.
Warner Home Video, 2008.

*Tim and Eric Awesome
Record, Great Songs! Vol. 1*.
CD. Williams Street, 2008.

Tim and Eric Nite Live. Web
talk show, SuperDeluxe.com.
Various episodes, 2007–2008.

*Time Out New York: Bars and
Restaurants*. Luna Lounge
capsule. www.timeout.com/
newyork/bars-clubs/lower-east-
side/4745/luna-lounge-closed.

*Tom Goes to the Mayor: The
Complete Series*. 3-disc DVD.
Turner Home Entertainment, 2007.

Tompkins, Paul F. *Impersonal*.
CD. AST Records, 2007.

Tool. *Vicarious*. DVD. Jive, 2007.

UnitedMusicians.com. Online
biography for Acoustic Vaudeville.
www.unitedmusicians.com/
temp/artists/vaude.html.

*Upright Citizens Brigade: The
Complete First Season*. 2-disc
DVD. Comedy Central, 2007.

*Upright Citizens Brigade: The
Complete Second Season*. 2-disc
DVD. Comedy Central, 2007.

*Upright Citizens Brigade: Asssscat!
Renegade Improv Comedy*.
DVD. Shout Factory, 2008.

Ventre, Michael. "Standup
Comedy Didn't Die with Carlin."
MSNBC.com, July 28, 2008. www.
msnbc.msn.com/id/25875719.

Waggoner, Eric. "Laugh, Riot: Neil
Hamburger Died for Your Grins."
Phoenix New Times, August 2, 2001.

Wenzel, John. "Mock Stars." *The
Denver Post*, November 12, 2006.

———. "Chelsea Handler:
Happy to Be a Joke." *The
Denver Post*, April 27, 2007.

———. "Comic Neil Hamburger
Loves to Make 'em Cringe." *The
Denver Post*, November 9, 2007.

———. "Stand-Up Comics Schaal,
Notaro Share Colorado Ties,
Oriental Stage." *The Denver
Post*, December 28, 2007.

———. "Comic Christian Finnegan:
'Week' Guy's Strengths." *The
Denver Post*, January 10, 2008.

———. "Tommy Chong: Time in Joint Fired Up Comic's Literary Side." *The Denver Post*, January 22, 2008.

———. "Happy Now, Bob Mould Is as Strong as Ever." *The Denver Post*, March 21, 2008.

———. "The Wild Wild Wrist: Stand-Up Comics Plug Energy into Denver's Graying Laugh Scene." *The Denver Post*, April 20, 2008.

———. "Lizz Winstead: Comedy Writer Stages a Return." *The Denver Post*, April 25, 2008.

———. "Stand-Up Comic Cho Is Beautiful (Just Ask Her)." *The Denver Post*, May 2, 2008.

———. "Don't Let the Dress Fool You: Lampanelli's No June Cleaver." *The Denver Post*, June 27, 2008.

———. "Comedy's No Sweat for Laid-Back Barry." *The Denver Post*, July 4, 2008.

———. "Denver-Born Comic on the Rise in LA." *The Denver Post*, August 1, 2008.

———. "Hipster Comics Black, Showalter Come to Gothic." *The Denver Post*, September 7, 2008.

Westhoff, Ben. "1,440 Minutes: An MTV Takeover Results in Better Bands, Random Absurdity and...vVdeos." *The Village Voice*, May 22, 2007.

Wheat, Alynda. "The Comedians of Comedy." *Entertainment Weekly*, review, November 11, 2005.

Wolf, Zoë. "A Beautiful Duet." *The New York Times*, August 19, 2007.

Wolinsky, David. *Neil Hamburger Sings Country Winners*, by Neil Hamburger. *The Onion A. V. Club*, April 29, 2008.

Wonder Showzen: Season 1. 2-disc DVD. Paramount/MTV, 2006.

Wonder Showzen: Season 2. 2-disc DVD. Paramount/MTV, 2006.

Yo La Tengo. *Sugarcube.* Music video. Matador Records, 1997.

Zoglin, Richard. *Comedy at the Edge: How Stand-Up in the 1970s Changed America.* New York: Bloomsbury, 2008.

Index

Nirvana, 11, 30, 104, 107
The Nitty Gritty Dirt Band, 31
Notaro, Tig, 25, 177,
    270, 272, 280–81

O

O'Brien, Conan, 13–14, 71
O'Brien, Michael, 99
Odenkirk, Bill, 73
Odenkirk, Bob, 65, 70–72, 78, 137,
    149, 150; *Arrested Development*,
    124; *The Ben Stiller Show*, 96,
    97–98; *Comedians of Comedy*,
    173; *Human Giant*, 198; and
    the indie-comedy movement,
    8, 26–27; *Mr. Show*, 3, 4, 64–66,
    72–73, 74–76, 78; *Tim and Eric
    Awesome Show, Great Job!*,
    204, 206, 207; *Tom Goes to
    the Mayor*, 209, 210, 211
Odenkirk, Naomi, 63–64, 72, 76, 88
Of Montreal, 156, 231
Ogunnaike, Lola, 197
Old Curtis Street Bar, 274
Oldham, Will, 169, 202, 252
100 Club, 125
The Onion, 78, 122, 215,
    216, 219, 249, 263
*Opening Night at Rodney's
    Place*, 50–61, 73, 142–43
Orange Cat Studios, 268,
    271–72, 274, 275–76
Oriental Theater, 268, 270
The Original Kings of Comedy, 160
Orvedahl, Andrew, 271
Oswalt, Patton, 42, 45, 104, 119,
    128–29, 152–53, 154–59, 166, 167,
    259; Acoustic Vaudeville, 153,
    159; CDs and DVDs, 114–15, 144,
    146, 157–58, 178–83; *Comedians
    of Comedy*, 16, 114–15, 143–44,
    159–65, 168, 171, 172–75, 177,
    178–79, 184, 186–87; Comedy
    Central, 148, 221; *Comedy
    Central Presents* special, 151,
    158; *Comedy Death-Ray*, 137;
    Disney, 187; *HBO Comedy

Half-Hour special, 151; *Human
    Giant*, 197; and the indie-
    comedy movement, 8, 26, 42;
    interview with author, 135, 142,
    178; *The King of Queens*, 143,
    158, 161; *MadTV*, 150; *Mr. Show*,
    74, 77, 150; music festivals,
    230, 232; *Ratatouille*, 143; Sub
    Pop Records, 144, 179–82, 220;
    TV, films, game shows and DC
    Comics, 143, 150–51, 154–55;
    Un-Cabaret, 71–72, 149
Ottobar, 114
Owings, Henry, 16, 109, 155–56,
    167–68, 169, 171, 179–80, 182,
    183; *Comedians of Comedy*,
    159–60, 165; Comedy on the
    Music Circuit, 234, 235, 236; *Mr.
    Show*, 76; music festivals, 237

P

Paesel, Brett, 74
Paley Center for Media, 203
Panda Bear, 116
Papa, Tom, 44
Pardo, Jimmy, 137
Paste Magazine, 45, 121–22, 219
Pavement, 46, 107, 193
Paxton, Tom, 31
Pearl Jam, 74
Penn, Michael, 152, 153
Penn & Teller, 33
Pepitone, Eddie, 138, 139
Peretti, Chelsea, 18
*Perfect from Now On: How Indie
    Rock Saved My Life* (Sellers), 11
Petrusich, Amanda, 121
Phillips, Emo, 145
Phoenix Theater, 148
phone-call comedy, 218–23
Pianos, 117
The Pick of Destiny, 252
Pinback, 251
Pitchfork (website), 47,
    112, 121, 131, 182
Pleaseeasaur, 260
Plug Awards, 126

For a complete catalog of our books, please contact us at:

speck press

4690 Table Mountain Drive, Suite 100
Golden, Colorado 80403
e: books@speckpress.com
t: 800-992-2908
f: 800-726-7112
w: speckpress.com

Our books are available through your local bookseller.